FINANCIAL ACCOUNTING

THE 360 DEGREE SERIES

Series Editor: Paul E. Smith, University of Hertfordshire
Other titles in the 360 Degree Series include:

Organizational Behaviour
Paul E. Smith, Wendy Yellowley, Marilyn Farmer
ISBN 978 1 444 1353 36

Business Economics (forthcoming)
Rob Dransfield
ISBN 978 1 444 1704 50

360°
series

FINANCIAL ACCOUNTING

PARMINDER JOHAL
BEVERLY VICKERSTAFF

Routledge
Taylor & Francis Group

LONDON AND NEW YORK

First published 2012 by
Hodder Education, a member of the Hodder Headline Group

Published 2014 by Routledge
2 Park Square, Milton Park, Abingdon, Oxon OX14 4RN
711 Third Avenue, New York, NY, 10017, USA

Routledge is an imprint of the Taylor & Francis Group, an informa business

British Library Cataloguing in Publication Data
A catalogue record for this book is available from the British Library

Library of Congress Cataloging-in-Publication Data
A catalog record for this book is available from the Library of Congress

ISBN 13: 978-1-444-17041-2 (pbk)

Typeset in 10/12pt Minion pro-Regular by Datapage (India) Pvt. Ltd.
Printed and bound by CPI Group (UK) Ltd, Croydon, CR0 4YY

Cover image © aquariagirl 1970–Fotolia

CONTENTS

Acknowledgements		viii
Series preface		ix
Preface		x
Guide to the book		xi

1   INTRODUCTION TO ACCOUNTING   1

Introduction	2
Accounting information systems	2
Information needs of stakeholders	3
Types of entity	6
Legislation	8
Underlying accounting concepts	9
Fundamental accounting concepts	10
The statement of principles	13
Audit and corporate governance	14
Summary	15

2   RECORDING TRANSACTIONS   18

Introduction	19
The accounting equation	19
T-accounts, debits and credits	21
Balancing the accounts	24
The trial balance	26
More T-accounts	27
Summary	31

3   THE STATEMENT OF FINANCIAL POSITION   35

Introduction	36
The basic statement of financial position	36
Understanding the terminology	38
The accounting equation	39
Preparing a statement of financial position	40
Company statements of financial position	45
Published statements of financial position	49
Limitations of the statement of financial position	49
Summary	50

4   THE INCOME STATEMENT   55

Introduction   56
The basic income statement   56
Understanding the terminology   57
Preparing an income statement   58
Service organizations   65
Company income statements   67
Published income statements   70
Limitations of the income statement   72
Summary   72

5   CURRENT ASSETS: VALUATION OF INVENTORY, BAD DEBTS AND BANK RECONCILIATIONS   77

Introduction   78
Inventory   78
Receivables   83
A bank   88
Summary   92

6   ADJUSTMENT TO ACCOUNTS I: ACCRUALS AND PREPAYMENTS   98

Introduction   99
What is an accrual?   99
Accounting treatment for accruals   100
What is a prepayment?   101
Accounting treatment for a prepayment   101
Relating accruals and prepayments to real company accounts   104
Summary   106

7   ADJUSTMENT TO ACCOUNTS II: NON-CURRENT ASSETS AND DEPRECIATION   108

Introduction   109
Valuing non-current assets on the Statement of Financial Position   109
Depreciation   113
Calculating depreciation   116
Accounting for the sale of a non-current asset   123
Summary   125

8   CASH FLOW STATEMENTS   128

Introduction   129
The importance of cash   129
Cash versus profit   132
The purpose of the cash flow statement   133

Presentation of the cash flow statement   135
Interpreting cash flow statements   146
Cash flow budgets   148
Summary   150

9 INTERPRETATION OF ACCOUNTS   156

Introduction   157
Users of financial statements   157
The interpretation process   159
Ratio analysis   159
Interpreting published financial statements   164
Other analytical measures   174
Limitations of ratio analysis   176
Summary   177

Glossary of terms   187
Answers to questions   190
Index   238

ACKNOWLEDGEMENTS

The authors and publishers would like to thank the following for their permission to reproduce copyrighted material:

Vodafone plc

Venturenavigator (University of Essex)

SERIES PREFACE

The 360 Degree Series is an exciting new range of textbooks that provides students with a clear introduction to business and management at undergraduate level. The books are very much written with the university and college student in mind, including those who are relatively unfamiliar with this particular field of study and are seeking a clear and accessible text to help them get up to speed with the subject quickly.

The 360 Degree Series aims to inspire students' interest in the subject and to motivate them to explore further by setting out the key topics, important ideas and essential debates required for study. Relevant theories and concepts are clearly explained and applied to practice using case studies and real-life examples. Current trends are outlined and up-to-date material provided.

Within each book, chapters include an outline and objectives and are clearly structured with headings and sub-headings, so they are easy to follow and can readily be applied to lectures and seminars. Key terms are defined and case study boxes and activity questions include real-life examples that help to put learning into context. Key themes are explored, giving students a more rounded view of the subject. Students are encouraged to check their understanding at regular intervals throughout via a number of reflective questions, reinforcing the point being made and creating a solid basis for further learning. For revision, review questions and a key ideas table are included at the end of each chapter, together with recommended reading, useful websites and references to encourage further exploration of the subject.

All this, together with the free online support materials, combine to make titles in The 360 Degree Series essential companions for students studying the dynamic and exciting world of business today.

As editor of The 360 Degree Series, I hope the books will help to boost your understanding and enjoyment of the subject, and thus lead to success in your studies.

Paul E. Smith
University of Hertfordshire
Series Editor

PREFACE

Whether you are an accounting student or studying for a business degree and coming to accounting for the very first time, this book has been written to help you develop a full understanding of financial accounting. Focusing as it does on the recording and reporting function of financial accounts, this book introduces you to ways to interpret and analyse financial data as it appears in financial statements. In this way you are prepared for, and are able to develop, financial analysis skills for yourself.

In *Financial Accounting* we have deliberately adopted internationally accepted accounting terminology. For example, although it is recognized that in the UK companies use the term 'Balance Sheet', in *Financial Accounting* the preferred term is 'Statement of Financial Position' (SoFP), as advocated by the International Accounting Standards Inventory (IAS1). Also, the financial statements will reflect the layout and terminology as recommended by the IAS1, e.g. the use of terms such as 'inventory' rather than 'stock', 'receivables' rather than 'debtors', etc. This is important as *Financial Accounting* is forward-looking and strongly reflects the increasingly global markets in which companies operate. Gaining familiarity with the way in which accounting is embracing internationalization will help you in your future career.

Financial Accounting is targeted at students such as you who want to know how to construct and interpret financial statements accurately. The clarity of the text makes it an ideal tool for both beginners and international students embarking on introductory financial accounting modules. Complex concepts and terminology are explained assuming no prior knowledge.

Financial Accounting takes you step-by-step through the financial function of a business, starting with how to record a basic transaction and ending up with how that transaction forms part of a company's published financial statements. The book then proceeds to make sense of what appears in the published accounts.

To reinforce this journey the chapters follow the logical sequence of:

- Recording of transactions
- Construction of a trial balance
- Feeding data from the trial balance into the income statement and the statement of financial position
- Adjusting accounts
- Addressing the importance of cash and the cash flow statement
- Interpreting the accounts to analyse company performance and position.

Financial Accounting makes it easier for you to understand the often complex nature of transactions and accounting terminology. It is recommended for students such as you at any stage of your study, whether you are a first-year accounting, business, marketing, or HR student, a UK-based student or an overseas student, or a postgraduate student coming to accounting for the first time.

Parminder Johal
University of Derby

Beverly Vickerstaff
De Montfort University

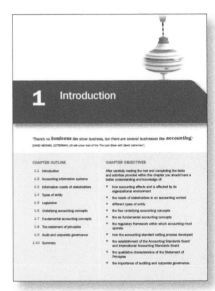

Chapter outlines and objectives Main topics and ideas are listed clearly at the start of each chapter to guide you carefully through the subject

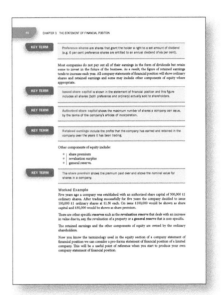

Key terms Terminology is both explained as you need it and gathered together as a glossary at the back of the book for reference

Case studies Relevant, real-world case studies highlight financial accounting principles, bringing theory to life

Worked examples Worked examples take you step-by-step through the process and principles of financial accounting

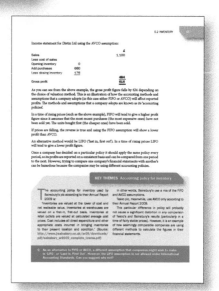

Key themes These boxes provide different perspectives and a more rounded view of particular topics

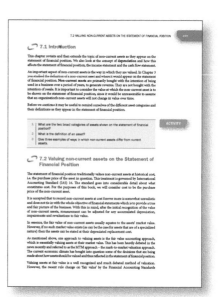

Activities Activities are located throughout each chapter to facilitate comprehension

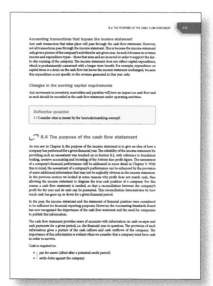

Reflective questions Frequent and challenging questions help you apply, analyse and evaluate what you've read to reinforce your understanding and promote critical thinking skills

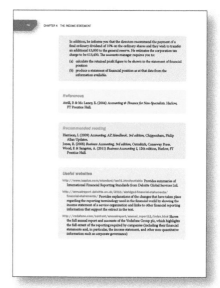

Revision support Chapter summaries, review questions, recommended reading lists and references are provided to help you revise, and additional support materials are available at http://cw.tandf.co.uk/360/

1 Introduction

*'There's no **business** like show business, but there are several businesses like **accounting**.'*

(DAVID MICHAEL LETTERMAN, *US talk show host of the 'The Late Show with David Letterman'*)

CHAPTER OUTLINE

1.1 Introduction

1.2 Accounting information systems

1.3 Information needs of stakeholders

1.4 Types of entity

1.5 Legislation

1.6 Underlying accounting concepts

1.7 Fundamental accounting concepts

1.8 The statement of principles

1.9 Audit and corporate governance

1.10 Summary

CHAPTER OBJECTIVES

After carefully reading the text and completing the tasks and activities provided within this chapter you should have a better understanding and knowledge of:

- how accounting affects and is affected by its organizational environment

- the needs of stakeholders in an accounting context

- different types of entity

- the four underlying accounting concepts

- the six fundamental accounting concepts

- the regulatory framework within which accounting must operate

- how the accounting standard setting process developed

- the establishment of the Accounting Standards Board and International Accounting Standards Board

- the qualitative characteristics of the Statement of Principles

- the importance of auditing and corporate governance.

1.1 Introduction

Modern accounting is widely recognized as a basic component of business management. **Accounting** is the means by which managers are informed of the financial status and progress of their companies, thus contributing to the continuing process of planning, control of operations and decision-making. Accounting provides a method of systematically recording and evaluating business activities.

KEY TERM	**Accounting** the process of recording, summarizing, communicating and analysing the financial transactions of a business.

A large proportion of the information that a business manager requires is derived from **accounting data**. The ability to analyse and use this data helps managers accomplish their objectives. Through your study of accounting, you will discover the types of business activities that can be accounted for usefully, the methods used to collect accounting data, and the implications of the resulting information. Furthermore, and often as important, you will become aware of the limitations of accounting reports and data.

KEY TERM	**Accounting data** all the data contained in the accounting records that underpins the preparation of the financial statements, e.g. the data contained in the ledgers and journals

Another useful definition of accounting is the process of *recording, classifying* and *reporting and interpreting* the financial data. While it is important for accountants to have a sound knowledge of the recording and classifying of the accounting process, it is often a relatively minor part of their total responsibility. Accountants direct most of their attention to the reporting and interpretation of the meaningful implications of the data.

Accounting has expanded greatly from its intuitive beginnings. It is now heavily regulated and controlled and there are well-established procedures for virtually all the traditional accounting tasks. The environment within which accounting exists is known as the **accounting information system** (often referred to as the 'accounting system'). In the next section we will look at accounting information systems.

KEY TERM	**Accounting information system** a computer-based collection of accounting records maintained by a business; the collection, storage, processing and analysing of accounting data

> *Reflective question*
>
> 1 | What do you think is the main objective of accounting?

1.2 Accounting information systems

A system is defined as a group of elements that are formed and interact to achieve goals or objectives. An organization is a system in which a number of people work together to achieve particular objectives. Organizations are increasingly dependent on information.

However, they must be able to get information when it is needed, where it is needed and in the form it is needed. Moreover, this information must complement the collection, analysis and communication of the information management process. The choice of approach to the management of information is driven, in part, by the sorts of decisions being undertaken.

An accounting information system collects, processes, stores, analyses and disseminates information for a specific purpose. At its simplest level, an accounting information system collects and processes a set of inputs (e.g. invoices) and produces a variety of outputs (e.g. reports and calculations) within a business.

For example, a manager who is in charge of ordering materials will use the accounting information system to determine how much material the organization holds and how much it will need. The manager will then decide how much material to order and who to order it from. That decision is entered into the accounting information system by the manager, the order is sent to the supplier by the accounting information system and the accounting information system is updated to show that an order has been placed.

Whereas the information system (e.g. human resources, marketing) will process a mixture of qualitative (i.e. non-numerical) data, the accounting information system focuses almost entirely on processing quantitative (i.e. numerical) data. For a business, the traditional means of communicating accounting information has been the issue of a balance sheet – or, as is more commonly used internationally, the statement of financial position (SoFP) – income statement and additional statements referred to collectively as the **financial statements.**

Reflective Questions

2 | Think of an organization you know and list examples of input to its accounting information system.
3 | Thinking again of the same organization you know, list examples of the output from its accounting information system.

1.3 Information needs of stakeholders

In today's society, many people and agencies outside of management are involved in the economic life of an organization. They are known as **stakeholders** – people who have an interest in the business – and the one thing they have in common is that they all use accounting information produced by the business.

Stakeholders frequently require financial data. For example, shareholders must have financial information in order to measure management's performance and to evaluate their own holdings. Potential investors need financial data to compare prospective investments. Creditors consider the financial strength of an organization before permitting it to borrow funds. Labour unions and financial analysts often require a considerable amount of reliable financial data. Finally, many regulations require that extensive financial information be reported to the various levels of government. As an information system, the accounting process serves people both inside and outside of an organization.

ACTIVITY

1 | List as many different classes (or groups) of users of accounting information that you can think of. Obvious ones would be the owners and the managers of the business — now add more of your own.

Types of stakeholders

Let us consider each stakeholder in more detail.

Competitors

Competitors want to find out as much information as they can about a business, particularly internal financial information concerning costs. However, they will usually have to rely on the published financial reports, newspaper reports and analysts' commentaries to carry out various analyses to evaluate strategic advantages.

Government

Various government bodies will wish to examine a business's financial statements. They want to know how much tax a business should be paying and whether it is complying with the tax laws and regulations.

Employees

Employees are interested in knowing about those aspects of the company most relevant to themselves, for example, their job security, potential for wage rises, pension issues and redundancies. They are, therefore, interested in the long-term survival of a business.

Lenders

Lenders want to know that the funds they have lent are safe. Often lenders will not just want to see the business's published financial statements but, also, the internal (management) accounts. There are different kinds of lenders providing various types of financing, ranging from banks to individual and institutional investors.

Owners

Owners want to see whether the business is profitable. They also want to know the financial resources of the business. The owners place a lot of reliance on the auditor's report and, in many cases, they rely on stockbrokers, analysts, and newspapers to guide them and interpret the information they have available to them. Of course, while the vast majority of owners are individuals with relatively small investments and levels of ownership, the 'man-in-the-street' is not the only type of owner. Large companies, insurance companies and pension funds, for example, invest heavily in companies. They employ analysts who are knowledgeable of both the companies in which they invest and the industries in which those companies are operating.

Analysts

Analysts generally know more about a company than any other external stakeholder group. Their job is to assess whether it is advisable to invest in a business. Analysts will want to know everything possible about a business. They will use financial statements, newspaper reports, commentaries from other analysts and anything else that may be relevant to make an analysis of a business.

Managers

Managers are mainly interested in the internal management accounts, to which few other stakeholders (except lenders) have access. They are interested in information relevant to budgeting, planning, decision-making and control. Since this form of accounting information is not generally available to outsiders, there is no external regulation or control over management accounting and no universally agreed way in which management accounting reports should be prepared.

Suppliers

Suppliers want to know that they will be paid what is owed to them, so they will be interested in a business's financial stability. Because suppliers are less interested in profit and more interested in cash flow, they will commonly monitor the financial reports. Suppliers often seek assurance about credit ratings and information about payment patterns before agreeing to supply goods to a business.

Customers

Customers want to know if their suppliers are going to be able to continue to supply them with the goods they require. They rely mainly upon the business's financial reports.

The public

The general public will wish to assess the effect of a business on the economy at local, national, and international levels. Businesses contribute to a local economy by creating employment and obtaining goods from local suppliers. Some businesses actively support communities by sponsoring events, providing education, and so on.

FIGURE 1.1 The users (stakeholders) of financial information produced by a business.

Reflective questions

4 | In which category of users or stakeholders do you think the following fit?
  (a)   The managing director of Smart Ltd.
  (b)   Mr Taylor, who is thinking about buying some shares in Sainsbury.
  (c)   Mr Harris, who is one of Smart Ltd's sales representatives.

5 | Which stakeholder is likely to be most interested in the growth in wealth of an organization and the profit relative to the money tied up in the organization?
  (a)   lenders
  (b)   investors
  (c)   employees
  (d)   none of the above.

1.4 Types of entity

So far we have examined the basic principles of accounting and their interpretation. We now go on to look at different types of **entity** in business, such as **sole traders**, **partnerships** and **limited companies**, and their capital structure. The accounts of the sole trader are a simple example of the capital structure. However, whether the capital structure is of a sole proprietorship or ten partners or a million shareholders, the interpretation of the basic principles remains the same. What is required as the number of owners multiply is an extension of the form of presentation of accounting information. We will now examine the changing capital structure as ownership of a business is extended, and the effect this has on the accounting information.

Sole traders

Sole traders are entities owned by one person and are the simplest form of business entity. A sole trader's major source of finance is his own savings and his ability to borrow often depends on the security of his business assets or private property. While borrowing makes possible a greater scale of operations, it subjects the borrower to limitations that creditors may impose. A sole trader is personally liable for any debts incurred by the business, so if the business does not generate enough cash to pay bills as they fall due, the sole trader's personal resources and assets will be used to satisfy debts.

KEY TERM

> **Sole trader** a business structure where an individual runs the organization on their own; there are numerous sole traders, e.g. driving instructors, wedding photographers

Partnership

A partnership exists between two or more people engaged in any activity in common with a view to profit. The greater the number of owners means that, in contrast to a sole trader, more finance becomes available, and this is a common reason for forming a partnership. Partnership is also a means of both sharing and managing the risks of business. Profits are divided among partners, often in accordance with the proportions in which they contributed capital to the business, though the partners can agree to divide profits in any way they wish. The rights and obligations of partners are usually defined by a written partnership agreement or oral agreement, and the existence of a partnership may be inferred from the conduct of the individuals concerned.

KEY TERM

> **Partnership** a business structure where two or more individuals run the organization together, e.g. accountants, solicitors

Limited company

A limited company is regarded as an entity that is separate from the parties who contribute capital to it. In the UK, companies are created and regulated by the Companies Act and have a legal personality of their own, distinct from the various groups – employees, owners, directors, managers – who have an interest in them.

KEY TERM

> **Limited company** a business structure where the business organization is separate from its owners, who invest in the organization by buying shares; the liability of the shareholders is limited to what they have invested or guaranteed to invest

Individuals (**shareholders**) contribute capital in agreed units usually referred to as **shares**, which have a **nominal value**, i.e. the price below which they cannot be issued, for example, £1, £10, etc. Where shareholders pay more than the nominal value of a share, the excess over the nominal value is called **share premium** and is recorded separately by the company. The amount of capital provided (or subscribed) by shareholders is referred to as **share capital**. The concept of being **limited by shares** means that the liability of the shareholders to creditors of the company is limited to the capital shareholders invest, that is, the nominal value of the shares and any premium paid in return for the issue of the shares by the company. A shareholder's personal assets are protected if the company cannot generate enough cash to pay its bills and becomes insolvent, but money already invested in the company may be lost.

A limited company may be private or public. A **private limited company** is not required by law to disclose as much about its activities and operations as a **public limited company**, and can only issue its shares privately. This is the major distinguishing feature between a private limited company and a public limited company, which can issue shares to the general public and trade them on a public **stock exchange**, though it is not compelled to do the latter. Table 1.1 below summarizes the different types of business.

TABLE 1.1 Different types of business

	Sole trader	Partnership	Limited company
Type of ownership	One owner	• Can have from 1 to 20 partners • Rights and duties are fixed by agreement • Subdivision of ownership interest requires agreement of all partners	• Can be divided into any number of shares • Each share carries defined legal rights and duties • Shares may be divided into classes with different legal attributes • A shareholder may hold any number of shares
Risk to owners	Unlimited	• Unlimited • Any partner is responsible for all the debts of the business	• Limited to a fixed amount per share, usually paid when the share is first issued
Management	At discretion of owner	• By agreement between partners	• In hands of directors elected by shareholders at annual meetings
Information available to public	None	• None	• The public can inspect registered information including annual accounting information which is registered with the Registrar of Companies • An annual audit of the information is made by qualified accountants
Withdrawal of funds	At discretion of owner	• By agreement among partners	• Dividends may be paid to shareholders only out of profits
Financing	Relatively restricted	• Relatively restricted	• Limited risk • The subdivision of interest and the law relating to borrowing makes financing simpler and cheaper than is the case with partnerships and sole traders
Constitution	None	• As agreed among partners • May be informal and need not be in writing	• Embodied in formal legal documents • Any alteration requires legal procedures, involving the consent of a specified proportion of the shareholders
Tax on income	Income tax	• Income tax	• Corporation tax
Termination	At will	• By agreement	• Perpetual succession unless liquidation

2 | List one advantage and one disadvantage of operating a business as a:
   (a) sole trader
   (b) partnership
   (c) limited liability company.

Reflective question

6 | Mr Smith has just opened a coffee shop and he and his wife have both put £10,000 into the business.
What form of business is the shop likely to be?

1.5 Legislation

The regulatory framework of accounting in the United Kingdom has been shaped by various factors, many of which are historical. The same is true of the accounting regulatory framework in other European countries. Attempts have been made to harmonize accounting across the European Union and the United States to ensure that financial statements are consistently prepared in accordance with a **true and fair view** no matter where the business entity is located.

In the United Kingdom the primary law relating to the disclosure of information in financial statements is the **Companies Act**, which contains detailed provisions regarding the applications of the basic accounting requirements. Accounts must reflect what has actually happened in the business and the information presented must not be misleading. The accounts are expected to be prepared on the basis of fundamental accounting principles and to comply with accounting rules.

The accounting rules are called the **accounting standards**, which are a set of professional declarations that establish the norms to be maintained for communicating accounting information, and are set, in the United Kingdom, by the **Accounting Standards Board (ASB).**

The Accounting Standard Board defines accounting standards as follows: 'Accounting standards are authoritative statements of how particular types of **transactions** and other events should be reflected in financial statements and accordingly compliance with accounting standards will normally be necessary for financial statements to give a true and fair view.'

The international financial reporting standards (IFRSs) are set by the **International Accounting Standards Board (IASB)**. The IASB is an independent establishment, whose objective is to standardize the accounting principles that are used in financial reporting throughout the world. The IASB committee consists of representatives of accountancy bodies from across the world. The members of IASB try to persuade the setters of national standards to publish accounting statements that are in accordance with the international standards. One of IASB's goals is to achieve international acceptance and recognition of the international standards.

In trying to achieve standardization of accounting statements, IASB aims to:

- make international investment decisions more compatible
- reduce the costs of converting financial statements made under one regime of accounting regulation to comply with those prepared under another (by multinational companies)

- encourage the growing number of national standard-making bodies to work in harmony
- provide accounting standards for countries that do not have their own standard-setting bodies.

We will now look at the underlying accounting concepts and the fundamental concepts contained in accounting standards that dominate the regulation of **financial statements**. Financial statements will include supporting information such as a report from the company chairman and another from the company auditor.

Reflective question

7 | Accounting standards are:
  (a) broad statements of guidance on accounting practice
  (b) effective mandatory statements of acceptable accounting practice
  (c) rules set out in the Companies Acts governing accounting practice
  (d) a particular form of accounting statement.

1.6 Underlying accounting concepts

A number of accounting concepts have been applied ever since financial statements were first produced for external reporting purposes. We will now look briefly at the following concepts:

- historical cost concept
- money measurement concept
- business entity concept
- time interval concept.

Historical cost concept

Assets of a company (e.g. a building owned by a company) are normally shown in the financial statements at a value based on their original cost. This approach is relatively objective because it is based on the actual invoices and other documents. For example, when a business entity buys a PC for £1,000, it receives an invoice or receipt for £1,000. This receipt is objective evidence of the cost of the PC.

Money measurement concept

Accounting information has traditionally been concerned only with those facts that can be measured in financial terms (i.e. expressed in terms of money) and most people agree to the financial value of a transaction. The advantage of such an approach is that a number of widely differing facts can be expressed in terms of a common measurement.

Reflective question

8 | What disadvantages can you think of in using the money measurement concept to prepare financial statements?

Business entity concept

The affairs of a business are totally separate from the non-business activities of its owners.

The items recorded in the accounting records of the business are therefore restricted to the transactions of the business. No matter what activities the proprietor(s) engage in outside the business, they are completely disregarded in the accounting records kept by the business. It is for this reason that funds or goods taken out of a business by its owners are treated as a reduction in their investment in the business, not as an expense of the business.

Time interval concept

One of the underlying principles of accounting is that financial statements are prepared at regular intervals of one year. For internal management purposes the financial statements may be prepared far more frequently, possibly on a monthly basis or even weekly.

1.7 Fundamental accounting concepts

Fundamental accounting concepts are enforced through regulation and legislation. These comprise a set of concepts considered so important that they have been enforced through accounting standards and the Companies Act. We now go on to look at the following fundamental concepts:

- going concern
- accruals concept (also known as matching concept)
- consistency
- prudence
- substance over form
- materiality.

Going concern

When preparing financial statements, values are based on the assumption that the business will continue into the foreseeable future. Therefore, the accounts are based on the assumption that there is neither the intention, nor the need, to reduce the scale of the company's operations or go into liquidation. The use of the **going concern** concept means that it is considered sensible to keep to the use of the historical cost concept when arriving at valuations of the company's funds, i.e. its assets.

ACTIVITY

3 | The annual report of a major public limited company included the following statement:

'The directors consider that the group and the company have adequate resources to remain in the operation for the foreseeable future and have therefore continued to adopt going concern basis in preparing the financial statements. As with all business forecasts the directors' statement cannot guarantee that the going concern basis will remain appropriate given the inherent uncertainty about the future events.' (Tesco plc Annual Report, 2008)

Explain why the going concern concept is of importance to a user of an annual report.

Accruals (matching) concept

Expenditure should be charged to the period that benefited from the expense incurred. This concept suggests that all revenue or other benefit received should be matched to the expenditure incurred in generating that revenue or benefit. Where expenditure has been incurred during a period for which revenue or benefit has not yet been received, the expenditure should be omitted from the calculation of profit for that period and accrued until the period when the revenue or benefit results. An example would be annual buildings insurance paid mid-period that is valid for the first six months of the next period. The accruals concept also applies in reverse when the benefit is received before expenditure occurs. An example would be electricity consumed before a period end not yet charged for as the billing date for electricity is after the period end.

Consistency

Each item should be treated in the same way in every period. There are a number of different ways in which some concepts can be applied. Each business must choose the approach that gives the most reliable picture of the business, not just for the current period, but also over time consistency. This is impossible if the approach is changed every year. The consistency convention suggests that when a method has been adopted for the accounting treatment of an item, the same method will be adopted for all subsequent occurrences of similar items.

Prudence

The accountant should be prudent when preparing financial statements. In other words, if something is in doubt, plan for the worst and, if a transaction has not yet been completed ignore any possible benefits that may arise from it. It is the accountant's duty to endeavour to present accurate facts in the financial statements. Assets must not be valued too highly. Nor should amounts owed by a business be understated. Otherwise, people might be misled into lending to or granting credit to a business when they would not have done had they known the true facts.

The prudence concept requires that all losses (costs) are recognized immediately they become known whereas all gains (revenue) should be recognized only when they are realized (certain to be received). As a result, profits will normally be understated.

A number of criteria must be observed before revenue may be recognized as having been realized:

- goods or services have been provided for the buyer
- the buyer accepts liability to pay for the goods or services
- the monetary value of the goods or services has been established
- the buyer is able to pay for the goods or services.

This is not necessarily going to be the same as either the time when the order is received or when the customer pays for the goods.

Substance over form

Each transaction should be included in the financial statements so as to show its true economic impact on the business. The legal form of a transaction can differ from its real substance. Where this happens, accounting should show the transaction in accordance with its real substance; that is, on the basis of how the transaction affects the economic situation of the firm. This means that accounting may not reflect the exact legal position concerning that transaction. This most frequently applies to leases and hire purchase transactions. Hire purchase is used by businesses to purchase assets in stages. Take the example of a machine being acquired by hire purchase. Legally, it does not belong to the business until the last instalment is paid and an option has been taken up by the business to become the owner of the machine. Effectively, the business has used the machine since it first acquired it in the same way as it would have done had it paid for it in full at that time. The substance over form concept says that the business should show the full value of the machine being bought on hire purchase in its financial statements as though it were legally owned by the business (as an asset), and show the full amount still owing to the supplier of the machine separately as a liability.

Materiality

The accounting concepts already discussed have become accepted in the business world, their assimilation having taken place over many years. However, there is one overriding rule applied to anything that appears in a financial accounting statement – it should be material. That is, it should be of interest to the stakeholders – those people who make use of financial accounting statements. It need not be material to every stakeholder, but it must be material to a stakeholder before it merits inclusion.

Accounting does not serve a useful purpose if the effort of recording a transaction in a certain way is not worthwhile. Thus, if a box of paper clips was bought it would be used up over a period of time, and a cost is incurred every time someone uses a paper clip. It is possible to record this as an expense every time it happens, but obviously the price of a box of paper clips is so little that it is not worth recording it in this fashion. The box of paper clips is not a material item, and therefore would be charged in full as an expense in the period it was bought, irrespective of the fact that it could last for more than one accounting period. In other words, do not waste time in the elaborate recording of trivial items.

Accountants distinguish between what they call **revenue expenditure** (expenditure on items that are not intended to be kept for very long, such as goods for resale and raw materials; or the benefits of which only last a short time, such as labour costs) and **capital expenditure** (expenditure on non-current assets, i.e. items purchased to be used in the business, such as machines, motor vehicles and buildings which are not intended to be resold). The definition of revenue expenditure is unhelpful, given that labour is not kept at all but wages are paid.

However, if an item is not material, it will always be treated as revenue expenditure. For example, a stapler would normally be classified as a non-current asset – it is likely to be used for a long time – and, therefore, as an item of capital expenditure. However, in reality, it would be treated as an expense in the period in which it was bought because it is not a material item.

Businesses operate their own individual rules to determine what is material and what is not. There is no law or regulation in the UK that defines these rules – the decision as to what is material and what is not is dependent upon judgement. A business may decide that all items under £200 should be treated as expenses in the period in which they were bought, even though they may be used for the following ten years. Another business may fix the limit at £500. Different limits may be set for different types of item.

1.8 The statement of principles

The Statement of Principles describes fundamental rules but does not contain requirements on how financial statements should be prepared or presented. Company accounts are prepared under the requirements of company law and accounting standards.

The primary purpose of the Statement of Principles is to provide a frame of reference to help the Accounting Standards Board to develop new accounting standards and review existing ones. The Statement of Principles contains and deals with the following key issues:

- the objectives of financial statements
- the qualitative characteristics of financial information
- the elements of financial statements
- recognition in financial statements
- measurement in financial statements
- presentation of financial information
- accounting for interests in other entities.

In deciding what information should be included in financial statements, when it should be included and how it should be presented, the aim is to ensure that financial statements yield useful information. Figure 1.2 outlines the key characteristics of useful financial information.

FIGURE 1.2 The characteristics of useful financial information

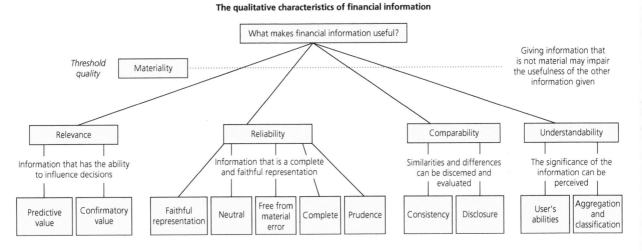

Financial information is useful if it is:

- **relevant** – information has the ability to influence the economic decisions of users and is provided in time to influence those decisions
- **reliable** – information can be depended upon to represent faithfully what it either purports to represent or could reasonably be expected to represent, and therefore reflects the substance of the transactions and other events that have taken place
- **comparable** – information enables users to discern and evaluate similarities in, and differences between, the nature and effects of transactions and other events over time and across different reporting entities
- **understandable** – information can be perceived by users that have a reasonable knowledge of business and economic activities and accounting and a willingness to study with reasonable diligence the information provided.

The ASB Statement of Principles is one of several national conceptual frameworks. Documents produced by leading accounting standard setters, such as in Australia, Canada, New Zealand and the USA, all utilize similar principles and explanations, though there are differences between them, some more significant than others. The US Financial Accounting Standards Board (FASB) pronouncements (a series of 'Concepts Statements') have been of particular importance in a worldwide context, given the USA's dominance in the global economy.

1.9 Audit and corporate governance

Company law subjects the management of a business to severe legal controls, including external audit, for the purposes of protecting the interests of the business's stakeholders, particularly its investors and creditors, and all others who deal with the business in one way and another. With the exception of small businesses, the financial statements will include a report from auditors. There are two types of **audit** – external audit and internal audit.

External audit

An external audit is carried out by professionals from outside the organization, who should be independent experts. They investigate the business's accounting systems and transactions and ensure that the financial statements have been prepared in accordance with the underlying concepts, and within the law and accounting standards. The purpose of an external audit is to investigate whether the financial statements being reported reflect a true and fair view. A satisfactory audit report provides considerable reassurance to the users of the accounts that those accounts are reliable. The auditor's report is addressed, not to the management of an organization, but to the shareholders.

Internal audit

An internal audit is a management tool which aims to verify that accounting procedures are being carried out as they should be. It often has the incidental benefit of recommending improvements to the system. Standards and procedures in an internal audit are thus a matter for the management of individual organizations.

In addition to the audit of accounts, the auditors of a company are required to review the director's statement on the company's compliance with the code of best practice and to draw any attention to any non-compliance. The term **corporate governance** is used to describe the ways in which companies are directed and controlled. The corporate governance system promotes qualified, honest people and structures employees' financial incentives to motivate them to maximize the value of a business.

An optimal corporate governance system is difficult to develop in practice, not least because the interests of shareholders, managers and other stakeholders often conflict. A firm's shareholders want managers to work hard and to protect shareholders' interests, which may lead managers to run the company to benefit the shareholders at the expense of creditors or other stakeholders who do not have a direct say in corporate governance.

1.10 Summary

Key ideas

Accounting information systems

- provide a method of systematically recording and evaluating business activities
- a large portion of the information that stakeholders require is derived from accounting data.

Stakeholders

- stakeholders are the various groups who usually have a need to access financial information about an organization
- stakeholders include owners, managers, employees, lenders, suppliers, customers, competitors, analysts, government and the public.

Types of business organization

- the principal forms of business organization are sole trader, partnership and limited company
- although sole traders, or single-owner businesses, are probably the most numerous, the corporate form of business is the most important to the economy
- the partnership form is often used when two or more sole traders merge into one business
- a company is a corporation that has an existence, rights and duties that are completely separate from its shareholders. This means that liability of shareholders is usually limited in some way.

Legislation

- Companies Act – law requires companies to publish annual audited accounts containing a number of required disclosures. All companies have a legal requirement to prepare statements that are true and fair.
- Accounting Standards Board (ASB) – the UK accounting standards-setting body
- International Accounting Standards Board (IASB) – the international accounting standards-setting body.

Accounting concepts

- certain underlying and fundamental accounting concepts provide a framework for recording and reporting business transactions
- these concepts have been developed over time to provide general guides to making financial statements as objective and as useful as possible
- there are six fundamental principles: matching, prudence, consistency, going concern, substance over form and materiality.

Statement of Principles

- the Statement of Principles reflects on the principles that affect the way that the financial statements are prepared
- it defines the attributes that information must have if it is to be included in the financial statements
- it describes how information should be presented in financial statements.

Audit

- auditors are required to report to shareholders whether the financial statements of an organization have been properly prepared in accordance with the Companies Act and the relevant accounting standards
- auditors must ascertain whether the financial statements give a true and fair view of the organization's financial position.

Corporate governance

- this refers broadly to the rules, processes or laws by which businesses are operated, regulated and controlled
- the company's auditors are required to review compliance to certain aspects of the code of best practice.

Review questions

1. Imagine a business recorded what it had sold, to whom, the date it was sold, the price it was sold at, and the date it received payment from the customer, along with similar data concerning the purchases made by the business. What information do you think could be produced from this data?

2. Which stakeholders will be using audited financial statements?

3. Once internal audit work has been found to be satisfactory there is no further need to review its work in the future. Would you agree with this statement? Explain your reasons.

Recommended reading

Laider, J. and Donaghy, P. (2008) *Understanding UK Annual Reports & Accounts, A Case Study Approach.* London: International Thompson Business Press.

Millichamp, A. (2009) *Auditing*, 9th edition, London: Thomson Learning.

Solomon, J. (2007) *Corporate Governance and Accountability*, 2nd edition, Chichester: John Wiley & Sons.

Useful websites

http://www.frc.org.uk/asb — describes the role of the Financial Reporting Council (FRC) in setting accounting standards

http://www.iasb.org/Home.htm — describes the role of the International Accounting Standards Board (IASB) in setting accounting standards

Recording transactions   2

'You have to know accounting. It's the **language of practical business** *life. It was a very useful thing to deliver to civilization. I've heard it came to civilization through Venice which of course was once the great commercial power in the Mediterranean. However,* **double-entry bookkeeping** *was a hell of an invention.'* (CHARLES THOMAS MUNGER (b.1924), Vice-chairman of Berkshire Hathaway Corporation, the diversified investment corporation chaired by investor Warren Buffett)

CHAPTER OUTLINE

2.1 Introduction

2.2 The accounting equation

2.3 T-accounts, debits and credits

2.4 Balancing the accounts

2.5 The trial balance

2.6 More T-accounts

2.7 Summary

CHAPTER OBJECTIVES

After carefully reading the text and completing the tasks and activities provided in this chapter you should have a better understanding and knowledge of:

- the need for financial records and financial statements

- the business entity and the dual aspect concepts

- the accounting equation

- the relationship between the accounting equation and double-entry bookkeeping

- recording transactions in the appropriate ledger accounts

- balancing off accounts at the end of an accounting period

- the preparation of a trial balance.

2.1 Introduction

An accounting transaction is a business activity or event that requires accounting recognition. The transactions of most businesses are numerous and complex, affecting many different items that appear on the financial statements. Therefore, a formal system of classification and recording is required so that data may be gathered for day-to-day management and for timely accounting reports. The system that accountants use to record transactions is known as **double-entry bookkeeping**. Double-entry bookkeeping is based on the **dual aspect** rule, i.e. a recognition that every transaction has a twofold effect which requires each transaction to be recorded in two locations within accounting records of the business.

> **KEY TERM**
>
> **Double-entry bookkeeping** a system of recording financial transactions that records each transaction as both a debit and a credit

Double-entry is a method of cross-checking accounting transactions. It is also an accounting process that one could describe as simply writing things down twice. That does not mean that when a company buys something it needs to write two cheques. It means that the accountant writes down the value of goods bought and the value of cheques that were given to the supplier. The two values should be the same because the accountant is entering the same amount twice, i.e. making a **double entry**.

> **Reflective question**
>
> 1 | What is meant by 'dual aspect'?

2.2 The accounting equation

When a business starts it has no money. The owner puts money in (known as **owner's capital**) and perhaps borrows money as well. This money is used to buy assets that are expected to bring financial benefits for the business in the future. If it were a manufacturing business, these assets might be premises, equipment and goods for sale.

> **KEY TERM**
>
> **Capital** is the value of the investment in the business by the owners. It is that part of the business that belongs to the owner; hence it is often described as the owner's interest. Capital must equal what the business owns (its assets) minus what is owes (its liabilities).

The accounting records separate out the finance put into the company by the owner (owner's capital) and the finance borrowed (a **liability** that needs to be repaid). The accounting records also separate out the **assets** bought from the finance used to buy the assets. The business can have assets only to the value of the finance it has available. The accounting records consequently will always reflect this fact in the following manner:

Assets		Liabilities
Resources	=	Sources of finance
(**owned** by an organization)		(**owed** by an organization)

Assets are the economic resources belonging to a business and can include *physical* or *tangible* possessions, e.g. property, fixtures and furniture, and *intangible assets*, i.e. non-physical possessions, e.g. copyright and patent rights.

However, the above equation ignores what the owners have invested in the business. In order to make it clear how the accounting equation relates to the owners' capital, it is usually shown as:

$$\text{Capital} = \text{Assets} - \text{Liabilities}$$

Liabilities are the opposite of assets. These are the amounts owed by the firm to outside parties.

When an owner contributes cash or other assets to a business, the business will experience an increase in assets and an increase in owners' capital. Conversely, when an owner withdraws assets from the business, both assets and owner's equity decrease.

Trade receivables is money owed to a business by customers. This in an important intangible asset in businesses that sell goods or services on credit.

Now that we have described the basic concepts underlying the accounting equation, let us illustrate its application with an example. (Remember that Capital = Assets – Liabilities!)

Worked Example

Transaction (1) On 1 June, you decide to invest your personal funds in a business. You do so by transferring £2,000 in cash from your private bank account. The business now has £2,000 invested in it. This is its capital. The business also has £2,000 in cash. So the £2,000 asset equals the £2,000 capital. This relationship between the assets and the capital can be expressed as an equation:

$$\text{£2,000 (capital)} = \text{£2,000 (cash)}$$

The equation captures the dual aspect of the transaction. The assets of the business have been increased by the capital that has been invested by the owner. There are no liabilities involved in this transaction.

Transaction (2) On 5 June, you decide to transfer £1,500 of the cash to a business bank account. The effect on the accounting equation is:

$$\text{£2,000 (capital)} = \text{£2,000} - \text{£1,500 (cash)} + \text{£1,500 (bank)}$$

You can see there has been a change on the asset side of the equation.

Transaction (3) On 6 June you borrow £500 in a loan from a bank to provide further financial help to the business. The assets will be increased by an inflow of £500 in cash, but £500 will be owed to the bank. The £500 owed is a liability and the bank has become a creditor of the business. The business has total assets of £2,500 (£1,500 in the bank account and £1,000 in cash). Its capital is £2,000 and it has a liability of £500. The equation reflects the borrowing as follows:

$$\text{£2,000 (capital)} = \text{£2,000} - \text{£1,500} + \text{£500 (cash)} + \text{£1,500 (bank)} - \text{£500 (loan)}$$

Again, you can see that there has been a change on the asset side of the equation.

ACTIVITY

1   Fill in the missing words in the following sentences.

     (a)   The accounting equation is reflected by _____ = _____ +

         _____ .

     (b)   Every transaction must be recorded _____ .

2.3 T-accounts, debits and credits

The basic component of the formal accounting system is the **account**, which is an individual record of increases and decreases in specific assets, liabilities and capital. A change to the accounting system is called an **entry** which is made in a **ledger**, which is a collection of individual records known as accounts.

The effect of entering a particular transaction once in one ledger account and again in another ledger account is to cause the balance on each of the two accounts either to increase or decrease (like in the accounting equation). Therefore, a transaction can either increase or decrease the total amount held in an account.

Account Name	
debit (dr) £	**credit (cr)** £

If a transaction increases an asset account, then the value of this increase must be recorded on the **debit** or left side of the asset account. If, however, a transaction decreases an asset account then the value of this decrease must be recorded on the **credit** or right side of the asset account. The converse of these rules applies to liability accounts and the capital account, as shown in the **T-accounts** below:

Asset Account	
debit (dr) £	**credit (cr)** £
Increases asset	Decreases asset

Liability Account	
debit (dr) £	**credit (cr)** £
Decreases liability	Increases liability

Capital Account	
debit (dr) £	**credit (cr)** £
Decreases capital	Increases capital

It will now be useful to work through the following example.

Worked Example

Transactions:

1   John Taylor who is an owner starts the business John Taylor Trading by investing £10,000. It is paid into a business bank account on 1 January 20X1.

2 | The business buys furniture for £800 on credit from Office Equip Ltd on 2 January 20X1.

3 | The business buys a computer with a cheque for £1,200 on 3 January 20X1.

4 | The business borrows £10,000 on loan from a bank on 4 January 20X1. The money is paid into the business bank account.

5 | The business pays Office Equip Ltd £400 by cheque on 5 January 20X1.

6 | The owner takes £100 from the bank for personal spending on 6 January 20X1.

Transaction (1): The owner starts the business with £10,000 paid into a business bank account on 1 January 20X1. (Following the rules we learned above, we need to debit an asset account and credit the capital account.)

Bank (asset account)

dr	£	cr	£
1/01/20X1 Capital*	10,000		

Capital Account

dr	£	cr	£
		1/01/20X1 Bank*	10,000

*Each T-account, when recording a transaction, names the corresponding T-account to show that the transaction reflects a double entry in the ledger.

Transaction (2): The business buys furniture for £800 on credit from Office Equip Ltd on 2 January 20X1. (We need to debit an asset account and credit a liability account.)

Furniture (asset account)

dr	£	cr	£
2/01/20X1 Office World Ltd	800		

Office Equip Ltd (liability account)

dr	£	cr	£
		2/01/20X1 Furniture	800

Transaction (3): The business buys a computer with a cheque for £1,200 on 3 January 20X1. (We need to debit an asset account and credit an asset account.)

Computer (asset account)

dr	£	cr	£
3/01/20X1 Bank	1,200		

Bank (asset account)

dr	£	cr	£
1/01/20X1 Capital	10,000	3/01/20X1 Computer	1,200

Transaction (4): The business borrows £10,000 on loan from a bank on 4 January 20X1. The money is paid into the business bank account. (We need to debit an asset account and credit a liability account.)

Bank (asset account)

dr		£	cr		£
1/01/20X1	Capital	10,000	3/01/20X1	Computer	1,200
4/01/20X1	Bank loan	10,000			

Bank loan (liability account)

dr		£	cr		£
			4/01/20X1	Bank	10,000

Transaction (5): The business pays Office Equip Ltd £400 by cheque on 5 January 20X1. (We need to debit a liability account and credit an asset account.)

Bank (asset account)

dr		£	cr		£
1/01/20X1	Capital	10,000	3/01/20X1	Computer	1,200
4/01/20X1	Bank loan	10,000	5/01/20X1	Office Equip Ltd	400

Office World Ltd (liability account)

dr		£	cr		£
5/01/20X1	Bank	400	2/01/20X1	Furniture	800

Transaction (6): The owner takes £100 from the bank for personal spending on 6 January 20X1. (We need to debit the capital account and credit an asset account.)

Bank (asset account)

dr		£	cr		£
1/01/20X1	Capital	10,000	3/01/20X1	Computer	1,200
4/01/20X1	Bank loan	10,000	5/01/20X1	Office Equip Ltd	400
			6/01/20X1	Capital	100

Capital

dr		£	cr		£
6/01/20X1	Bank	100	1/01/20X1	Bank	10,000

As there were only six transactions, it was probably not too difficult to record them. However, many businesses have to record hundreds of transactions per day. Having individual T-accounts within the ledger makes it much easier to collect the information from many different types of transactions. The next section explains how to balance each of these accounts.

Reflective questions

2 | In one sentence describe what is meant by each of the following terms:

   (a)   An account is _____.

   (b)   A ledger of accounts is _____.

   (c)   Debit is _____.

   (d)   Credit is _____.

3 | What is the purpose of a ledger account? Mr Jones is considering running a small shop which will sell newspapers and confectionery. List the accounts you consider he should keep. What factors have influenced your choice?

ACTIVITY

2 | The data below relate to the business of commodity dealer Mr Smith.
   Mr Smith starts a business with cash of £2,000.
   - Buys furniture for shop with cash of £300.
   - Pays £500 cash into the business bank account.
   - Buys a computer paying by cheque £200.
   - Invests £500 into the business bank account.
   - Buys a printer on credit from Office Equip Ltd.

Required:

Make a list of the names of the ledger accounts required to record these transactions. Write up the transactions in the T-accounts you have identified.

2.4 Balancing the accounts

At the end of an accounting period after entering numerous transactions, the ledger accounts may need to be balanced. Accounts are straightforward to balance off if they consist of only one type of entry, i.e. only debit entries or only credit entries. In this case, all the account entries are simply added up to get the balance on the account. However, when accounts consist of both debit and credit entries, the following procedure should be used to balance off the ledger accounts:

- Add up the amounts on each side of the account to find the totals.
- Enter the larger figure as the total for both the debit and credit sides.
- For the side that does not add up to this total, calculate the figure that makes it add up by deducting the smaller from the larger amount. Enter this figure so that the total adds up, and call it the balance carried down.
- This is usually abbreviated as **Balance c/d**.
- Enter the balance brought down (abbreviated as **Balance b/d** on the opposite side below the total figure. (The balance brought down is usually dated one day later than the balance carried down as one period has closed and another one has started.)

Worked Example

Using the rules above, we can now balance off all of John Taylor Ltd's ledger accounts starting with the bank account.

Bank

dr		£	cr		£
1/01/20X1	Capital	10,000	3/01/20X1	Computer	1,200
4/01/20X1	Bank loan	10,000	5/01/20X1	Office Equip Ltd	400
			6/01/20X1	Capital	100
			6/01/20X1	Balance c/d*	18,300
		20,000			**20,000**
7/01/20X1	Balance b/d	18,300			

*The balance on the bank account reflects that £20,000 has come into this asset account and £1,700 (£1,200 + £400 + £100) has gone out to leave a debit balance of £18,300. This is why on the opposite side to the 'Balance c/d' figure, a 'Balance b/d' figure is needed to represent a closing debit balance.

We balance off the capital account in the same way as we did the bank account.

Capital

dr		£	cr		£
6/01/20X1	Bank	100	1/01/20X1	Bank	10,000
6/01/20X1	Balance c/d	9,900			
		10,000			**10,000**
			7/01/20X1	Balance b/d	9,900

The Furniture account has a single entry on one side. This amount is the total as well as the balance in the account.

Furniture

dr		£	cr		£
1/01/20X1	Office Equip Ltd	**800**	6/01/20X1	Balance c/d	**800**
7/01/20X1	Balance b/d	800			

The account for the creditor Office Equip Ltd has a debit and a credit entry so we will use the method we used for the bank and the capital accounts.

Office World Ltd

dr		£	cr		£
5/01/20X1	Bank	400	2/01/20X1	Furniture	800
6/01/20X1	Balance c/d	400			
		800			**800**
			7/01/20X1	Balance b/d	400

The Computer and Bank loan accounts have single entries on one side like the Furniture account.

Computer

dr		£	cr		£
3/01/20X1	Bank	**1,200**	6/01/20X1	Balance c/d	**1,200**
7/01/20X1	Balance b/d	1,200			

Bank loan

dr		£	cr		£
6/01/20X1	Balance c/d	**10,000**	4/01/20X1	Bank	**10,000**
			7/01/20X1	Balance b/d	10,000

Reflective question

4 | For each of the transactions described below, indicate which accounts will be debited and credited.

- Payment to a creditor.
- Purchase of office equipment on credit.
- Purchase of motor vehicle, paying by cheque.

2.5 The trial balance

A **trial balance** is a list of all the balances in the ledger accounts. It does not form part of the double-entry process. It simply serves as a check to ensure that for every transaction, a debit recorded in one ledger account has been matched with a credit in another. The total of the debit balances should always equal the total of the credit balances.

The trial balance assists in the preparation of the main financial statements; the statement of financial position (SoFP) and the income statement.

The preparation of a trial balance is illustrated in the example below which is based on the balancing figures from the previous section. Making a list of the above balances brought down produces a trial balance as follows.

Worked Example

John Taylor Ltd
Trial balance as at 6 January 20X1

	dr	cr
	£	£
Bank	18,300	
Capital		9,900
Furniture	800	
Office Equip Ltd (a creditor)		400
Computer	1,200	
Bank loan		10,000
Total	**20,300**	**20,300**

It is always reassuring when a trial balance does balance. However, even when a trial balance is in balance, the accounts may still contain errors. A trial balance simply proves that, as recorded, debits equal credits. The following errors may not be detected by producing a trial balance:

- missing the recording or entering of a particular transaction
- entering a transaction more than once
- entering amounts in the wrong accounts
- making an error that offsets the effect of another error.

Several types of errors will cause a trial balance to be out of balance and often the only way to find them is to retrace each entry, check the arithmetic performed in balancing accounts, and make certain that no error has occurred in transcribing amounts or in adding the trial balance.

2.6 More T-accounts

Now we understand how to record capital, assets and liabilities, we can expand the main accounting equation:

$$Capital = Assets - Liabilities$$

The main goal of any business is to increase the owner's capital by earning income. The profit of a business is determined by subtracting the purchases and expenses incurred from the revenue earned. The owner's capital is increased by revenue and decreased by purchases and expenses. Therefore, a revised accounting equation can be shown as:

$$Capital + (Revenue - Purchases - Expenses) = Assets - Liabilities$$

Revenue the money a business earns by selling goods and services to its customers.

The owner of a business introduces capital at various times. There will always be some assets (usually cash) introduced into the business when the business is initially set up, called 'opening capital', but there may also be some amounts invested in the business at a later date, called 'capital introduced'. The owner many also withdraw assets from the business (usually cash) as it progresses and makes a profit. The accounting equation can now be extended further:

$$(Opening\ Capital + Capital\ Introduced - Drawings + (Revenue - Purchases - Expenses) = Assets - Liabilities$$

Transactions involving opening capital, capital introduced and drawings are all recorded in the capital account.

Expenses, otherwise known as costs in the accounting world, are incurred by the business in the process of earning revenue. Examples include rent and rates, lighting and heating, repairs and renewals, and employees' salaries.

Now we understand the concepts underlying the extended accounting equation, let us illustrate its application with an example that includes the use of revenue (sales) accounts and expense accounts. The example also shows how to deal with sales on credit and purchases on credit. Rent is used as an example of an expense account.

Worked Example

Ray Tailor decided to open a shop selling wooden gifts. During his first month of trading (January 20X6) Ray had the following transactions:

01 Jan	Started in business by putting £9,000 of his own money into the business bank account.
05 Jan	Bought a van, paying by cheque (£2,000).
10 Jan	Purchased goods for resale, paying by cheque (£3,000).
12 Jan	Transferred £200 from the bank account to the cash account.
15 Jan	Sold goods on credit, valued at £1,300, to Mr Hill.
20 Jan	Purchased goods on credit from Tree Ltd, costing £4,500.
22 Jan	Sold goods for £5,500 cash.
25 Jan	Paid Tree Ltd the sum of £2,800, paying by cheque.
30 Jan	Paid rent (£700) by cheque.

We can start by entering the transactions in the relevant accounts, in date order. Each transaction must have both a debit and a credit entry. Once all the transactions are complete the accounts can be balanced off.

Capital Account

		£			£
31 Jan X6	Bal c/d	**9,000**	1 Jan X6	Bank a/c	**9,000**
			1 Feb X6	Bal c/d	9,000

Bank Account

		£			£
1 Jan X6	Capital a/c	9,000	5 Jan X6	Van a/c	2,000
			10 Jan X6	Purchases a/c	3,000
			12 Jan X6	Cash a/c	200
			25 Jan X6	Tree a/c	2,800
			30 Jan X6	Rent a/c	700
					8,700
			31 Jan X6	Bal c/d	300
		9,000			**9,000**
1 Feb X6	Bal b/d	300			

Van Account

		£			£
10 Jan X6	Bank a/c	**2,000**	31 Jan X6	Bal c/d	**2,000**
1 Feb X6	Bal b/d	2,000			

Purchases Account

		£			£
10 Jan X6	Bank a/c	3,000	31 Jan X6	Bal c/d	7,500
20 Jan X6	Tree a/c	4,500			
		7,500			**7,500**
1 Feb X6	Bal b/d	7,500			

Cash Account

		£			£
12 Jan X6	Bank a/c	200	31 Jan X6	Bal c/d	5,700
22 Jan X6	Sales a/c	5,500			
		5,700			**5,700**
1 Feb X6	Bal b/d	5,700			

Sales (revenue) Account

		£			£
			15 Jan X6	Mr Hill a/c	1,300
31 Jan X6	Bal c/d	6,800	22 Jan X6	Cash a/c	5,500
		6,800			**6,800**
			1 Feb X6	Bal b/d	6,800

Mr Hill (receivables) Account

		£			£
15 Jan X6	Sales	**1,300**	31 Jan X6	Bal c/d	**1,300**
1 Feb X6	Bal b/d	1,300			

Tree Ltd (payables) Account

		£			£
25 Jan X6	Bank a/c	2,800	20 Jan X6	Purchases a/c	4,500
31 Jan X6	Bal c/d	1,700			
		4,500			**4,500**
			1 Feb X6	Bal b/d	1,700

Rent (expense) Account

		£			£
30 Jan X6	Bank a/c	**700**	31 Jan X6	Bal c/d	**700**
1 Feb X6	Bal b/d	700			

Once the accounts have been balanced off at the end of the period (31 January X6) and the balances have been brought down at the start of the next period (1 February X6), you can produce a trial balance to help check the accuracy of the entries.

Trial Balance at 31 January X6

	£	£
Capital		9,000
Bank	300	
Van	2,000	
Purchases	7,500	
Cash	5,700	
Sales		6,800
Mr Hill	1,300	
Tree Ltd		1,700
Rent	700	
	17,500	**17,500**

ACTIVITY

3 | The following question will aid your understanding of how to write up transactions into T-accounts.

On 1 March 20X5, Peter Davidson started a business selling multi-coloured walking sticks. Please write up the following transactions into the relevant T-accounts.

01 Mar X5	Peter invested £1,000 into his business bank account.
02 Mar X5	Peter bought some walking sticks for resale, costing £450, paying by cheque.
03 Mar X5	Peter sold six walking sticks at a price of £10 each, being paid in cash.
04 Mar X5	He transferred £50 from the cash account to the bank account.

Once you have finished entering the transactions, balance off the accounts at 5 March 20X5.

You are now able to produce a trial balance for Peter as at 5 March 20X5.

Reflective question

5 | State whether each of the following errors would be discovered as a result of preparing a trial balance:

(a) £765 has been entered in both ledger accounts instead of £675.

(b) £1,000 has been put in the Cash account instead of the Purchases account.

(c) The debit column in an account has been overstated by £100.

2.7 Summary

Key ideas

Transactions
- a transaction is an event carried out in any business
- all transactions have a twofold effect. A double-entry system records that twofold effect.

Accounting equation
- the accounting equation is represented by the formula: Capital = Assets – Liabilities
- the accounting equation underpins the dual aspect rule and forms the basis for accounting records.

Rules of debit and credit
- the left side of an account is always the debit side; the right is always the credit side
- for every debit entry there must be a credit entry
- increases in assets are debit entries; increases in liabilities and capital are credit entries
- the normal balance of any account appears in the side for recording increases.

Accounts
- an account is a recorded history of a particular transaction
- a book of accounts is known as a ledger.

Balancing accounts
- accounts are balanced periodically
- balancing an account requires adding the entire respective debit and credit entries, subtracting one total from the other, and arriving at the net balance.

Trial balance
- the accuracy of the bookkeeping is tested by preparing a trial balance
- the trial balance lists the debit balances and all the credit balances extracted from each of the accounts throughout the ledger. If the two totals agree, it means that the bookkeeping procedures have been carried out accurately.

Review questions

1. Here are some transactions in respect of a new business that was started on Day 1:

Day	Transaction
1	Started business by paying a cheque for £80,000 into the business bank account.
2	Purchase of machinery by cheque £20,000.
3	Purchase of inventory on credit £46,000.
4	Goods are sold for £10,000. The customer pays by cheque.
5	Payment of £30,000 to the supplier of the goods purchased on Day 3. This is a part-payment of the total amount due.
6	Goods are sold on credit for £10,500.
7	The owner of the business writes a cheque to withdraw £3,000 from the business.
8	A business loan of £100,000 is received by cheque.

Required

(a) Make a list of the names of the accounts required to record these transactions.

(b) Write up the transactions in the T-accounts you have identified in part (a) above:

You will need to create an account for drawings to record the removal from the business of £1,500 by the owner. Drawings are recorded in the account as debit entries.

2. Miss Samphire has started a business as a jeweller. Her transactions for the first ten days of trading are as follows:

Day	Transaction
1	£300,000 is paid into the business bank account.
2	Miss Samphire spends £250,000 buying a retail shop.
3	Miss Samphire buys inventory of £40,000 on credit.
4	Miss Samphire spends £20,000 on fittings for her shop.
5	A watch is sold for £500. The sale proceeds are paid into the bank account.
6	£2,000 is paid to the payables of the business (the people and businesses to whom money is owed).
7	A ring is sold on credit for £1,500.
8	Miss Samphire writes herself a cheque for £5,000.
9	Miss Samphire borrows £100,000 from the bank for the business.
10	A cheque for £7,000 is paid to the creditors.

Required

Write up these transactions in T-accounts, extract the balances and produce a trial balance.

3. The following are some of the accounts of Williamson Ltd.:

Mr Smith

	£		£
Balance	28,000		
Sales	36,000		

Mr Johnson

	£		£
Balance	93,000		
Sales	29,000		

Office equipment

	£		£
Balance	213,000		
Cash	98,000		
Cash	1,300		

Office expenses

	£		£
Balance	129,000		
Sales	9,000		

Wages

	£		£
Balance	100,000		
Sales	50,000		

Some additional information was discovered:

(i) The goods debited to Mr Smith's account (£36,000) had been sold to Mr Johnson.

(ii) Mr Smith has recently been declared bankrupt. (You can use a bad debts account to reflect this.)

(iii) The £1,300 debited to office equipment had been for a supply of stationery.

(iv) The £50,000 debited to the wages account was cash drawn by Mr Williamson.

Required:

(a) Prepare the entries necessary to reflect these facts.

(b) Show the correct accounts.

4. A trial balance extracted from the accounting records of a trader did not balance and the following errors were discovered (in the original trial balance the credits exceeded the debits by £260,000):

(a) Sales account undercast by £20,000.

(b) Office wages of £180,000 shown on credit side of the trial balance.

(c) Credit sales of £90,000 completely omitted from the accounts.

(d) Credit purchases for £60,000 included in the purchase account but omitted from the personal account.

(e) Goods bought on credit for £40,000 credited to wrong receivables account.

(f) Office equipment bought for £2,100 debited to the purchases account.

Required:

Prepare a new trial balance which corrects the discovered errors.

5. Fatima has been in a business for some years. The following balances were brought forward in her accounts as at 1 January 20X1.

	Dr	Cr
	£	£
Bank	10,000	
Capital		40,000
Cash	2,000	
Jeremy		4,000
Michael	12,000	
Furniture	20,000	
	£44,000	**£44,000**

During the year to 31 December 20X1 the following transactions took place:
- Goods bought from Jeremy on credit for £60,000.
- Cash sales of £40,000.
- Cash purchases of £30,000.
- Goods sold to Michael on credit for £100,000.
- Cheques sent to Jeremy totalling £58,000.
- Cheques received from Michael totalling £90,000.
- Cash received from Michael amounting to £14,000.
- Office expenses paid in cash totalling £18,000.
- Purchase of delivery van paid by cheque £24,000.
- Cash transfers to bank account totalling £6,000.

Required:
(a) Compile Fatima's accounts for the year 31 December 20X1, balance off the accounts and bring down the balances as at 1 January 20X2.
(b) Extract a trial balance as at 31 December 20X1.

Recommended reading

Cox, D. & Fardon, M. (2005) *Accounting: The Basics of Financial and Management Accounting,* Worcester: Osborne Books Limited.

Harrison, I. (2009) *Accounting, AZ Handbook,* 3rd edition, Chippenham: Philip Allan.

Jones, R. (2008) *Business Accounting,* 3rd edition, Ormskirk: Causeway Press.

Wood, F. & Sangster, A. (2008) *Business Accounting 1,* 11th edition, Harlow: FT Prentice-Hall.

3 The Statement of Financial Position

'It sounds extraordinary but it's a fact that **balance sheets** *can make* **fascinating** *reading.'* (MARY ARCHER)

CHAPTER OUTLINE

3.1 Introduction

3.2 The basic statement of financial position

3.3 Understanding the terminology

3.4 The accounting equation

3.5 Preparing a statement of financial position

3.6 Company statements of financial position

3.7 Published statements of financial position

3.8 Limitations of the statement of financial position

3.9 Summary

CHAPTER OBJECTIVES

After carefully reading the text and completing the tasks and activities provided in this chapter you should have a better understanding and knowledge of:

- the purpose of the statement of financial position

- the contents of the statement of financial position

- the terminology used in a statement of financial position

- the presentation of the statement of financial position

- the limitations of the statement of financial position

3.1 Introduction

A business needs to know what it owns, where it got the money from to buy what it owns and the amount it owes to others. It does this formally in a financial statement. In the UK many companies call this financial statement a **balance sheet,** but increasingly the term statement of financial position (SoFP) is used in the UK and elsewhere. A business could produce a statement of financial position every day, but this would be time-consuming and expensive. Therefore, most businesses produce a statement of financial position annually, at the end of each accounting year.

KEY TERM

> **Balance sheet** a term widely used in the UK to refer to a financial statement that shows the assets, liabilities and capital of a business at a given point in time; another term used for balance sheet is **statement of financial position (SoFP).**

A statement of financial position is a useful statement for stakeholders who have an interest in the business, including the owner, managers who run the business on a daily basis and banks who may lend the business money.

As the statement of financial position summarizes the progress of a business at a given point in time, it is the key document used by businesses to support requests for external funding.

CASE STUDY   Here's how a good balance sheet can help to improve a business

Sandeep Sud is a qualified solicitor who also runs a school uniform business in partnership with his parents. The business is based in Hounslow and has four full-time employees. To gauge how the business is progressing, Sandeep uses a balance sheet. It has also been a key factor in securing a bank loan for the improvement and expansion of the company premises. Sandeep used the balance sheet to secure a loan.

"Having a strong balance sheet helped when it came to borrowing. When we first applied for a refurbishment loan we couldn't provide up-to-date accounts to the bank manager. This could have been a problem, but we quickly got our accounts in order and the loan was approved straightaway. Because our balance sheet was strong, the bank thought we were a good risk. Although we decided not to draw down on the loan – because we used cash flow instead – it did open our eyes to the importance of a strong balance sheet."

Source: http://www.businesslink.gov.uk/bdotg/action/ detail?type=CASE%20STUDIES&itemId=1075431500

 ## 3.2 The basic statement of financial position

The statement of financial position is a snapshot of the financial position of the business at a given point in time. It shows the value of all assets (the things that the business owns) including cash, the value of all liabilities (the amounts the business owes) and the value of the capital (the owner's investment in the business).

KEY TERM

> **Capital** of the business is used to buy **assets** that can be used to generate revenue. Assets can be divided into two categories: **non-current assets** and **current assets.** Non-current assets are likely to be kept for more than a year whereas current assets are likely to be changed into cash within a year.

Liabilities can also be divided into two categories: **current liabilities** and **non-current liabilities**. Current liabilities are debts that need to be paid within a year, whereas non-current liabilities are debts that need to be paid after more than one year.

There is a standard format for preparing a statement of financial position that contains some technical terminology. We will start by having a look at the basic layout of a statement of financial position for a sole trader and then we will look at the meaning of the wording used.

A.N. Individual
Statement of Financial Position as at 31 December 20X1

	£	£
Assets		
Non-current assets		
Equipment	4,000	
Fittings	500	
Motor vehicles	7,400	11,900
Current assets		
Inventory	2,300	
Receivables	1,500	
Bank and cash	1,200	5,000
Total assets		**16,900**
Capital		15,600
Current liabilities		
Payables		1,300
Capital plus liabilities		**16,900**

All statements of financial position must balance and show that the total assets equal the capital plus liabilities. You can see in the above example that both total £16,900.

Net assets = Capital

1 | Alex provides you with the following information:

	£
Non-current assets	23,400
Current assets	13,800
Current Liabilities	12,450

Calculate the value of Alex's net assets and the capital.

3.3 Understanding the terminology

KEY TERM

Non-current assets are assets that are primarily bought with the intention of being used in the business over a period of years to generate revenue — not with the intention of resale. Examples include land and buildings. (Note that the terminology used may vary: for example, land and buildings may also be referred to as freehold premises.) Non-current assets are usually shown in order, showing the assets that are going to be held in the business for the longest first.

Examples of non-current assets:

- land and buildings
- plant and machinery
- fixture and fittings
- motor vehicles.

KEY TERM

Current assets are assets that are expected to be sold or converted into another form within one year.

Current assets include items such as **inventory.** A retail business will bulk-buy, i.e. buy large quantities of goods such as baked beans, and re-sell them in smaller quantities. In a manufacturing business the inventory may include raw materials, work-in-progress and finished goods. A car manufacturer would have an inventory including parts, cars on the assembly line and new cars. Another word used for inventory is **stock**.

KEY TERM

Inventory is made up of goods purchased by the business for resale at a profit.

When the inventory is sold the customer is usually given a period of time (e.g. 28 days) in which to pay for the goods. During this time the amount owing by the customer is shown in the **accounts receivable**. Once the customer pays, the accounts receivable is converted into cash. (Some older texts may refer to the accounts receivable as debtors.) Current assets are listed in liquidity order, showing the movement through the trade cycle.

KEY TERM

Accounts receivable shows the money owed to the business.

Current assets (in liquidity order) are:

- inventory
- accounts receivable
- cash at bank
- cash in hand.

A **liability** is an amount of money owed by the business that must be paid at some future date. The statement of financial position shows the value of all of the debts the business is responsible for. Liabilities can be divided into two categories: current liabilities and non-current liabilities.

KEY TERM

Current liabilities are debts that the business must pay within one year. They include items such as a **bank overdraft**, that are technically repayable on demand (although, in reality many businesses use an overdraft on a more or less permanent basis).

Current liabilities:

- bank overdraft
- loans
- accounts payable
- taxation.

KEY TERM

Accounts payable shows the total value of any money owed by the business to suppliers or service providers, such as an outstanding electricity bill. Other current liabilities include any amount owed to HM Revenue and Customs for taxation and loans due for repayment within twelve months. Some older texts may refer to the accounts payable as creditors.

Non-current liabilities:

- Loans

KEY TERM

Non-current liabilities are amounts owing that are not due for repayment in the next twelve months. At this stage of your studies a more in-depth look at non-current liabilities is not required.

Reflective questions

1 Which of the following are assets?
   - inventory
   - sales
   - fixtures
   - expenses
   - buildings.

2 Which of the following are liabilities?
   - buildings
   - loan from E Smith
   - motor vehicles
   - accounts payable
   - accounts receivable.

 3.4 The accounting equation

We can see from the above examples that there are two parts to every statement of financial position: the assets minus the liabilities and the capital. In every example these two parts are equal, i.e. they balance. This can be written in the form of an equation:

Assets – Liabilities = Capital

Capital and liabilities are sources of finance that are used to buy assets. Therefore the equation is sometimes written in the format:

$$\text{Assets} = \text{Capital} + \text{Liabilities}$$

Worked Example

A has assets of £20,000 and liabilities of £7,000. What is the value of the capital?

Solution:
20,000 – 7,000 = 13,000
The capital will be valued at £13,000

ACTIVITY

2 | B has capital valued at £10,000 and knows the liabilities are £2,000. Calculate the value of the assets.

3.5 Preparing a statement of financial position

At the end of each accounting period a trial balance is prepared, which is a list of all the balances in the accounting records of the business. A trial balance is used to check that the double-entry bookkeeping has been carried out accurately. You were shown how to prepare a trial balance in Chapter 2.

A trial balance

	£	£
Motor vehicles	8,900	
Cash at bank	4,000	
Loan		11,000
Inventory	8,000	
Accounts receivable	2,700	
Capital		12,600
	23,600	**23,600**

The column on the left contains what are referred to as the debit balances (e.g. motor vehicles £8,900) and the column on the right contains the credit balances (e.g. loan £11,000). The trial balance provides a useful summary of the accounting records, from which a statement of financial position can be produced.

Having looked at the basics of the statement of financial position, we will now consider a more detailed pro-forma statement of financial position. This will be a useful point of reference when you start to produce your own statements of financial position.

M.Y. Name
Statement of Financial Position as at 31 December 20X2

	£	£
Assets		
Non-current assets		
Land and buildings	110,000	
Plant and equipment	46,000	
Fixtures and fittings	3,100	
Motor vehicles	15,200	
		174,300
Current assets		
Inventory	9,600	
Accounts receivable	4,100	
Cash at bank	5,300	
Cash in hand	200	19,200
Total assets		**193,500**
Capital		65,400
Non-current liabilities		
Loan		100,000
Current liabilities		
Bank overdraft	27,000	
Accounts payable	1,100	**28,100**
		193,500

The following steps can be used when preparing a statement of financial position:

1 Start by writing the title, stating the name of the individual the statement of financial position is being prepared for and the statement of financial position as at the relevant date.

2 Then you need to list the assets. Start with the non-current assets and total them.

3 Next list the current assets in order of liquidity, total them and add them to the total for the non-current assets. This gives the *total assets* figure. Double-underline this as it is the end of the first part of the statement of financial position.

4 Then show the capital.

5 Next show the liabilities, starting with the current liabilities which you need to list and total.

6 Then list the non-current liabilities. Total them and add them to the total of the current liabilities. This gives you the *total liabilities* figure.

7 If the total assets do not equal the total of the capital plus the liabilities, the SoFP does not balance and therefore you must have made a mistake. At this point, you need to go back through your work and find out where you have gone wrong.

It will now be useful to work through the following example.

Worked Example

Wendy produced the following trial balance for her beauty clinic on 30 September 20X9.

	£	£
Buildings	68,000	
Equipment	14,000	
Motor vehicles	11,000	
Inventory	2,400	
Cash at bank	1,000	
Accounts payable		800
Bank loan		70,000
Capital		25,600
	96,400	96,400

In addition Wendy provided the following information:

The bank loan is due for repayment in three years' time. There are no accounts receivable as all customers pay in cash.

The solution will show a statement of financial position for Wendy as at 30 September 20X9.

Solution:

Wendy

Statement of Financial Position as at 30 September 20X9

	£	£
Assets		
Non-current assets		
Buildings	68,000	
Equipment	14,000	
Motor vehicles	11,000	
		93,000
Current assets		
Inventory	2,400	
Cash at bank	1,000	3,400
Total assets		96,400
Capital		25,600
Non-current liabilities		
Loan		70,000
Current liabilities		
Accounts payable	800	
		800
		96,400

In the statement of financial position we have looked at so far we have shown the capital as one figure. However, more details may be given including the opening balance, any capital introduced, the profit or loss for the year and any drawings.

> **KEY TERM**
>
> **Opening balance** shows the capital that had been invested in the business at the start of the accounting period; this will be the same as the closing balance on the capital account at the end of the previous accounting period.

> **KEY TERM**
>
> **Capital introduced** shows the value of all assets the owner has invested in the business during the accounting period. This is likely to be in the form of cash but may include an asset such as a motor vehicle. If there is sufficient capital in the business the owner may not need to introduce any more during the accounting period and, therefore, in some examples there will be no capital introduced.

> **KEY TERM**
>
> **Drawings** show the value of any assets that the owner has taken out of the business during the accounting period, which is usually in the form of cash.

The profit or loss the business makes during an accounting period is calculated in an income statement, which you will find out about in Chapter 4. If the business has made a profit, this is added to the value of the capital; if the business has made a loss, this will be deducted.

Worked Example

Charlotte runs a hairdressing salon and has provided the following trial balance for the year end 31 March 20X3.

	£	£
Fixtures and fittings	24,000	
Loan		15,000
Profit for the year		14,800
Inventory	3,300	
Accounts receivable	100	
Accounts payable		500
Bank balance	1,700	
Motor vehicles	13,000	
Capital introduced 01.04.X2		20,000
Cash	200	
Drawings	8,900	
Tax due to HMRC		900
	51,200	**51,200**

Charlotte has also provided the following information: the loan is due for repayment in 20X8.

The solution will show a statement of financial position for Charlotte as at 31 March 20X3.

In this example, the assets, liabilities and capital are shown in a random order in the trial balance. Therefore, you need to think about the layout of the statement of financial position (refer to the previous M.Y. Name example) and look through the trial balance to see if you can find the items to go in each section. It may be worthwhile ticking off each item in the trial balance as it is used to ensure nothing is missed out.

Solution:

Charlotte
Statement of Financial Position as at 31 March 20X3

	£	£
Assets		
Non-current assets		
Fixtures and fittings	24,000	
Motor vehicles	13,000	
		37,000
Current assets		
Inventory	3,300	
Accounts receivable	100	
Cash at bank	1,700	
Cash in hand	200	5,300
Total assets		**42,300**
Capital		
Opening balance		20,000
Add profit for the year		14,800
		34,800
Less drawings		8,900
Non-current liabilities		25,900
Loan		**15,000**
Current liabilities		
Accounts payable	500	
Taxation	900	1,400
Net assets		**42,300**

Reflective question

3 | Which of the following assets are current assets?
- Inventory
- Offices
- Office furniture
- Current account at bank
- Accounts receivable
- Vans
- Machinery
- Cash kept in a tin
- Factory

3.6 Company statements of financial position

So far in this chapter you have been learning how to prepare a statement of financial position for a sole trader. Being a sole trader is a risky business because the individual running the business is personally liable for the debts and in times of difficulty this could cause bankruptcy. In contrast, a company has **limited liability** and, therefore, the owners will never be required to input more than an agreed amount of capital.

> **Sole trader** is an individual in business on his or her own.

KEY TERM

Much of the detail in the statement of financial position of a limited company is the same as in the statement of financial position of a sole trader, although the statement of financial position of a company is usually more extensive. The sub-headings of the non-current assets, current assets, current liabilities and non-current liabilities remain the same, but the capital account in a sole trader's statement of financial position is replaced by **equity** in the company statement of financial position. A company is owned by shareholders who own **share capital,** which is part of the equity.

> **Share capital** is part of the capital in a business and is made up of ordinary shares or preference shares, or both.

KEY TERM

We will start by looking at the equity section of the company statement of financial position. Equity includes:

- share capital
- share premium account
- retained earnings
- other reserves.

> **Shareholder** Someone who owns (i.e. 'holds') shares in a company.

KEY TERM

For the shareholder, there are two main advantages gained by investing in shares in a company:

- the annual dividend
- the increase in value of the shares year upon year.

Of course, buying shares in a company involves risk. Any shareholder should be aware that the value of shares can go down as well as up!

> **Ordinary shares** are the most common type of share; they carry no dividend rights, but entitle the shareholder to a proportion of the profits after the preference share has been paid.

KEY TERM

There are two main types of share that a shareholder can invest in. These are:

- ordinary shares
- preference shares.

KEY TERM

Preference shares are shares that grant the holder a right to a set amount of dividend (e.g. 6 per cent preference shares are entitled to an annual dividend of six per cent).

Most companies do not pay out all of their earnings in the form of dividends but retain some to invest in the future of the business. As a result, the figure of retained earnings tends to increase each year. All company statements of financial position will show ordinary shares and retained earnings and some may include other components of equity where appropriate.

KEY TERM

Issued share capital is shown in the statement of financial position and this figure includes all shares (both preference and ordinary) actually sold to shareholders.

KEY TERM

Authorized share capital shows the maximum number of shares a company can issue, by the terms of the company's articles of incorporation.

KEY TERM

Retained earnings include the profits that the company has earned and retained in the company over the years it has been trading.

Other components of equity include:

- share premium
- revaluation surplus
- general reserve.

KEY TERM

The share premium shows the premium paid over and above the nominal value for shares in a company.

Worked Example

Five years ago a company was established with an authorized share capital of 500,000 £1 ordinary shares. After trading successfully for five years the company decided to issue 100,000 £1 ordinary shares at £1.50 each. On issue £100,000 would be shown as share capital and £50,000 would be shown as share premium.

There are other specific **reserves** such as the **revaluation reserve** that deals with an increase in value due to, say, the revaluation of a property or a **general reserve** that is non-specific.

The retained earnings and the other components of equity are owned by the ordinary shareholders.

Now you know the terminology used in the equity section of a company statement of financial position we can consider a pro-forma statement of financial position of a limited company. This will be a useful point of reference when you start to produce your own company statement of financial position.

A Company Ltd
Statement of Financial Position as at 31 December 20X3

	£	£	£
Assets			
Non-current assets			
Land and buildings		130,000	
Plant and equipment		46,000	
Fixtures & fittings		3,100	
Motor vehicles		20,200	
			199,300
Current assets			
Inventory		10,600	
Accounts receivable		7,100	
Cash at bank		8,300	
Cash in hand		200	
			26,200
Total assets			225,500
Equity			
Share capital			10,000
Share premium account			1,000
Retained earnings			47,200
Revaluation surplus			1,400
Other reserves			5,800
			65,400
Non-current liabilities			
Long-term borrowings			
(e.g. 5% debentures)	90,000		
Long-term provisions	30,000		
		120,000	
Current liabilities			
Trade and other payables	35,000		
Short-term borrowings			
(e.g. bank overdraft)	2,100		
Current tax payable	2,000		
Short-term provisions	1,000		
		40,100	
Total liabilities			160,100
			225,500

Worked Example

The accountant of Holywell Ltd extracted the following balances from the accounting records as at 31 December 20X5.

	£000
Total assets	44,500
Total liabilities	23,100
Ordinary share capital	2,000
Retained earnings	18,900
Other reserves	500

The following solution will show extracts from the statement of financial position for Holywell Ltd as at 31 December 20X5.

Solution:

Holywell Ltd

Statement of Financial Position extracts as at 31 December 20X5

	£000
Total assets	44,500
Total liabilities	23,100
	21,400
Equity	
Share capital	2,000
Retained earnings	18,900
Other reserves	500
	21,400

ACTIVITY

3 | Waltz Ltd supplies you with the following information:

	£000s
Current assets	14,300
Ordinary share capital	10,000
Revaluation surplus	1,000
Non-current liabilities	5,000
Current liabilities	6,400
Retained earnings	11,800
Non-current assets	19,900

Produce a statement of financial position (SoFP) using the above information.

3.7 Published statements of financial position

In the real world you may come across the financial statements of a public limited company (plc) that is quoted on a stock exchange. The financial statements of these quoted companies are governed by an International Accounting Standard IAS 1 Presentation of Financial Statements. The non-quoted companies we have been dealing with above have the option to adopt this international accounting standard but at present few are choosing to do this.

The equity section can be seen in the following extract of the published accounts of Vodafone plc. At this stage of your studies there is no need to go into any more detail regarding the statement of financial position of a public limited company. However, it should now be interesting to look at an extract from the statement of financial position of Vodafone plc, as shown in Figure 3.1.

 ## 3.8 Limitations of the statement of financial position

The statement of financial position is a useful document that aids decision-making and summarizes the position of the business to enable users to assess its performance. However, if you were going to buy a business, you would not base your decision solely on the information contained in the statement of financial position, as a statement of financial position does have its limitations:

- The statement of financial position only contains numerical data and is purely a summary of the financial position of the business. It does not include non-numerical information such as the quality of the staff, levels of customer satisfaction, business location, local competition or the economic conditions at the time the statement of financial position was prepared.
- The statement of financial position is produced on a given day of the year, which provides the opportunity for a business to manipulate the information to present a better picture. Potentially, if the statement of financial position was prepared not long before or not long after a different picture could be presented.
- The statement of financial position is based upon historical cost, which may not represent the income that could be raised if a particular asset was sold, for instance, property is valued at cost and may therefore be shown in the statement of financial position at below market value.
- A time period elapses between the statement of financial position date and the time the information becomes available. Consequently, the information is often out of date before it becomes available and therefore may not be very useful in helping to predict the future.
- Personal opinions and judgements are used in calculating the statement of financial position values of some of the assets. You will consider the use of these personal judgements in the calculation of depreciation and provisions later in this book.

FIGURE 3.1 Consolidated Statement of Financial Position of Vodafone plc

Consolidated statement of financial position

at 31 March

	Note	2011 £m	2010 £m
Non-current assets			
Goodwill	9	45,236	51,838
Other intangible assets	9	23,322	22,420
Property, plant and equipment	11	20,181	20,642
Investments in associates	14	38,105	36,377
Other investments	15	1,381	7,591
Deferred tax assets	6	2,018	1,033
Post employment benefits	23	97	34
Trade and other receivables	17	3,877	2,831
		134,217	**142,766**
Current assets			
Inventory	16	537	433
Taxation recoverable		281	191
Trade and other receivables	17	9,259	8,784
Other investments	15	674	388
Cash and cash equivalents	18	6,252	4,423
		17,003	**14,219**
Total assets		**151,220**	**156,985**
Equity			
Called up share capital	19	4,082	4,153
Additional paid-in capital		153,760	153,509
Treasury shares		(8,171)	(7,810)
Retained losses		(77,661)	(79,655)
Accumulated other comprehensive income		15,545	20,184
Total equity shareholders' funds		**87,555**	**90,381**
Non-controlling interests		2,880	3,379
Put options over non-controlling interests		(2,874)	(2,950)
Total non-controlling interests		**6**	**429**
Total equity		**87,561**	**90,810**
Non-current liabilities			
Long-term borrowings	22	28,375	28,632
Taxation liabilities		350	–
Deferred tax liabilities	6	6,486	7,377
Post employment benefits	23	87	237
Provisions	24	482	497
Trade and other payables	25	804	816
		36,584	**37,559**
Current liabilities			
Short-term borrowings	22	9,906	11,163
Taxation liabilities		1,912	2,874
Provisions	24	559	497
Trade and other payables	25	14,698	14,082
		27,075	**28,616**
Total equity and liabilities		**151,220**	**156,985**

The consolidated financial statements were approved by the Board of directors and authorised for issue on 17 May 2011 and were signed on its behalf by:

Vittorio Colao   Andy Halford
Chief Executive   Chief Financial Officer

Source: Vodafone (2011) Annual Report

 3.9 Summary

Key ideas

Statement of Financial Position (SoFP)

- a statement of financial position is a financial statement that summarizes the financial position of a company at a given point in time

- there are three main sections in a statement of financial position: assets (what a business owns), liabilities (what a business owes) and capital (the amount invested by the owner)
- the statement of financial position must balance – this is shown by the equation:

Total assets = Capital + Total liabilities

- the statement of financial position is a useful document but it has its limitations. It contains numerical information only; it is merely a snapshot of the financial position at a given point in time; and it is based on historical data.

Assets

- can be divided into two groups: non-current assets and current assets
- non-current assets are likely to be used in a business over a period of years, whereas current assets are likely to be converted into another form within 12 months
- current assets are shown in liquidity order in the statement of financial position, starting with the least liquid current asset – inventory – and ending with the most liquid current asset – cash
- examples of non-current assets include land and buildings, plant and machinery, fixtures and fittings and motor vehicles
- examples of current assets include inventory, accounts receivable and cash at bank.

Liabilities

- can be divided into two groups: current liabilities and non-current liabilities
- examples of current liabilities include bank overdraft, loans and accounts payable.

Accounting equation

- the accounting equation shows the relationship between the three main sections in the statement of financial position: asset, liabilities and capital
- it is shown by the following formula:

assets – liabilities = capital

Review questions

1. How would you define the following terms?
   (a) non-current assets
   (b) current liabilities
   (c) accounts receivable
   (d) accounts payable
2. Jessica runs a consultancy business from a rented office in the town centre. She would like you to state which heading in the statement of financial position (non-current assets, current assets, current liabilities or non-current liabilities) the following should be shown under:
   (a) VAT payable to HMRC
   (b) loan from E Green (repayable in three years' time)
   (c) bank overdraft

(d) accounts receivable

(e) rent owing to landlord

3. Faye's statement of financial position shows total assets of £40,000 and total liabilities of £18,400. What will be the total of Faye's capital?

4. James runs a sports injury clinic. His statement of financial position as at 31 December 20X8 contains the following assets and liabilities:

	£
Inventory	300
Accounts receivable	1,400
Accounts payable	700
Loan (repayable within 12 months)	10,000
Equipment	13,000
PAYE due to HMRC	500
Motor vehicle	8,000

You are required to state the value of the:

(a) current assets

(b) total assets

(c) current liabilities

(d) owner's capital

5. Akil has provided the following extracts from his accounting records:

	£
Total assets	30,000
Total liabilities	3,700
Capital introduced	22,000
Loss for the year	2,600
Drawings	11,300
Opening capital account balance	18,200

You are required to:

(a) Show the capital account extract as it would appear on the statement of financial position.

(b) Explain how you will know the closing balance figure on the capital account is correct.

6. David prepared the following trial balance from his accounting records for his carpentry business on 31 March 20X1. You are required to prepare a statement of financial position as at that date.

	£	£
Freehold premises	60,000	
Inventory	5,000	
Accounts receivable	3,000	
Accounts payable		2,500
Bank balance	1,000	
Motor vehicles	7,000	
Capital		73,500
	76,000	**76,000**

7. Amy produced the following trial balance for her letting agency on 30 September 20X4.

	£	£
Freehold shop	68,000	
Capital (01.10.X3)		36,000
Equipment	22,000	
Drawings	26,800	
Money due from clients	3,700	
Motor vehicles (Audi A3)	18,000	
Stationery inventory	1,400	
Cash at bank	6,500	
Bank loan (repayable 20X9)		70,000
Bank loan (repayable 20X4)		4,600
Accounts payable		1,100
Capital introduced		5,600
Profit for the year		27,800
Income tax owing		1,300
	146,400	**146,400**

You are required to produce a statement of financial position for Amy as at 30 September 20X4.

8. The accountant of Cubert Ltd produced the following trial balance as at 31 October 20X5:

	£	£
Freehold land and buildings	168,000	
Ordinary shares at £1 each		6,000
Plant and equipment	22,000	
Trade receivables	3,700	
Motor vehicles	18,000	
Inventory	21,600	
Bank overdraft		6,500
Bank loan (repayable 20X9)		80,000
Bank loan (repayable 20X5)		4,600
Trade payables		1,100
Share premium account		600
Retained earnings		127,800
Corporation tax owing		1,300
Short-term provisions		5,400
	233,300	**233,300**

You are required to produce a statement of financial position for Cubert Ltd as at 31 October 20X5.

9. The following information was extracted from the computerized records of Trencreek Ltd as at 30 April 20X7.

	£ 000
Issued share capital: Ordinary shares £1 each	50,000
10% debentures repayable in 10 years	20,000
Retained earnings	302,080
Share premium	5,000
General reserve	10,000
Land and buildings	280,500
Fixtures and fittings	60,800
Inventory	30,600
Trade receivables	15,600
Trade payables	12,540
Current tax payable	4,700

The above information includes all balances with the exception of the bank balance, which may show there is cash in the bank or there is an overdraft with the bank.

You are required to prepare a statement of financial position for Trencreek Ltd, as at 30 April 20X7 and find the balancing figure for the balance with the bank.

Reference

http://www.businesslink.gov.uk/bdotg/action/detail?type=CASE%20STUDIES& itemld=1075431500 (Accessed 3 August 2012).

Recommended reading

Dyson, J.R. (2007) *Accounting for Non-accounting Students*, 7th edition, Harlow: FT Prentice-Hall.
Growthorpe, C. (2005) *Financial Accounting for Non-Specialists*, 2nd edition, London: Thomson Learning.
Jones, M. (2002) *Accounting for Non Specialists*, Chichester: J Wiley & Son Ltd.

Useful websites

ASB statement of principles. Available from: http://www.frc.org.uk/documents/ pagemanager/asb/Statement%20-%20Statement%20of%20Principles%20 for%20Financial%20Reporting.pdf (accessed 25/09/09).

J Sainsburys Annual report and financial statements 2009. Available from: http:// www.j-sainsbury.co.uk/ar09/downloads/pdf/sainsbury_ar2009_complete_ lowres.pdf (accessed 03/10/09)

Next Annual Report and Accounts. Available from: http://www.investis.com/ nextplc/financialinfo/reportsresults/2008/Next_RA.pdf (accessed 05/10/09)

4 The income statement

'If there is **excitement** in their lives, it is contained in the figures on the **profit and loss sheet**. What an indictment.' DAME ANITA RODDICK, British entrepreneur and founder of the Body Shop

(Source: *Body and Soul* co-written with Russell Miller, 1991)

CHAPTER OUTLINE

4.1 Introduction

4.2 The basic income statement

4.3 Understanding the terminology

4.4 Preparing an income statement

4.5 Service organizations

4.6 Company income statements

4.7 Published income statements

4.8 Limitations of the income statement

4.9 Summary

CHAPTER OBJECTIVES

After carefully reading the text and completing the tasks and activities provided in this chapter you should have a better understanding and knowledge of:

● the purpose of the income statement

● the contents of the income statement

● the terminology used in the income statement

● the presentation of the income statement

● the limitations of the income statement.

4.1 Introduction

When an individual sets up in business they generally do so to make a profit. Consequently, the owner needs to know how to make sure the business is actually making a profit and how much profit it is making. This is done formally in a financial statement called an **income statement**. Income statements are usually prepared for a period covering a year, coinciding with the annual accounting date, but they can be prepared for any length of time.

An income statement is a financial statement that shows the **revenue**, **expenses** and **profit** or **loss** of a business for a given period of time. The calculation of the profit is one of the most interesting accounting functions. The income statement is a useful statement for the stakeholders as it shows them how well the business is performing. It can be used to assist the business externally in applying for a bank loan or showing a potential buyer the details of the business's performance. It may also be used internally to assist with future planning and controlling expenses, by making comparisons to previous years. The **net profit** calculated in the income statement is used as the basis for calculating the owner's tax liability.

Note that the term 'income statement' is used today although you may still come across the term 'profit and loss account'.

4.2 The basic income statement

The income statement summarizes the revenue (the amount received from sales), expenses (the amount spent to generate the sales) and the profit or loss of the business. There is a standard format for preparing an income statement that contains some technical terminology. We will start by looking at the basic layout of the income statement and then consider the meaning of the wording used.

A.N. Individual
Income Statement for the year ended 31 December 20X1

	£
Revenue (sales)	91,450
Less cost of sales	59,450
Gross profit	32,000
Less expenses	14,170
Net profit	**17,830**

---

1 | For the year ended 31 January 20X2, Chris has sales of £24,350, cost of sales of £20,050 and expenses of £1,980.
    Prepare an income statement for Chris for the year ended 31 January 20X2.

Reflective question

1 | Eloise has extracted the following information from her accounting records:

	£
Revenue	42,900
Expenses	3,200
Cost of sales	31,800

Calculate Eloise's gross profit and net profit.

4.3 Understanding the terminology

Revenue shows the total value of goods or services sold. It may also be referred to as 'sales' or 'turnover'.

KEY TERM

Cost of sales shows the cost to the business of the goods sold during the period.

KEY TERM

Cost of sales = opening inventory + purchases − closing inventory

Gross profit shows the profit the business has made purely from manufacturing or buying and selling goods. It is found by taking the sales figure and deducting the cost of sales. For example, if a computer retailer purchases laptops at a cost of £195 each and sells them for £269 each, the gross profit per laptop on sale would be £74 (269 − 195).

KEY TERM

Gross profit = Revenue (sales) − cost of sales

Expenses are costs incurred in running a business, such as rent, electricity and bank charges. They are necessary to generate the revenue. Sometimes, these costs may be referred to as 'overheads'. Expenses are costs that a company incurs while functioning as a business.

KEY TERM

Net profit shows the profit the business has made after all costs involved in the running of the business have been deducted. It may also be referred to as 'the profit for the year'. The net profit is found by taking the gross profit and deducting the expenses.

KEY TERM

Net profit = gross profit − expenses

It can also be calculated by taking the revenue and deducting both the cost of sales and the expenses.

Net profit = revenue − cost of sales − expenses

Not all businesses make a profit; some make a loss. If the cost of sales figure is greater than the revenue the business will make a gross loss and if the expenses exceed the **gross profit** the business will make a net loss.

Cost of sales > revenue = gross loss

Expenses > gross profit = net loss

ACTIVITY

2 | For the year ended 31 March 20X3, Dee has the following results:

	£
Revenue	19,800
Cost of sales	8,400
Expenses	11,800

You are required to prepare an income statement for Dee for the year ended 31 March 20X3.

4.4 Preparing an income statement

Now you have an understanding of some of the basics we can begin to expand the detail in the income statement. The first section of the income statement – revenue minus cost of sales equals gross profit – is called the **trading account**. It shows how much profit is made during the manufacturing or buying and selling process. This section is required by all businesses that carry out a manufacturing function or trade by buying and selling goods.

Due to the accruals or matching concept (explained in Chapter 1), the **cost of sales** figure needs to show the actual cost of the goods sold during the period. The cost of sales is therefore adjusted to take into consideration the inventory held at the beginning and end of the period. The inventory held at the beginning of the period is added to the purchases figure as these goods may be sold during the year. The inventory held at the end of the period is deducted from the purchases figure as it consists of goods that remain in the business as they have not been sold during the period. The closing inventory becomes the opening inventory for the following period. A business has to carry out a stock take to value the inventory at the end of each accounting period. The cost of sales is found by taking the opening inventory, adding on the purchases and deducting the closing inventory.

Cost of sales (example)

	£
Opening inventory	4,800
Add purchases	22,600
	27,400
Less closing inventory	(5,300)
Cost of sales	**22,100**

The trading account can now be shown in more detail.

Trading account (example)

	£	£
Revenue		83,200
Opening inventory	4,800	
Purchases	22,600	
	27,400	
Closing inventory	(5,300)	
Cost of sales		(22,100)
Gross profit		**61,100**

Worked Example

Ann runs a small business selling garden ornaments. She has supplied the following information for the period ended 30 April 20X4: revenue £29,600, purchases £12,100, inventory at the start of the period £3,800 and inventory at the end of the period £2,700. The solution shows a trading account for Ann for the period ended 30 April 20X4.

Solution:

Ann
Trading account for the period ended 30 April 20X4

	£	£
Revenue		29,600
Opening inventory	3,800	
Purchases	12,100	
	15,900	
Closing inventory	(2,700)	
Cost of sales		(13,200)
Gross profit		**16,400**

Now you have worked through this example it will be useful for you to prepare your own trading account.

ACTIVITY

3 | Fred has extracted the following information from his accounting records for the year ended 30 September 20X5:

	£
Revenue	54,800
Expenses	11,620
Opening inventory	3,740
Purchases	46,500

Fred valued his closing inventory at £3,570. Prepare an income statement for Fred for the year ended 30 September 20X5.

> **Reflective question**
>
> 2 | Daniel sold goods that totalled £36,420. His opening inventory was £2,210 and his purchases cost £28,050. At the end of the period he valued his inventory at £2,860. Calculate Daniel's gross profit.

The section of the income statement following the trading account is called the **profit and loss account**. In this section the expenses are deducted from the gross profit to arrive at the net profit. There are all sorts of costs that may be included as expenses (see below) and these will vary from business to business. Remember, purchases are included in the cost of sales and not in the list of expenses.

Examples of expenses:

- rent and rates
- telephone
- light and heat
- bank charges
- repairs and renewals
- insurance

- motor expenses
- training and conferences
- salaries and wages
- professional fees
- administrative costs

We can now consider a more detailed pro-forma for an income statement. This will be a useful point of reference when you start to produce your own income statements.

A.N. Individual
Income Statement for the year ended 31 December 20X1

	£	£
Revenue		91,450
Opening inventory	6,750	
Purchases	59,800	
	66,550	
Closing inventory	(7,100)	
Cost of sales		(59,450)
Gross profit		32,000
Less expenses		
Rent and rates	9,800	
Light and heat	1,200	
Repairs and renewals	860	
Motor expenses	790	
Telephone	340	
Bank charges	90	
Insurance	75	
Training and conferences	120	
Professional fees	850	
Miscellaneous expense	45	(14,170)
Net profit		**17,830**

The following steps should be followed when preparing an income statement:

1 | Start by writing the title, stating the name of the individual the income statement is being prepared for and 'Income Statement for the period or year ended on X date'.

2 | Now begin the numerical computation by showing the revenue figure.

3 | Then show the cost of sales. Start with the opening inventory, add on the purchases and sub-total the two figures before deducting the closing inventory. The resulting figure is the cost of sales and it is shown directly below the revenue.

4 | Next deduct the cost of sales figure from the revenue to find the gross profit figure.

5 | Now put a sub-heading 'less expenses' and make a list of all the expenses you have been given. Once you complete the list you need to add them all together and show the total directly below the gross profit.

6 | You then deduct the total of the expenses from the gross profit to give the net profit figure.

It will now be useful to work through the following example.

Worked Example

Paresh is a sole trader who has a retail outlet that sells jewellery in a town centre. The following is a list of balances that have been extracted from his accounting records for the year ended 30 September 20X9.

	£
Revenue	138,400
Purchases	76,800
Opening inventory	6,900
Rent and business rates	14,500
Wages	22,000
Motor expenses	1,200
Telephone and broadband	750
Insurance	620
Accountancy	450
Repairs	340

At the end of the year Paresh valued the closing inventory at £7,100.

The solution on page 62 shows an income statement for Paresh for the year ended 30 September 20X9.

Solution:

Paresh

Income Statement for the year ended 30 September 20X9

	£	£
Revenue		138,400
Opening inventory	6,900	
Purchases	76,800	
	83,700	
Closing inventory	(7,100)	
Cost of sales		(76,600)
Gross profit		61,800
Expenses		
Rent and business rates	14,500	
Wages	22,000	
Motor expenses	1,200	
Telephone and broadband	750	
Insurance	620	
Accountancy	450	
Repairs	340	(39,860)
Net profit		**21,940**

Reflective question

3 | Jenny extracted the following information from her computerized accounting records for the year ended 31 May 20X5:

	£
Revenue	28,780
Purchases	14,350
Inventory (01.06.X4)	1,740
Rent and rates	3,860
Light and heat	490
Motor expenses	840
Repairs	210
Professional fees	450

At the end of the year Jenny valued her inventory at £1,870.

Prepare an income statement for Jenny for the year ended 31 May 20X5.

The trial balance provides a useful summary of the accounting records, from which the the income statement and the statement of financial position can be prepared. All the figures shown in the trial balance are used once in the preparation of an income statement and statement of financial position. The closing inventory is not usually shown in the trial balance but as a note. Any information provided by way of a note is used twice in the preparation of the income statement and statement of financial position. The closing inventory is used in both financial statements. Other examples of information given by way of a note include accruals, prepayments and impairments and these will be dealt with in

Chapters 6 and 8. The accounts payable appears in the statement of financial position and shows the total value of any money owed by the business to suppliers or service providers, for example, an outstanding telephone bill.

When preparing financial statements from a trial balance it is sensible to get into the habit of ticking off each item as it is used, to prevent missing out any of the figures. At the end of the income statement the net profit is the amount earned by the business for the owner and the figure is transferred from the income statement to the capital section of the statement of financial position as profit for the year.

Worked Example

Nick is a sole trader who runs a lighting warehouse. The following is a trial balance extracted at the end of a year's trading, on 30 June 20X8.

	£	£
Premises	158,000	
Purchases	148,090	
Revenue		236,135
Opening inventory	17,035	
Business rates	15,870	
Salaries and wages	35,685	
Accounts receivable	6,805	
Accounts payable		6,915
Telephone	810	
Motor expenses	9,505	
Bank account	15,490	
Bank loan		210,000
Advertising	2,530	
Administration expenses	6,750	
Motor vehicles	45,700	
Fixtures	8,880	
Capital (01.07.X7)		50,100
Capital introduced		2,000
Drawing	34,000	
	505,150	**505,150**

At the year end Nick valued the inventory at £21,200.

The solution will:

1 | Identify which items on the trial balance will be shown on the income statement and which items will be shown on the statement of financial position

2 | Show an income statement for the year ended 30 June 20X8

3 | Show a statement of financial position as at 30 June 20X8.

Solution:

(a) The trial balance, identifying items that go on the income statement (IS) and the SoFP.

	£	£	
Premises	158,000		SoFP
Purchases	148,090		IS
Revenue		236,135	IS
Opening inventory	17,035		IS
Business rates	15,870		IS
Salaries and wages	35,685		IS
Accounts receivable	6,805		SoFP
Accounts payable		6,915	SoFP
Telephone	810		IS
Motor expenses	9,505		IS
Bank account	15,490		SoFP
Bank loan		210,000	SoFP
Advertising	2,530		IS
Administration expenses	6,750		IS
Motor vehicles	45,700		SoFP
Fixtures	8,880		SoFP
Capital (01.07.X7)		50,100	SoFP
Capital introduced		2,000	SoFP
Drawing	34,000		SoFP
	505,150	**505,150**	

(b) Income Statement for the year ended 30 June 20X8

	£	£
Revenue		236,135
Opening inventory	17,035	
Purchases	148,090	
	165,125	
Closing inventory	(21,200)	
Cost of sales		(143,925)
Gross profit		92,210
Expenses		
Business rates	15,870	
Salaries and wages	35,685	
Telephone	810	
Motor expenses	9,505	
Advertising	2,530	
Administration expenses	6,750	
		(71,150)
Net profit		**21,060**

(c) Statement of Financial Position as at 30 June 20X8

	£	£
Assets		
Non-current assets		
Premises	158,000	
Motor vehicles	45,700	
Fixtures	8,880	
		212,580
Current assets		
Inventory	21,200	
Accounts receivable	6,805	
Cash at bank	15,490	**43,495**
Total assets		**256,075**
Capital		
Opening balance		50,100
Add capital introduced		2,000
Add profit for the year		21,060
		73,160
Less drawings		(34,000)
		39,160
Current liabilities		
Accounts payable	6,915	
Non-current liabilities		
Bank loan	210,000	216,915
		256,075

 ## 4.5 Service organizations

Service organizations do not trade by manufacturing or buying and selling but by performing services. Accountants, lawyers, beauticians and gardeners are examples of businesses that provide a service to their customers or clients. These organizations do not need to prepare a trading account, as they do not hold inventory or buy goods for resale, but they do invoice customers for the services they provide. An income statement for a service organization is shown below.

Service organization
Income Statement for the year ended 31 December 20X6

	£	£
Income		18,700
Less expenses		
Rent and rates	4,690	
Light and heat	1,250	
Training	300	
Stationery	1,380	
Miscellaneous expenses	900	(8,520)
Net profit		**10,180**

4 | Charlotte offers consultancy services to businesses. For the year ended 31 May 20X8 she extracted the following balances from her accounting records.

	£
Consultancy income	32,400
Office expenses	2,300
Telephone and broadband	990
Light and heat	1,020
Use of house as office	3,800

You are required to prepare an income statement for Charlotte for the year ended 31 May 20X8.

FIGURE 4.1 The published income statement of Deloitte LLP.

	2011	2010
	£m	£m
Revenue	2,098	1,953
Operating expenses		
Expenses and disbursements on client assignments	(322)	(277)
Staff costs	(859)	(750)
Depreciation and amortisation	(48)	(41)
Other operating expenses	(326)	(292)
Share of results of joint venture	(1)	-
Profit from operations	542	593
Other income	2	23
Finance income	38	30
Finance cost	(72)	(103)
Profit before tax	510	543
Tax	(1)	1
Profit for the year before provision for annuities and remuneration for current members	**509**	**544**
Provision for annuities and remuneration for current members	(101)	(128)
Profit for the financial year	**408**	**416**

Source: Deloitte (2011) Annual Report

Reflective question

4 | Eve established a letting agency in a small market town. Her income comprised of commission received from clients when she successfully rented out their properties. For the year ended 31 December 20X2 she extracted the following balances from her accounting records:

	£
Commission received	38,760
Office expenses	4,870
Telephone	970
Motor expenses	1,140
Rent & rates	3,870
Light & heat	1,320

Prepare an income statement for Eve for the year ended 31 December 20X2.

4.6 Company income statements

So far in this chapter you have been learning how to prepare the income statement for a sole trader. We are now going to move on and introduce the layout of an income statement for a limited company. The first part of the income statement of a company is similar to that of a sole trader, although the income statement of a company continues beyond the net profit.

We will start by looking at the additional items that are shown on the income statement of a limited company. To understand how the retained earnings in the statement of financial position are calculated, companies prepare a Statement of Changes in Income and Equity. However this statement is beyond the scope of this book and therefore the following layout summarizes how the retained earnings in the income statement are arrived at.

A Ltd
Income Statement extract for the year ended 30 June 20X3

	£	£
Net profit/profit for the year before taxation		435,900
Less corporation tax		(75,800)
Profit for the year after taxation		360,100
Add retained profits brought forward		221,020
		581,120
Less appropriations		
Transfer to general reserve	10,000	
Transfer to revaluation reserve	65,300	
Preference dividend	4,800	
Ordinary dividend	12,600	
		(92,700)
Retained profit carried forward		**488,420**

Companies pay taxation called **corporation tax** on their profits. Although you do not need to have a detailed understanding of taxation at this stage of your studies, you do need to know where to show the corporation tax liability in the income statement. Technically, the corporation tax liability is an appropriation of profit, but to provide the users of the income statement with useful data it is shown separately, to enable the income statement to highlight the profit *before* taxation and the profit *after* taxation. We then add on the **retained profits** brought forward from previous years as these are also available for appropriation.

Each year a company may decide to transfer some of its profits to a reserve account. There are specific reserves such as the **revaluation reserve** that deals with an increase in value, due for example to the revaluation of a property, or a **general reserve** that is non-specific. After deducting the taxation and the transfers to the reserve accounts, any balance remaining is available to be paid to shareholders in the form of **dividends**. The preference shareholders have a prior right to a dividend payment.

Questions that ask you to deal with the payment of corporation tax, the transfer to reserves and the payment of dividends will require you to deal with the items by a double entry. There will be one entry made in the income statement and a further entry made in the statement of financial position, as you will see in the following example.

Worked Example

Newlyn Ltd manufactures chocolates. The following trial balance was extracted from the accounting records as at 30 June 20X8.

	£000	£000
Retained profits brought forward		14,560
Premises	68,000	
Purchases	38,090	
Revenue		86,130
Opening inventory	7,030	
Business rates	5,630	
Salaries and wages	5,000	
Accounts receivable	6,050	
Accounts payable		10,395
Motor expenses	9,505	
Bank account	8,480	
Bank loan (repayable in five years)		47,000
Administration expenses	6,750	
Motor vehicles	4,900	
Fixtures	2,800	
Issued ordinary shares of 50p each		2,000
Issued preference shares of £1 each		200
Share premium account		150
General reserve		1,800
	162,235	**162,235**

At the year end Newlyn Ltd provided the following information:

- The value of the closing inventory was £3,200,000.
- The directors recommend that £1,000,000 is transferred to the general reserve.
- The corporation tax charge for the year is £4,000,000.
- The directors wish to pay an ordinary dividend of £16,000,000, after paying the preference dividend, of 5%.

The solution will:

1. Show an income statement for the year ended 30 June 20X8
2. Show a statement of financial position as at 30 June 20X8
3. Highlight in italics the items that require you to deal with a double-entry adjustment.

Solution:

Newlyn Ltd
Income statement for the year ended 30 June 20X8

	£000	£000
Revenue		86,130
Opening inventory	7,030	
Purchases	38,090	
	45,120	
Closing inventory	(3,200)	
Cost of sales		(41,920)
Gross profit		44,210
Expenses		
Business rates	5,630	
Salaries and wages	5,000	
Motor expenses	9,505	
Administration expenses	6,750	
		(26,885)
Profit for the year before taxation		17,325
Corporation tax		(4,000)
Profit for the year after taxation		13,325
Add retained profits brought forward		14,560
		27,885
Less:		
Transfer to general reserve	1,000	
Preference dividend (5% x £200,000)	10	
Ordinary dividend	16,000	(17,010)
Retained profit carried forward		**10,875**

Newlyn Ltd
Statement of Financial Position as at 30 June 20X8

	£	£
Assets		
Non-current assets		
Premises	68,000	
Motor vehicles	4,900	
Fixtures	2,800	
		75,700
Current assets		
Inventory	3,200	
Accounts receivable	6,050	
Cash at bank	8,480	17,730
Total assets		**93,430**
Equity		
Issued ordinary shares of 50p each		2,000
Issued preference shares of £1 each		200
Share premium account		150
Retained earnings		10,875
General reserve (1,800 + *1,000*)		2,800
		16,025
Non-current liabilities		
Bank loan		47,000
Current liabilities		
Accounts payable	10,395	
Corporation tax payable	*4,000*	
Dividends payable	*16,010*	
		30,405
		93,430

4.7 Published income statements

A public company must publish its financial statements. The detail in the income statement of a public company is the same as in the income statement of a limited company, although the income statement of a public company is published in a summarized format as you can see in the following extract taken from the annual report and accounts of Vodafone plc.

FIGURE 4.2 Vodafone Group plc Consolidated Income
Statement for the years ended 31 March 2011

	2011	2010
	£m	£m
Revenue	**45,884**	**44,472**
Cost of sales	(30,814)	(29,439)
Gross profit	**15,070**	**15,033**
Selling & distribution expenses	(3,067)	(2,981)
Administrative expenses	(5,300)	(5,328)
Share of result in associates	5,059	4,742
Impairment losses	(6,150)	(2,100)
Other income & expense	(16)	114
Operating profit	**5,596**	**9,480**
Non-operating profit & expense	3,022	(10)
Investment income	1,309	716
Financing costs	(429)	(1,512)
Profits before taxation	**9,498**	**8,674**
Income tax expense	(1,628)	(56)
Profit for the financial year	**7,870**	**8,618**
Attributable to:		
–Equity shareholders	7,968	8,645
–Non-controlling interests	(98)	(27)
	7,870	8,618
Basic earnings per share	**15.20p**	**16.44p**
Diluted earnings per share	**15.11p**	**16.36p**

Source: Vodafone (2011) Annual Report

The profit before taxation equates to the net profit of a sole trader. In the annual report and accounts of a public limited company, in addition to the three main financial statements – statement of financial position, income statement and cash flow statement – there are extensive notes, which include a breakdown of some of the information shown in the summarized income statement.

You can see that the expenses are not listed separately, as they are when preparing the income statement for a sole trader or a limited company, but instead are summarized in two categories: distribution costs and administration expenses. Expenses such as salaries and wages are split between the two categories.

At this stage of your studies you do not need to go into any great detail regarding public limited companies. However, we hope you found it interesting to look at the income statement and supporting note contained in the annual report and accounts of Vodafone plc. You will be asked to analyse a set of published accounts in Chapter 9.

4.8 Limitations of the income statement

The income statement is a useful document that aids decision-making and shows the performance of the business for a given period. However, all financial statements have their limitations, as explained below.

- The income statement only contains numerical data. It does not put this numerical information into context by including non-numerical information about external factors such as the economic environment or internal factors such as staff morale.

- The income statement is produced for a given year end and could be dishonestly manipulated by including sales that take place after the end of the accounting period.

- A time period elapses between the accounting period end and the time the information becomes available. Consequently, the information is often out of date before it is available to use for future planning.

- In times of inflation the figures on the income statement are distorted by inflationary rises in prices during the accounting period.

- Personal opinions and judgements are used in calculating the asset values. These personal judgements will have an impact on the calculation of depreciation and provisions that you will come across later in this book.

 4.9 Summary

Key ideas

Income statement

- the income statement is one of the three main financial statements

- it shows the performance of a business over a given period of time

- there are two sections in an income statement – the trading account and the profit and loss account

- the income statement is a useful document but it has its limitations since it only contains numerical information, it may be dishonestly manipulated and it is based on historical data.

Trading account

- the trading account is used to calculate the gross profit

    Gross profit = revenue – cost of sales

- the cost of sales is calculated to ensure the sales are matched with the relevant purchases

    Cost of sales = opening inventory + purchases – closing inventory.

Profit and loss account

- the profit and loss account calculates the net profit

    Net profit = gross profit – expenses.

Business expenses

- there are many examples of business expenses, including rent and rates, light and heat, wages and salaries.

Service organizations

- the income statement of a service organization is different to that of a manufacturing business or a business that trades by buying and selling goods

- a service organization does not need a trading account and does not calculate a gross profit figure. It simply shows the income received less the expenses to give the net profit.

Review questions

1. Parag runs a shop selling sports equipment and a range of sports clothing. Trading times have been difficult and he is not sure whether his business is still profitable. He has provided the following balances for the year ended 31 August 20X2.

	£
Revenue	102,800
Wages	10,980
Purchases	68,760
Cleaning	1,420
Light and heat	1,380
Inventory (01.09.X1)	17,895
Rent and rates	9,640
Van expenses	2,320
Staff uniforms	840
Office expenses	960

At the end of the year Parag valued the closing inventory at £11,230.

Prepare an income statement for the year ended 31 August 20X2.

2. Nagin set up a new business on 1 January 20X9, producing fresh cookies to sell to cafes in his local area. He wants to confirm his new venture is making a profit and extracted the following balances from his computerized records for the six months ending 30 June 20X9:

	£
Revenue	68,470
Purchases	14,350
Bank charges	280
Staff wages	12,000
Protective clothing	450
Cleaning materials	345
Rent and rates	3,540
Light and heat	1,130

Nagin valued his inventory at £1,470 on 30 June 20X9.

You are required to produce an income statement for Nagin for the six months ending 30 June 20X9. Indicate whether or not he is making a profit.

3. Lee is a sole trader who runs Window Advertising. He extracted the following trial balance from his accounting records for the year ended 30 April 20X4:

	£	£
Revenue		78,750
Purchases	38,280	
Motor vehicles	7,900	
Property	82,800	
Motor expenses	1,110	
Bank balance	10,420	
Opening inventory	3,540	
Office furniture	1,570	
Business rates	6,490	
Business loan		60,000
Light and heat	1,480	
Stationery	430	
Training	100	
Wages	10,380	
Accounts payable		9,480
Opening capital		31,270
Drawings	15,000	
	179,500	**179,500**

On 30 April 20X4 Lee valued his inventory at £4,140. The business loan is repayable in ten years' time.

You are required to prepare:

(a) an income statement for Lee for the year ended 30 April 20X4

(b) a statement of financial position for Lee as at 30 April 20X4.

4. Justin is a sole trader who has been in business for many years. He manufactures retail refrigeration equipment. The following trial balance has been extracted from his accounting records for the year ended 31 December 20X3:

	£	£
Factory	148,000	
Revenue		293,350
Motor vans	14,870	
Purchases	186,050	
Inventory (01.01.X3)	24,600	
Accounts receivable	29,480	
Accounts payable		22,300
Rent and rates	9,470	
Light and heat	2,860	
Wages and salaries	30,400	
Equipment	16,310	
Bank overdraft		5,400
Capital (01.01.x3)		35,810
Motor expenses	4,950	
Professional fees	1,250	
Drawings	36,000	
Loan		150,000
Bank charges	1,110	
Insurance	230	
Sundry expenses	1,280	
	506,860	**506,860**

Justin also provides the following information:

- The loan is repayable in five years' time.
- The closing inventory was valued at £28,700 on 31 December 20X3.

You are required to prepare:

(a) an income statement for Justin for the year ended 31 December 20X3
(b) a statement of financial position for Justin as at 31 December 20X3.

5. Trevone Ltd has an issued share capital of 500,000 ordinary shares of £1 each. The accounts manager prepared the first part of the income statement for the year ended 30 April 20X9, which showed a profit before taxation of £77,540. The following balances remained on the trial balance:

	£
Non-current assets	640,800
Current assets	197,890
Trade payables	12,350
Share premium account	5,000
Revaluation reserve	10,000
General reserve	12,000
Retained profits brought forward	221,800

In addition, he informs you that the directors recommend the payment of a final ordinary dividend of 10% on the ordinary shares and they wish to transfer an additional £3,000 to the general reserve. He estimates the corporation tax charge to be £13,400. The accounts manager requires you to:

(a) calculate the retained profit figure to be shown in the statement of financial position

(b) produce a statement of financial position as at that date from the information available.

Reference

Atrill, P. & Mc Laney, E. (2004) *Accounting & Finance for Non-Specialists*. Harlow, FT Prentice Hall.

Recommended reading

Harrison, I. (2009) *Accounting, AZ Handbook, 3rd edition*, Chippenham, Philip Allan Updates.
Jones, R. (2008) *Business Accounting, 3rd edition*, Ormskirk, Causeway Press.
Wood, F. & Sangster, A. (2011) *Business Accounting 1*, 12th edition, Harlow, FT Prentice Hall.

Useful websites

http://www.iasplus.com/standard/ias01.htm#puttable Provides summaries of International Financial Reporting Standards from Deloitte Global Services Ltd.

http://annualreport.deloitte.co.uk/2011/abridged-financial-statements/financial-statements/ Provides explanations of the changes that have taken place regarding the reporting terminology used in the financial world by showing the income statement of a service organization and links to other financial reporting information that support the extract in the text.

http://vodafone.com/content/annualreport/annual_report11/index.html Shows the full annual report and accounts of the Vodafone Group plc, which highlights the full extent of the reporting required by companies (including their financial statements and, in particular, the income statement, and other non-quantitative information such as corporate governance)

5 Current assets: Valuation of inventory, bad debts and bank reconciliations

'Any *measurement* must take into account the position of the observer. There is no such thing as measurement absolute, there is only *measurement relative*.' JEANETTE WINTERSON, GUT SYMMETRIES (1997)

CHAPTER OUTLINE

5.1 Introduction

5.2 Inventory

5.3 Receivables

5.4 Bank

5.5 Summary

CHAPTER OBJECTIVES

After carefully reading the text and completing the tasks and activities provided in this chapter you should have a better understanding and knowledge of:

- the main methods of inventory valuation and how they are applied

- adjustments needed when receivables will certainly never be paid, and when there is merely doubt whether they will ever be paid

- the purposes and importance of the bank reconciliation process

- how to prepare a very simple bank reconciliation statement.

5.1 Introduction

In this chapter we look at issues connected with current assets on the statement of financial position. As you know, the three main categories of current asset are inventory, receivables and bank and we shall look at each in turn. We will see that how they are valued (or 'measured') depends on the different methods and assumptions that different companies adopt. As with many figures in the financial statements, the values placed on inventory, receivables and bank cannot always be said to be a matter of unquestionable, absolute fact.

Before we start, remember that inventory is also sometimes known in the UK as 'stock' and that receivables can also be called 'debtors'. Some accountants and some textbooks will still use these alternative terms.

 ## 5.2 Inventory

As you have learnt, inventory is the goods that a business holds with the intention of reselling to its customers. The nature of inventory will vary between different types of business:

1 | For a sportswear retailer, it will be all the clothes and trainers in its stores and in its warehouses.
2 | For a car manufacturer, it will be all the parts it holds to build more cars (raw materials); all the finished cars ready to sell (finished goods); plus all the part-finished cars the company is working on at that moment (work in progress).
3 | A business that only offers services (like an advertising agency) may have no inventory whatsoever.

For many companies, inventory will be a very significant item. On 28 February 2009, Tesco plc held £2.7 billion of inventory, while at 31 March 2009, the Toyota Corporation held $15 billion.

Moreover, as you know, inventory appears twice in the financial statements: once in the statement of financial position as a current asset, and again in the income statement as a reduction in cost of sales (being the costs of purchasing and producing goods that have not yet been sold to customers). The valuation of inventory will therefore have a direct effect on the profits that a business reports. We will demonstrate this with an example:

Worked Example

ZX Ltd made sales of £20,000 during the year. The opening inventory was valued at £4,000 and the company's purchases totalled £10,000.

Calculate the gross profit of ZX Ltd if closing inventory is valued at:

(a) £3,000

(b) £6,000

Solution:

	Solution (a) £		Solution (b) £
Sales		20,000	20,000
Less cost of sales			
Opening inventory	4,000		4,000
Add purchases	10,000		10,000
Less closing inventory	(3,000)		(6,000)
		11,000	8,000
Gross profit		**9,000**	**12,000**

Valuing inventory in the financial statements

The simple example above demonstrates the direct impact of inventory valuation on reported profits. It is essential that inventory is valued fairly, so how should it be valued?

The answer is that inventories should be valued at cost price, unless for some reason they have reduced in value and are now worth less than what they originally cost. This is known as the rule of 'the lower of cost and net realizable value'.

Let's have a look at what 'cost' and **net realizable value** actually mean.

The cost of inventory

At first sight, 'cost' seems straightforward: we simply value inventory at what the company originally paid to acquire it. However, this cost figure must include all costs incurred in bringing inventories to their present location and condition, which may include a wide variety of costs depending on whether the inventory is raw materials, finished goods, or work-in-progress.

So, for example, with the inventory of raw materials, the cost will be their purchase price plus all the costs of getting the goods delivered, including import duties if the goods came from overseas.

The 'cost' of finished goods will represent the cost of raw materials that have gone into the goods, plus the wages costs of staff that have worked directly on making the goods, plus a 'fair share' of the factory costs incurred in making the goods (e.g. factory rent, rates, power and so on). These calculations (particularly the fair share of factory costs) become quite complex and are beyond the scope of this book.

For work-in-progress the calculation is even more difficult. The cost must include raw materials used so far, direct wages so far, plus a fair share of overheads in proportion to how far the work is finished. For example, keeping track of the costs incurred by a ship builder on its inventory of part-finished ships at any one time is a major exercise.

Again, complex inventory costing techniques are beyond the scope of this book. However, even aspects of inventory valuation that appear straightforward, such as the cost of raw materials purchased, are not always as simple as they seem, as we will see in the next section.

Different assumptions in costing raw materials

A practical problem is that the cost price of raw materials tends to go up (and down) over time. A company may buy several batches of a particular item throughout the course of a period, with some batches costing more than others. At the end of the period, there may be no way of knowing which ones are left in stock – is it the cheaper ones or the more expensive ones? Most companies will not know and will have to make some sort of assumption.

We will demonstrate this with an example.

Worked Example

Distin Ltd starts business on 1 June with a plan to import and then sell a new type of energy-saving light bulb. Unfortunately the cost price is rising rapidly due to short supply. It imports three batches of bulbs in June:

		Total cost £
8 June	100 bulbs at £1.80 each	180
15 June	100 bulbs at £2.30 each	230
20 June	100 bulbs at £2.50 each	250
		660

On 25 June, Distin Ltd sells 220 bulbs to a retailer for £1,100 (a selling price of £5 per bulb).

At the end of June, Distin Ltd has 80 bulbs still in stock. The company does not know which ones have been sold. How should the remaining inventory be valued?

Solution 1:
Distin Ltd could assume that it sold the oldest bulbs first (the 'First in, First Out' or FIFO assumption).

Closing inventory therefore consists of the most recent purchases: 80 bulbs at £2.50 each = £200.

Income statement for Distin Ltd using the FIFO assumption:

		£
Sales		1,100
Less cost of sales		
Opening inventory	0	
Add purchases	660	
Less closing inventory	200	
		460
Gross profit		**640**

Solution 2:
Alternatively, Distin Ltd could apply an average cost (the AVCO assumption).

Distin bought 300 bulbs paying a total of £660, so the average cost per bulb is £2.20.

Therefore, under this assumption closing inventory consists of 80 bulbs at £2.20 each = £176.

Income statement for Distin Ltd using the AVCO assumption:

	£
Sales	1,100
Less cost of sales	
Opening inventory 0	
Add purchases 660	
Less closing inventory 176	
	484
Gross profit	**616**

As you can see from the above example, the gross profit figure falls by £24 depending on the choice of valuation method. This is an illustration of how the accounting methods and assumptions that a company adopts (in this case either FIFO or AVCO) will affect reported profits. The methods and assumptions that a company adopts are known as its 'accounting policies'.

In a time of rising prices (such as the above example), FIFO will tend to give a higher profit figure since it assumes that the most recent purchases (the most expensive ones) have not been sold yet. The units bought first (the cheaper ones) have been sold.

If prices are falling, the reverse is true and using the FIFO assumption will show a lower profit than AVCO.

An alternative method would be LIFO ('last in, first out'). In a time of rising prices LIFO will tend to give a lower profit figure.

Once a company has decided on a particular policy it should apply the same policy every period, so its profits are reported on a consistent basis and can be compared from one period to the next. However, trying to compare one company's financial statements with another's can be hazardous because the companies may be using different accounting policies.

KEY THEMES Accounting policy for inventory

The accounting policy for inventory used by Sainsbury's plc according to their Annual Report 2009 is:

'Inventories are valued at the lower of cost and net realisable value. Inventories at warehouses are valued on a first-in, first-out basis. Inventories at retail outlets are valued at calculated average cost prices. Cost includes all direct expenditure and other appropriate costs incurred in bringing inventories to their present location and condition.' (Source: http://www.j-sainsbury.co.uk/ar09/downloads/pdf/sainsbury_ar2009_complete_lowres.pdf)

In other words, Sainsbury's use a mix of the FIFO and AVCO assumptions.

Tesco plc, meanwhile, use AVCO only according to their Annual Report 2009.

This particular difference in policy will probably not cause a significant distortion in any comparison of Tesco's and Sainsbury's results (particularly in a time of fairly stable prices). However, it is an example of how seemingly comparable companies are using different methods to calculate the figures in their financial statements.

Q As an alternative to FIFO or AVCO, a different assumption that companies might wish to make is 'LIFO', or 'Last In, First Out'. However, the LIFO assumption is *not* allowed under International Accounting Standards. Can you suggest why not?

Net Realizable Value (NRV)

As referred to earlier, sometimes due to adverse circumstances the selling value of some of a company's inventory falls below what it originally cost.

For example, fresh food held in stock can easily deteriorate. If it is not sold quickly enough, its selling price can fall below what it originally cost, or even to zero.

Another example could be a business that held a lot of VHS video tapes in stock. In recent years, such a company may have found the tapes were worth less than the business originally paid for them. Such inventory can be called 'obsolete'.

Any inventory held whose selling value falls below original cost must be shown at 'net realizable value'.

KEY TERM

> **Net realizable value (NRV)** is the price that the inventory is now expected to fetch, minus any costs needed to complete the sale.

The value of inventory (as shown both in the statement of financial position and the cost of sales component of the income statement) must be reduced immediately. Any such downward adjustments are known as 'write downs'.

ACTIVITY

> 1 | Toomes Ltd runs a music shop and has a piano in stock which originally cost £800. It can be sold for £1,100. However, before it can be sold, it will have to be repaired at a cost of £500.
>
> How should the piano be valued in the inventory of Toomes Ltd?
> (a) £500
> (b) £600
> (c) £700
> (d) £800

Inventory in published financial statements

Large organizations like Next always comprise a 'group' of several companies so the financial statements for the whole group are said to be 'consolidated'. The Next plc Consolidated Income Statement, as seen in the extract below, shows that the group has made an operating profit of £478.3m for the year to January 2009.

Extract from Next plc consolidated income statement:

	2009	2008
	£m	£m
Revenue	3,271.5	3,329.1
Operating profit	478.3	537.1

As the name suggests, 'operating profit' basically means the profit that Next makes from its normal operations of selling clothes and other goods in its stores. It is essentially the profit before any interest payments and tax charges.

The income statement in published accounts is summarized, so we have to look at the notes to the accounts to get more information about inventory.

The accounting policies note, tells us:

> 'Stock is valued at the lower of standard cost or net realisable value. Net realisable value is based on estimated selling prices less further costs to be incurred on disposal.'
>
> Source: Next plc Annual Report January 2009, p.48

This policy is as we would expect, based on what we have discussed so far in this chapter.

The notes tell us that operating profit is stated after charging various items, including the following two which relate to Next's inventory:

	2009 £m	2008 £m
Cost of inventories recognized as an expense	1,167.2	1,205.7
Write down of inventories to net realisable value	**96.6**	**121.5**

A further note tells us the finished goods in stock on the Statement of Financial Position:

	2009 £m	2008 £m
Finished goods	**305.7**	**303.3**

Since finished goods levels are almost constant from one year to the next, the 'cost of inventories recognized as an expense' are pretty much equivalent to purchases.

It is interesting to note that 2009 write downs amounted to the equivalent of about 8 per cent of Next's purchases (£96.6m write downs/£1,167.2m inventory expense = 8%). The figure was even higher in 2008, at 10 per cent. Remember that these represent write-downs to expected selling price (NRV) when it falls *below the original purchase price of the stock*.

Without being an expert on Next's business it is difficult to comment authoritatively.

However, it would seem likely that Next incurs significant write-downs because it is in the fashion trade. Fashions are difficult to predict, particularly when buyers have to make their decisions months in advance. A buyer might predict that, say, green flared jeans will be the must-wear item this autumn, but if the public disagrees the jeans will end up being written down to whatever the company can get rid of them for – their net realizable value.

 5.3 Receivables

Most companies will show one figure for 'receivables' on the face of their statement of financial position. This will typically include:

- trade receivables: amounts of money due from credit customers
- prepayments: payments in advance made by the company
- other receivables: amounts due from other parties (not customers).

So for most companies, the single figure on the statement of financial position will contain elements of all three. You need to look at the notes to the accounts to see the breakdown.

Prepayments are normally a relatively straightforward calculation and are looked at in more detail in Chapter 6.

'Other receivables' tend to include amounts due from other companies in the group, any amounts due from governmental organizations and so on.

It is in the trade receivables where the assumptions and methods that each company applies will have the most impact.

With the exception of retail, most business in the UK is done on credit terms, so for most businesses trade receivables are a significant item in the statement of financial position.

The downside of selling on credit is that customers do not always pay. Some customers are declared bankrupt and cannot pay. Others will dispute the quality or specification of the goods supplied and will refuse to pay. Occasionally some credit customers are fraudulent and vanish without trace without paying for their goods.

Whatever the reason may be, receivable amounts that will not actually be received are commonly known as 'bad debts'.

There are two types of bad debts to consider:

1 | **Bad debts** – where it is known with reasonable probability that specific debts will not be received.
2 | **Doubtful debts** – where there is uncertainty; debts might be received but they might not.

Bad debts

If a debt is known to be bad, the accounting procedure is fairly straightforward. The debt must be 'written off' from the records:

- reduce the asset of trade receivables by the amount of the bad debt
- show a bad debt expense in the income statement for exactly the same amount.

The reduction in trade receivables is a credit entry (because an asset is being reduced) and the bad debt expense is a debit entry (because it is an increase in expenses).

Bad debt expense is also sometimes called 'receivable expense' or 'impairment of receivables'. As you may have realized already, a confusing aspect of looking at published accounts is that different companies use different phrases to describe the same thing!

KEY TERM

> **Bad debt** money owed to the company when it becomes reasonably certain that a credit customer will never pay.

Doubtful debts

Sometimes there is uncertainty as to whether some trade receivables might or might not be received. Maybe there are rumours that a particular customer is in financial difficulty. Or perhaps a customer is disputing a particular invoice and there is doubt over whether they will ever pay it.

KEY TERM

> **Doubtful debt** money owed to a company when it is not yet clear whether a credit customer will pay.

Since these debts are not yet definitely irrecoverable, they must remain on the trade receivables account. The entries that must be made are:

• | create a separate 'Provision for doubtful debts' that can be set off against the trade receivables figure in the statement of financial position (to cover the possibility that the amounts might not be received)

• | increase the bad debt expense in the income statement by the same amount as the increase in the provision.

The Provision for doubtful debts entry is a credit (because it will be offset against trade receivables so will effectively reduce the value of an asset). The bad debt expense entry is a debit (because it is an increase in expenses).

The Provision for doubtful debts is sometimes known as the 'Allowance for receivables' or 'Provision for credit losses' or something similar.

ACTIVITY

2 | Troy sells £900,000 of goods in his first year of trading to 31 December. His trade receivables are £80,000 as at that date. These receivables include:

(a) £7,000 due from V Ltd. This debt is outstanding since early September. V Ltd have told Troy that they will definitely pay their bill, and have given a variety of excuses for the delay. Troy has heard that several other of V Ltd's suppliers have been waiting for payments that are similarly overdue.

(b) £15,000 due from C Ltd. Troy learnt yesterday that C Ltd has gone into liquidation.

How should these figures appear in the financial statements of Troy Ltd for the year to 31 December?

General provisions for doubtful debts

Very often, past experience and history of a business will indicate that a certain percentage of its trade receivables will never be paid. The company doesn't know which ones, but on average a certain percentage are not recovered. In this case, the 'provision for bad/doubtful debts' may be calculated as a percentage of trade receivables.

Worked Example

On 31 December 20X8, Pienaar Ltd's trade receivables were £36,000. The company's past experience and history indicates that 5 per cent of its trade receivables will never be paid. Pienaar Ltd has never established a provision for bad debts before.

Solution:

£36,000 × 5% = £1,800, so Pienaar Ltd is assuming that £1,800 will never be recovered.

• | set up a provision for bad/doubtful debts of £1,800 (a credit)
• | record a bad debt expense of £1,800 (a debit).

The figure for receivables in the SoFP will be:

	£
Trade receivables	36,000
Less provision for bad debts	(1,800)
	34,200

Things become a little more complicated for Pienaar Ltd one year later.

Suppose on 31 December 20X9, Pienaar Ltd's trade receivables are now £44,000. The company still thinks that 5 per cent are doubtful.

Solution:

£44,000 × 5% = £2,200, so Pienaar Ltd is assuming that £2,200 will never be recovered.

A provision for bad debts of £1,800 already exists from last year, so the increase required is £400.

- increase the provision for bad debts by £400 (a credit)
- the increase in the provision is an additional bad debt expense of £400 (a debit).

The figure for receivables in the Statement of Financial Position will be:

	£
Trade receivables	44,000
Less provision for bad debts	(2,200)
	41,800

The fact that the figure of 5 per cent in the example above is merely an educated guess based on past experience and history is another small example of the many estimates and suppositions on which figures in the financial statements are based. Accountants try to make these estimates as accurately as possible, but of course no one can predict the future. Financial reports are not a statement of pure fact – they include estimates and assumptions which may or may not turn out to be accurate.

Moreover, less scrupulous companies may adjust or 'massage' their estimates in order to present a more favourable picture of their own financial affairs to the outside world. This is an example of 'creative accounting', a phrase you may have come across before.

Bad debts essentially lay at the centre of the 'credit crunch' of 2007–09, when it became clear that assets being traded by financial institutions were worth much less than previously thought because they were fundamentally based on loans that would never be repaid by their borrowers, i.e. they were based on bad debts. This fairly simple fact had been partly obscured hitherto by the complexity of the financial instruments being traded. The huge impact of these bad debts on the world economy does serve to highlight how important it is to assess the recoverability of all receivables and make immediate, accurate adjustments for bad and doubtful debts.

CASE STUDY RBS

The bad debt expense of the Royal Bank of Scotland plc for the year to 31 December 2008 was £6,973m in respect of loans to customers identified as bad or doubtful. By comparison, its bad debt expense was only(!) £1,946m in 2007 and £1,877m in 2006 (Annual Report 2008, Note 12, p.212, 'Impairment losses charged to the income statement (in respect of) Loans and advances to customers').

Meanwhile the provision for bad debts of RBS plc rose from £3,935m at 31 December 2006 to £11,016m at 31 December 2008 (Annual Report 2008, Note 12, p.212, 'Provision for Impairment losses for loans and advances').

The dramatic increases in these 'impairment' figures for RBS highlights how bad debt problems for banks came to a head in 2008.

Q As we have seen, a company will write off a debt as bad in one accounting period when it *appears* reasonably certain the money will never be recovered. However, very occasionally, such a debt may actually be paid in a subsequent accounting period (in whole or in part). How should such a receipt be dealt with in the accounts?

Receivables in published accounts

Vodafone Group plc can be used to investigate receivables in published accounts.

To obtain details of how trade receivables have been treated, we need to examine the 'Notes to the Consolidated Financial Statements', shown below.

The 'Significant Accounting Policies' note explains how Vodafone accounts for its Trade Receivables:

'Trade receivables

Trade receivables do not carry any interest and are stated at their nominal value as reduced by appropriate allowances for estimated irrecoverable amounts. Estimated irrecoverable amounts are based on the ageing of the receivable balances and historical experience. Individual trade receivables are written off when management deems them not to be collectible.'

This policy is exactly in line with the principles outlined earlier in this chapter. The three sentences of the policy above are saying, in other words:

- trade receivables are stated net of provisions for bad and doubtful debts
- Vodafone's provision for bad debts is estimated based on a combination of how long Vodafone has been waiting for the money and its past experience
- individual debts are written-off completely when it appears reasonably certain that the customer will not pay.

Vodafone's Statement of Financial Position shows 'Trade and other receivables' of £7,662m in 2009 and £6,551m in 2008 under 'Current assets', and refers us to a note which provides a breakdown as follows:

	2009 £m	2008 £m
Trade receivables	3,751	3,549
Amounts owed by associated undertakings	50	21
Other receivables	744	494
Prepayments and accrued income	2,868	2,426
Derivative financial instruments	249	61
	7,662	**6,551**

In this chapter we are looking at trade receivables, so we shall focus our attention on the first row of the above table (trade receivables of £3,751m and £3,549m for 2009 and 2008 respectively).

The notes go on to state how Vodafone's provision (or 'allowance') for bad debts is analysed:

'The Group's trade receivables are stated after allowances for bad and doubtful debts based on management's assessment of creditworthiness, an analysis of which is as follows:

	2009 £m	2008 £m
1 April	664	473
Exchange movements	101	73
Amounts charged to administrative expenses	423	293
Trade receivables written off	(314)	(175)
31 March	**874**	**664**

To explain the terminology used in the above table:

1. | The 'Exchange movements' arise because Vodafone operates throughout the world. Some of its doubtful receivables will be denominated in foreign currency and will therefore be affected by fluctuations in exchange rates.

2. | 'Amounts charged to administrative expenses' represent the total bad debt expense charged to the income statement, whether as a result of bad debts written off completely or through increases in the bad debt provision.

3. | 'Trade receivables written off' represent amounts previously deemed to be doubtful and now felt to be definitely irrecoverable.

It is interesting to note that the amounts charged to administrative expenses (total bad debts) was £293m in 2008 and £423m in 2009, an increase of some 44 per cent, calculated as follows:

$$\frac{423 - 293}{293} \times 100 = 44\%$$

You will revisit calculations similar to this in Chapter 9. There will be various business reasons for this, but one factor is probably the increasing economic pressures facing Vodafone's customers in the recession that followed the 'credit crunch'.

5.4 Bank

Some companies will have a positive bank balance so this will appear as a current asset on the statement of financial position. Others, of course, will be overdrawn, in which case the overdraft will be shown as a current liability. However, all the comments that follow apply whether the company is in credit or overdrawn.

Cash at the bank is easily the most straightforward of the current assets to value: it is simply the amount of money in the bank account according to the business records.

However, how does the business know that its records are correct? After all, many businesses will have thousands of receipts every day and likewise make thousands of payments. How does the business know that they have all been recorded correctly?

The answer is a **bank reconciliation**.

Bank reconciliations

A bank reconciliation is simple in principle. It means checking all receipts and payments according to the business's books against all the receipts and payments shown on the business bank statement.

Traditionally this was done manually by 'ticking off' every item on the business records against the corresponding item on the bank statement.

Nowadays, businesses can bank online and bank statements can be received electronically. The 'ticking off' process can therefore be performed by reconciliation software.

Whether done manually or electronically, once the ticking off process has been finished:

- any errors or omissions in the business records can be corrected
- the bank can be notified of any mistakes that they may have made, and the bank statements will be amended
- there will remain certain timing differences between the business's records and the bank statement.

These timing differences are:

- payments, normally cheques, sent to suppliers which have not yet cleared on the bank statement ('uncleared payments')
- receipts that the business has deposited into its account but have not yet cleared on the bank statement ('uncredited deposits')

Bank reconciliation means the process of checking the information on the bank statement against the information on the nominal ledger account for Bank and identifying errors, omissions and timing differences.

We will now look at an example.

Worked Example

Hoggins Ltd receives its bank statement for the month of April:

		Withdrawals	Deposits	Balance	
April		**£**	**£**	**£**	
1	Balance b/f			841	Cr
6	Cheque 901452	181		660	Cr
14	Cheque 901453	478		182	Cr
15	Cheque 901454	123		59	Cr
21	Deposit		400	459	Cr
30	Standing Order – J Fox	80		379	Cr

Hoggins Ltd's nominal ledger account for 'Bank' for April shows the following:

		£			£
1 April	Bal b/f	841	2 April	W Wilkins	181
21 April	B Wilson	400	11 April	P Smith	478
30 April	A Jardine	223	12 April	L Wise	123
			28 April	K Jones	91
			29 April	L Pearson	55

Prepare a bank reconciliation for April for Hoggins Ltd.

Step 1: Tick off items that appear on the bank statement and on the nominal ledger:

Bank Statement for April

April		Withdrawals £		Deposits £		Balance £		
1	Balance b/f					841	✓	Cr
6	Cheque 901452	181	✓			660		Cr
14	Cheque 901453	478	✓			182		Cr
15	Cheque 901454	123	✓			59		Cr
21	Deposit			400	✓	459		Cr
30	SO – J Fox	80				379		Cr

Nominal ledger account for 'Bank' for April

		£				£	
1 April	Bal b/f	841	✓	2 April	W Wilkins	181	✓
21 April	B Wilson	400	✓	11 April	P Smith	478	✓
30 April	A Jardine	223		12 April	L Wise	123	✓
				28 April	K Jones	91	
				29 April	L Pearson	55	

The three unticked items (shown in italics above) represent a deposit and two payments that have not yet cleared on the bank statement.

Step 2: Update the nominal ledger for items that should have been recorded but have been omitted.

In this example, the only item that had been omitted is the standing order payment to J Fox (unticked on the bank statement above and shown in italics below).

Nominal ledger account for 'Bank' for April: updated for omissions identified

		£			£
1 April	Bal b/f	841	2 April	W Wilkins	181
21 April	B Wilson	400	11 April	P Smith	478
30 April	A Jardine	223	12 April	L Wise	123
			28 April	K Jones	91
			29 April	L Pearson	55
			30 April	SO – J Fox	80
			30 April	Balance c/f	456
		1,464			**1,464**

Step 3: Prepare a bank reconciliation statement that reconciles the bank statement balance with the nominal ledger balance:

Hoggins Ltd: Bank reconciliation as at 30 April

	£	£
Balance per bank statement		379
Less cheque payments not yet cleared		
K Jones	91	
L Pearson	55	(146)
Add deposits not yet credited		
A Jardine		223
Balance per nominal ledger		**456**

Exact reconciliation as demonstrated in the above example is very important: it gives the business confidence that the bank records are complete and accurate for April.

ACTIVITY

3 | Banner Ltd's nominal ledger account for Bank showed a positive bank balance of £2,000 as at 31 May, which did not match the bank balance shown by the bank statement.
Careful checking of the bank statement against the nominal ledger revealed:

(a) Cheque payments made by Banner Ltd of £13,000 had not yet cleared on the bank statements.

(b) Deposits made of £6,000 had not yet been credited on the bank statements.

(c) Bank charges of £200 had not yet been recorded in the nominal ledger.

Prepare a simple bank reconciliation statement as at 31 May.

The importance of bank reconciliation

The bank reconciliation process has three significant benefits:

1 | It will identify any errors or omissions in the business's bank records (whether caused by innocent error or by fraud).

2 | It will highlight any errors or omissions on the bank statement (banks make mistakes too!).

3 | It will give the business more confidence in the accuracy of many of its other accounts. Since many entries in various accounts in the nominal ledger are the other side of bank payments and receipts, then checking that the bank account is correct will give assurance that the other side of all those entries is also correct.

The bank reconciliation process is therefore a basic but very important check on the accuracy of the business records. The bank statement is one of the only independent sources of information that can be used to check the accounting records. All well-run businesses, from the very large to the very small, perform bank reconciliations regularly on all their business bank accounts.

Manipulation of the bank figure in the financial statements

Even the asset of money at the bank is not immune to a little bit of manipulation by companies to make them appear 'richer' at their financial year end. Companies can bring forward or delay certain transactions around the year end date purely to improve the position shown by the statement of financial position. This is sometimes known as 'window-dressing'.

In its most basic form, it could simply be a case of holding back payments to suppliers just before the year end so that its bank balance is artificially inflated. More sophisticated tricks are also used.

Once again, it is useful to remind ourselves that even figures in the financial statements that one might think were a straightforward matter (like the amount of money at the bank) are not beyond a little bit of distortion by clever accountants!

 ## 5.5 Summary

Key ideas

Inventory

- three types of inventory: raw materials, work in progress and finished goods

- inventory is valued at the lower of cost and net realizable value. This means that inventory in the statement of financial position is valued at the lower of (a) what it cost to buy and/or produce, and (b) the net proceeds it would fetch if it were sold now

- cost of inventory shown in the statement of financial position can depend on the assumption that the company makes about which of its purchases are still in stock. Companies can use (a) 'First In First Out' (FIFO) which assumes that the older purchases have been sold and the most recent remain in closing inventory, (b) Average Cost (AVCO) which values items at the average price paid for them, or (c) 'Last In First Out' (LIFO), which assumes the latest purchases are sold first

- value of inventory can fall below what it originally cost if it is damaged, becomes obsolete, or goes out of fashion. The value of such inventory must be 'written-down' to its NRV (the price it can now be sold for minus any expenses needed to complete the sale)

Bad debts

- sometimes a company learns that one of its trade receivables will never be received because it is clear that the customer cannot or will not pay – these are known as bad debts

- bad debts must be 'written-off' from the trade receivables figure in the statement of financial position and shown as a 'bad debt expense' in the income statement

- there may be doubt over some trade receivables: they may or may not be recovered. Doubtful debts continue to be included within the trade receivables figure. They are not 'written-off'. Instead, a 'provision for bad debts' is set up to cover the possibility that the money might not be received. Increases in the provision are shown as an expense in the income statement

- 'bad debt expense' is called different things by different companies. They may use phrases such as 'receivables expense' or 'impairment of receivables'

- different companies use different terms for the 'provision for bad debts'. Alternative phrases include 'allowance for receivables' and 'provision for credit losses'.

Bank reconciliation

- involves carefully checking of every item in the nominal ledger bank record against the corresponding item on the bank statement and identifying errors or omissions that have been made by the business or by the bank. It is a vital control procedure

- once any errors have been identified and corrected, the balance per the business's records can be 'reconciled' to the balance per the bank statement

- the reconciliation statement will normally include all the payments and deposits that the company has made that have not yet cleared on the bank statement. Exact reconciliation gives the business confidence that the bank records are complete and accurate

- some companies will bring forward or postpone certain transactions around their year end date in order to present an artificially high Bank figure on their statement of financial position. This is known as 'window dressing' and can be as simple as postponing payments to suppliers until just after the financial year end.

Review questions

1. Blonsky Ltd's year end trial balance reveals the following balances:

	£
Opening inventory	25,000
Trade receivables	86,000
Trade payables	59,000
Bank overdraft	13,000

Blonsky Ltd's closing inventory is valued at £20,000.

Based on the above figures, what is the total of Blonsky Ltd's current assets at the year-end?

(a) £106,000

(b) £111,000

(c) £93,000

(d) £119,000

2. Joylove is in the antiques business. He has a dining table in his shop that cost £2,000. He expects to spend £600 repairing it which means he will then be able to sell it for £3,000.

At what value should the table be recorded in Joylove's inventory?

(a) £1,400

(b) £2,400

(c) £2,000

(d) £2,600

3. Which of the following costs should be included in calculating the value of the inventory of a manufacturer?

(i) Carriage outwards

(ii) Carriage inwards

(iii) Salespersons' salaries

(iv) Factory equipment hire

    (a) (i) and (iv) only

    (b) (i), (ii) and (iv) only

(c) All of them

(d) (ii) and (iv) only

4. At the start of May, Sterns Ltd had an opening inventory of 20 calculators valued at £3 each.

    During May, the following occurred:

    6 May – sold 15 calculators for £7 each

    13 May – bought 15 calculators for £4 each

    21 May – sold 17 calculators for £8 each

    Using the FIFO method of inventory valuation, the closing inventory at the end of May is:

    (a) £9

    (b) £11.25

    (c) £12

    (d) £24

5. Osbourne Ltd starts business and buys 8 units of Product X at £5 each and then buys 12 more units of Product X for £6 each. During the year, Osbourne Ltd sells 15 units of Product X for £13 each.

    Assuming inventory is valued using the FIFO method, what is the gross profit of Osbourne Ltd for the year?

    (a) £105

    (b) £113

    (c) £83

    (d) £108

6. In the published financial statements of companies, 'Provision for bad debts' can also be called:

    (a) Provision for credit losses

    (b) Allowance for doubtful receivables

    (c) Provision for impairment of receivables

    (d) All of the above

7. Marie starts business on 1 January and makes total sales of £800,000 during the year to 31 December. However, this turnover includes a sale of £40,000 to Mr L Lucan, who has disappeared without trace and has not paid for his goods.

    Marie's business has total receivables of £170,000 at 31 December.

    No adjustments yet have been made as a result of the disappearance of Mr Lucan.

    How should this information be reflected in the final accounts of Marie's business for the year ended 31 December?

    (a) Sales £760,000; Receivables £170,000

    (b) Sales £760,000; Receivables £130,000

    (c) Sales £800,000; Receivables £170,000

    (d) Sales £800,000; Receivables £130,000

8. At 30 April 2009 XD Ltd's provision for bad debts was £26,000. At 30 April 2010 its trade receivables were £630,000. It was decided to write-off irrecoverable debts of £39,000 and adjust the provision for bad debts to the equivalent of 8 per cent of trade receivables on the basis of past events.

What is the total figure for bad debt expense that should appear in the income statement of XD Ltd for the year ended 30 April 2010?

(a) £86,280

(b) £63,400

(c) £60,280

(d) £89,400

9. On 31 July Joel Ltd was owed £68,000 by its customers. At the same date, its provision for doubtful debts was £3,000. How will these balances appear in Joel Ltd's statement of financial position as at 31 July?

(a) £65,000 current asset

(b) £71,000 current asset

(c) £68,000 current asset and £3,000 current liability

(d) £68,000 current asset and £3,000 current asset

10. The provision for doubtful debts in the books of Dunson Ltd at 30 November 20X8 was £3,000. During the year ended 30 November 20X9, bad debts of £9,000 were identified as irrecoverable and were written-off. Receivables at 30 November 20X9 were £80,000. Based on past experience, Dunson Ltd requires a provision for doubtful debts of 5 per cent.

The charge for bad debt expense in the income statement of Dunson Ltd for the year ended 30 November 20X9 should be:

(a) £9,550

(b) £10,000

(c) £12,000

(d) £13,000

11. Is a bank overdraft:

(a) Income?

(b) An expense?

(c) An asset?

(d) A liability?

12. Which of the following is NOT one of the objectives of performing regular bank reconciliations?

(a) To identify errors made by the bank

(b) To identify errors made by the business

(c) To ensure that the nominal ledger bank balance is exactly the same as the balance on the bank statement

(d) To help ensure that various nominal ledger accounts are accurate

13. A junior member of staff has produced the following bank reconciliation:

	£
Overdraft balance per bank statement	4,600
Unpresented cheques	7,800
	3,200
Uncredited deposits	14,300
	17,500

What is the correct figure you would expect to see on the statement of financial position in respect of bank?

(a) £1,900 current asset

(b) £17,500 current asset

(c) £26,700 current liability

(d) £11,100 current liability

14. Dillon Ltd's bank statement shows an overdraft balance of £3,100. Comparison with the nominal ledger account for bank shows that there are unpresented cheque payments totalling £1,300 and deposits not yet credited of £400. The figure for bank overdraft on the statement of financial position should be:

(a) £2,200

(b) £4,000

(c) £1,400

(d) £3,100

15. The following trial balance has been extracted at 30 November 2009 from the nominal ledger of Showroad Antiques Ltd. The company is owned and run by Fiona Scully, who asks you to help her prepare the final accounts for 2009.

	Dr £	Cr £
Bank interest paid	2,000	
Bank loan		20,000
Insurance	5,000	
Cash at bank	2,000	
Fixtures and fittings at cost	11,000	
Inventory as at 1 December 2008	88,000	
Motor vehicles at cost	30,000	
Provision for bad debts as at 1 December 2008		3,000
Purchases	380,000	
Rent and rates	14,000	
Retained earnings as at 1 December 2008		37,000
Sales		699,000
Share capital		28,000
Telephone	7,000	
Trade payables		27,000
Trade receivables	66,000	
Travel expenses	68,000	
Wages and salaries	141,000	
	814,000	**84,000**

Additional information:

(a) Inventory at 30 November 2009 was counted and valued at cost totalling £77,000. However, included in this figure are two items that Fiona is unsure about:

- A guitar that was once played by a very famous rock star is included at cost price of £2,200. However, the star's public image has just been ruined by a high-profile, unsavoury scandal. The guitar will probably now only fetch about £500 when it is sold.
- A tennis racket used by the great Fred Perry at Wimbledon is included at cost price £3,100. However, it will have to be repaired at a cost of £500 before it can be sold for £4,000.

(b) During December, Fiona learnt that a credit customer had gone into liquidation. The customer owed £16,000 to the company as at 30 November 2009, which is included in the trade receivables figure in the above trial balance. Additionally, the provision for bad debts is to be adjusted to 10 per cent of trade receivables based on past experience.

(c) The bank loan does not become repayable until 2012.

You are required to prepare the income statement for Showroad Antiques Ltd for the year ended 30 November 2009 and the statement of financial position as at that date.

Recommended reading

http://www.j-sainsbury.co.uk/ar09/downloads/pdf/sainsbury_ar2009_complete_lowres.pdf

Useful websites

http://www.guardian.co.uk/business/2008/jul/08/persimmon.housingmarket1?INTCMP=SRCH – A short article looking at the impact of inventory write-downs on a house-building company; the fall in house prices in recent years can cause the value of the stock of houses and land held by a house-builder to fall below the original cost. Published online on 8 July 2008 in *The Guardian*.

http://www.dailymail.co.uk/news/article-422685/Drop-bad-debts-puts-HBOS-record-year.html#ixzz21C7MGr1F – 'Drop in bad debts puts HBOS on a record year'; published on 14 December 2006 by *The Daily Mail*.

http://www.dailymail.co.uk/news/article-1094063/HBOS-shareholders-approve-Lloyds-takeover-bank-reveals-6bn-bad-debts.html#ixzz21C7oHGgl – 'HBOS shareholders approve Lloyds takeover as bank reveals £6billion of bad debts'; published on 12 December 2008 in *The Daily Mail*.

http://www.dailymail.co.uk/money/article-1199293/Lloyds-write-13billion-bad-debts.html#ixzz21C74XMax – 'Lloyds Banking Group to write off £13billion in bad debts'; published on 13 July 2009 by *The Daily Mail*.

Adjustments to accounts I: Accruals and prepayments

6

'Running a small **business** profitably requires **prudence**.' (ANONYMOUS)

CHAPTER OUTLINE

6.1   Introduction

6.2   What is an accrual?

6.3   Accounting treatment for accruals

6.4   What is a prepayment?

6.5   Accounting treatment for a prepayment

6.6   Relating accruals and prepayments to real company accounts

6.7   Summary

CHAPTER OBJECTIVES

After carefully reading the text and completing the tasks and activities provided in this chapter you should have a better understanding and knowledge of:

- what gives rise to an accrual and/or a prepayment

- how to adjust both the statement of financial position and the income statement for accruals and prepayments

- how the adjustments of accruals and prepayments affect a company's financial position.

6.1 Introduction

So far we have looked at the process by which financial data is recorded, fed into a trial balance and then ultimately reported in the form of financial statements, such as the statement of financial position and income statement. It is now necessary to go back to these statements and see how they need to be adjusted for transactions that have fallen outside of the trial balance.

Such transactions give rise to items known as accruals and prepayments. Let us start by looking at an accrual. You have already been introduced to the term 'accounts payable' in Chapter 3.

With accounts payable, an organization is aware that a sum of money is owed. In contrast, where the organization, at the statement of financial position date, is uncertain of the amounts that are owed, there will be an accrual rather than an accounts payable. One of the most likely reasons for this uncertainty is the absence of an invoice.

Cash versus accrual

Method of accounting	Expense incurred	Expense paid	Revenue earned	Revenue received
Accrual	✓		✓	
Cash		✓		✓

Accrual accounting is typical where a business has inventory items in excess of £5m. These are items that are intended for sale to the public. Under such circumstances, the Accounting Standards require a company to use the accrual method of accounting.

As the table above shows, accrual accounting means that revenue is recognized as soon as it has been earned. This is regardless of whether or not the cash has been received. Likewise, expenses are recorded as soon as they become an obligation, regardless of whether or not the expense has actually been paid.

> ### Reflective question
>
> 1 | (a) What is 'an accounts payable'?
> | (b) In which financial statement does it appear?

6.2 What is an accrual?

Accrual in accounting terms an acrrual is 'a liability in respect of goods and services provided to a business ..., consumed up to an accounting date but not billed by that date.' R Brockington (1993)	**KEY TERM**

With accruals, the point to note is that a liability relating to a particular period is recognized; it is the *amount* of that liability that is not known with certainty. A typical example of an **accrual** would be a telephone or electricity bill. Such bills are often received after the period of use, either monthly or quarterly. As such, the final month or quarter of the financial year ending for example on 31 March 2010 may not be billed until the next accounting period, that being the financial year ending 2011. As the service was not consumed in that period the bill does not actually relate to that period. Therefore an estimate is made and it is recorded as an accrual in the accounts of the period to which it relates; in our example this would be the year ending 31 March 2010.

Consider the following dates for payment of Ring Ltd's telephone bill. The company's year end is 31 March. The telephone is paid quarterly on the following dates:

- July 2009
- October 2009
- January 2010
- April 2010

The bill for the fourth quarter (Jan–Mar 2010) falls into the next financial year and has not yet been received by year end. However, because it relates to the accounts of the year ending March 2010, it should be accrued and shown in these accounts. The accrual amount may be an estimate or if the bill is received after the year end date but before the accounts are signed off, the actual amount of the bill can be shown in the accounts.

Put simply, an accrual is an expense that relates to a particular financial period, that, as yet, has not been paid. This supports the accruals concept of accounting whereby expenses are recognized by when they are incurred and not when they have been paid. It is clear, therefore, that if the accounts of a year are to give a complete picture of the company's financial position, then these accrual amounts must be included.

6.3 Accounting treatment for accruals

In order to account for an accrual the double-entry rules are applied – which you first looked at in Chapter 2. The accounting treatment of an accrual item can help reinforce the matching concept. We account for any accrual by recognizing it against the revenue that it earned. This provides us with accounts that deliver a better picture of the company's long-term profitability and liability position. However, this method does lack the ability to provide an accurate picture of the company's cash flow position.

With this in mind the accounting treatment needs to ensure that what is relevant to the current accounting period is in fact recorded in the financial accounts of that period, even if the payments and receipts have not yet physically been paid or received.

In summary, an accrual adjustment therefore requires an increase in the expenses on the income statement and an increase or a creation of an accrual on the statement of financial position, under the current liabilities section.

ACTIVITY

1   Consider the following dates for payment of Ring Ltd's telephone bill. The company's year end is 31 March. The telephone bill is paid quarterly on the following dates:

7 July 2009	£900	(Re. quarter Apr 09 – June 09)
10 October 2009	£700	(Re. quarter Jul 09 – Sept 09)
10 January 2010	£1,250	(Re. quarter Oct 09 – Dec 09)

The bill for the fourth quarter (re. Jan 10 – Mar 10) falls into the next financial year and has not yet been received. It is invoiced at £1,100 in April 2010 and received by Ring Ltd on 8 April 2010.

State how this last bill should be shown in Ring Ltd's accounts?

6.4 What is a prepayment?

KEY TERM

Prepayments For accounting purposes these are 'amounts already paid which will fall to be treated as expenses in a forthcoming period.' R Brockington (1993)

The way that prepayments are treated in the accounts is the opposite of an accrual. Where a prepayment has taken place, it is often the case that the product/service has yet to be provided or fulfilled. A typical example of this kind of arrangement is rental payment. It is usually the case that the rent for the agreed future period will be paid in advance. This may mean that the rent is actually paid in one accounting period even though it actually relates to the next accounting period, that being the period in which the service is consumed. Let us consider the following:

Lett Ltd's rental expenses for the calendar year are £1,200. The company's year end is 31 March. The rental expense is paid in full to the landlord at the start of the calendar year.

The £1,200 is paid on 1 January 2009 for the whole year. However, for the financial year ending 31 March 2009, only one quarter of the rental has been consumed for that year; the remainder relates to a future benefit to be received in the next accounting period. In this case only £300 of the £1,200 should appear as an expense in the accounts ending 31 March 2009. The remaining £900 is a prepayment and should be shown as such under the heading of current assets in the statement of financial position for the year ending 31 March 2009.

6.5 Accounting treatment for a prepayment

In order to account for a prepayment the same double-entry rules are applied, as described earlier in Chapter 2. Let us stay with the example of Lett Ltd.

As with an accrual, it is necessary to adjust for prepayments so that we end up with accounts that deliver a better picture of the company's long-term profitability and liability position. Again, we are reinforcing the matching principle, this time by taking the prepayments out of the period in which they were made and putting them against the revenue they actually relate to.

The accounting treatment needs to ensure that we only charge the current accounting period with costs that have been incurred to earn that period's revenue. If these payments relate to future anticipated revenues then they should be charged in the accounts that reflect those future revenues.

Reflective question

2 | The matching principle requires the revenues of a period to be matched against the costs incurred to earn these revenues. True or false?

A prepayment adjustment therefore requires a decrease in the expenses on the income statement and an increase or a creation of a prepayment on the statement of financial position, under the current assets section.

ACTIVITY

2 | Consider the following dates for rental payments of Lett Ltd. The company's year end is 31 March. The rental is paid quarterly in advance on the following dates:

30 June 2009	£300
30 September 2009	£300
28 December 2009	£300
31 March 2010	£300

In the accounts for the year ending 31 March 2010:
- (a) Calculate the rental expense in the income statement.
- (b) Calculate the prepayment amount under current assets in the statement of financial position.

Worked Example

Consider the following trial balance for Work It Out Ltd, for the year ending 31 March 2010:

	Dr £	Cr £
Capital		36,200
Drawings	31,000	
Payables		25,600
Receivables	31,800	
Bank overdraft		2,160
Cash	560	
Opening inventory	3,800	
Plant & machinery	8,000	
Purchases	66,400	
Sales		198,800
Rent & Rates	12,260	
General expenses	30,460	
Salaries	54,260	
Distribution expenses	24,220	
	262,760	**262,760**

At the year end the notes listed below have come to light:

1	Closing inventory	£3,060
2	Accrued salaries as at 31 March 2010	£2,160
3	Rates accrued as at 31 March 2010	£160
4	Prepaid general expenses	£240
5	Prepaid distribution expenses	£1,340

In view of the above notes prepare the statement of financial position and income statement for Work It Out Ltd for the year ending 31 March 2010.

Solution:

Work It Out Ltd

Income Statement for the year ending 31 March 2010

	£	£
Sales		198,800
Opening inventory	3,800	
Add purchases	66,400	
Less closing inventory	(3,060)	
Cost of sales		(67,140)
Gross profit		**131,660**
Less expenses:		
Rent and rates (12,260 + 160)	12,420	
General expenses (30,460 – 240)	30,220	
Salaries (54,260 + 2160)	56,420	
Distribution (24220 – 1,340)	22,880	
Total expenses		(121,940)
Net operating profit for the year		**9,720**

Statement of Financial Position as at 31 March 2010

	£	£
Non-current assets:		
Tangibles: Plant and machinery		8,000
Current assets:		
Inventory	3,060	
Receivables (31,800)	31,800	
Cash	560	
Prepayments (240 + 1,340)	1,580	
		37,000
Total assets		**45,000**
Financed by:		
Capital		36,200
Drawings		(31,000)
Profit for the year		9,720
		14,920
Current liabilities:		
Bank overdraft	2,160	
Payables	25,600	
Accruals (160 + 2,160)	2,320	30,080
		45,000

> **Reflective question**
>
> 3 | Under the revenue principle, businesses should record revenue when it is earned regardless of when payment is received from the customer. Is this true or false?

6.6 Relating accruals and prepayments to real company accounts

Although this chapter has provided you with a detailed look at what an accrual and a prepayment are, and how they should be accounted for, it is perhaps useful to look at some real company accounts and to see where these items appear. You will find that in most accounts accruals and prepayments will be included under a heading such as 'Other payables' or 'Other receivables'. In order to ascertain whether or not an accrual or a prepayment exists, you would normally have to read the note against this category.

ACTIVITY

3 | Figure 6.1 shows an extract from the accounts of Vodafone plc. Identify where in these accounts the accruals and prepayments are shown.

FIGURE 6.1 Extract from Vodafone accounts

Consolidated statement of Financial position at 31 March

	Note	2010 £m	2009 £m
Non-current assets			
Goodwill	9	51,838	53,958
Other intangible assets	9	22,420	20,980
Property, plant and equipment	11	20,642	19,250
Investments in associates	14	36,377	34,715
Other investments	15	7,591	7,060
Deferred tax assets	6	1,033	630
Post employment benefits	23	34	8
Trade and other receivables	17	2,831	3,069
		142,766	**139,670**
Current assets			
Inventory	16	433	412
Taxation recoverable		191	77
Trade and other receivables	17	8,784	7,662
Other investments	15	388	–
Cash and cash equivalents	18	4,423	4,878
		14,219	**13,029**
Total assets		**156,985**	**152,699**

	Note	2010 £m	2009 £m
Equity			
Called up share capital	19	4,153	4,153
Additional paid-in capital		153,509	153,348
Treasury shares		(7,810)	(8,036)
Retained losses		(79,655)	(83,820)
Accumulated other comprehensive income		20,184	20,517
Total equity shareholders' funds		**90,381**	**86,162**
Non-controlling interests		3,379	1,787
Put options over non-controlling interests		(2,950)	(3,172)
Total non-controlling interests		**429**	**(1,385)**
Total equity		**90,810**	**84,777**
Non-current liabilities			
Long-term borrowings	22	28,632	31,749
Deferred tax liabilities	6	7,377	6,642
Post employment benefits	23	237	240
Provisions	24	497	533
Trade and other payables	25	816	811
		37,559	**39,975**
Current liabilities			
Short-term borrowings	22	11,163	9,624
Current taxation liabilities		2,874	4,552
Provisions	24	497	373
Trade and other payables	25	14,082	13,398
		28,616	**27,947**
Total equity and liabilities		**156,985**	**152,699**

Source: Vodafone (2010) Annual Report

6.7 Summary

Key ideas

Accrual

- an expense that is recognized but not yet recorded due to there being no invoice
- it is shown as a credit on the statement of financial position, under current liabilities, because it provides a more accurate picture of the liabilities that relate to the financial year in question
- shown as a debit on the income statement, by adding to the existing expenses; This is because it provides a more accurate picture of the expenses that relate to the financial year in question.

Prepayment

- an expense paid in advance at the end of the financial year
- shown as a debit on the statement of financial position, under current assets, as it provides a more accurate picture of the assets (future economic benefit) that relate to the financial year in question
- shown as a credit on the income statement, by deducting from the existing expenses, as it provides a more accurate picture of the expenses that relate to the financial year in question.

Review questions

1. If an adjusting entry for accrued expenses is not made, which of the following items will be overstated?
   (a) Expenses
   (b) Assets
   (c) Profit
   (d) Liabilities
   (e) All of the above

2. A prepaid expense will appear under which of the following headings?
   (a) Non-current assets
   (b) Turnover
   (c) Current asset
   (d) Current liability
   (e) None of the above.

3. Which of the following is an example of an accruals account?
   (a) Rental income receivable
   (b) Fees receivable
   (c) Income tax payable
   (d) Wages payable
   (e) All of the above

4. If a company uses accrual accounting and then receives an electric bill, this would require an expense account to be debited. Is this true or false?

5. Call plc received a telephone bill on 11th December 2009. However, they did not pay the bill until 8th January 2010. Under the accrual basis of accounting, if the year end is 31st Dec the expense should appear on:
   (a) Neither the 2009 nor the 2010 income statement
   (b) Income statement for 2010
   (c) Income statements for both 2009 and 2010
   (d) Income statement for 2009

6. The trial balance shows insurance costs as £8,200, but there is a prepayment of £1,200. Therefore:
   (a) an expense of £9,400 will be shown in the income statement
   (b) an expense of £7,000 will be shown in the income statement
   (c) prepayments of £9,400 will be shown under current assets in the statement of financial position
   (d) prepayments of £1,200 will be shown under current liabilities in the statement of financial position

7. The trial balance shows electricity costs as £1,000, but there is an accrual of £300. Therefore:
   (a) an expense of £1,300 will be shown in the income statement
   (b) an expense of £700 will be shown in the income statement
   (c) accruals of £1,300 will be shown under current liabilities in the statement of financial position
   (d) accruals of £300 will be shown under current assets in the statement of financial position

8. Which of the following totals will an accrual increase?
   (a) Revenue in the income statement
   (b) Non-current assets in the statement of financial position
   (c) Non-current liabilities in the statement of financial position
   (d) Current liability in the statement of financial position

Recommended reading

Berry, A. and Jarvis, R. (2006) *Accounting in a Business Context*, London: Thomson Learning.

Black, G. (2009) *Introduction to Accounting and Finance*, Harlow: FT Prentice-Hall.

Brockington, R. (1993) *Dictionary of Accounting and Finance*, London: Pitman Publishing.

Davies, T. and Boczko, T. (2005) *Financial Accounting: An Introduction*, Maidenhead: McGraw-Hill.

Useful websites

http://www.realsmallbusiness.com/money/cash-flow/articles cash flow accrual/index.html

Will help to explain accrual accounting by highlighting the way in which accrual accounting differs from cash accounting – of further use to you in Chapter 8.

Adjustments to accounts II: Non-current assets and depreciation

7

'In **business** a reputation for keeping absolutely to the letter and spirit of an agreement, even when it is unfavourable, is the most **precious of assets**, although it is not entered in the balance sheet.' (LORD CHANDOS (1893–1972), British Statesman and industrialist)

CHAPTER OUTLINE

7.1 Introduction

7.2 Valuing non-current assets on the SoFP

7.3 Depreciation

7.4 Calculating depreciation

7.5 Accounting for the sale of a non-current asset.

7.6 Summary

CHAPTER OBJECTIVES

After carefully reading the text and completing the tasks and activities provided in this chapter you should have a better understanding and knowledge of:

- how to value non-current assets

- what is meant by depreciation and why it is necessary

- how to calculate a depreciation figure using different methods

- how depreciation is reflected in the financial statements

- accurately accounting for changes to the non-current assets because of a sale

- the impact on all financial statements of the sale of a non-current asset.

7.1 Introduction

This chapter revisits and then extends the topic of non-current assets as they appear on the statement of financial position. We also look at the concept of **depreciation** and how this affects the statement of financial position, the income statement and the cash flow statement.

An important aspect of non-current assets is the way in which they are valued. In Chapter 3 you studied the definition of a non-current asset and where it would appear on the statement of financial position. **Non-current assets** are primarily bought with the intention of being used in a business over a period of years, to generate revenue. They are not bought with the intention of resale. It is important to consider the value at which the non-current asset is to be shown on the statement of financial position, since it would be unreasonable to assume that an organization's non-current assets will not change in value over time.

Before we continue it may be useful to remind ourselves of the different asset categories and their definitions as they appear in the statement of financial position.

ACTIVITY

1	What are the two broad categories of assets shown on the statement of financial position?
2	What is the definition of an asset?
3	Give three examples of ways in which non-current assets differ from current assets.

7.2 Valuing non-current assets on the Statement of Financial Position

The statement of financial position traditionally values non-current assets at historical cost, i.e. the purchase price of the asset in question. This treatment is governed by International Accounting Standard (IAS) 16. The standard goes into considerable detail about what constitutes cost. For the purposes of this book, we will consider cost to be the purchase price of the non-current asset.

It is accepted that to record non-current assets at cost forever more is somewhat unrealistic and does not tie in with the whole objective of financial statements which is to provide a true and fair picture of the business. With this in mind, after the initial recognition of the value of non-current assets, measurement can be adjusted for any accumulated depreciation, impairments and revaluations to fair value.

In essence, the fair value of non-current assets usually equates to the assets' market value. However, if no such market value exists (as can be the case for assets that are of a specialized nature) then the assets can be stated at their depreciated replacement cost.

As mentioned above, one approach to valuing assets is the fair value accounting approach, which is essentially valuing assets at their market value. This has been heavily debated in the news recently and referred to as the MTM approach – the mark-to-market valuation approach. The current economic climate has bought into question some of the decisions that are being made about how assets should be valued and thus reflected in the statement of financial position.

Valuing assets at fair value is a well recognized and much debated method of valuation. However, the recent rule change on 'fair value' by the Financial Accounting Standards

Board (FASB) has sparked some debate, with some now questioning why should a recommended method of valuing assets not be adhered to? Although this is not the main focus of this chapter, it does make for interesting reading and is certainly relevant if you are seeking to grasp an understanding of the bigger picture.

The article below helps shed some light on this controversy.

KEY THEMES Warning on Fair Value

Accounting board calls U.S. changes 'crazy' by **Duncan Mavin and Eoin Callan**

Bank lobbyists and politicians are damaging the credibility of corporate reporting and hurting the interests of investors around the world by pulling back on mark-to-market accounting, one of the world's top international accountants warned.

The comments from Tom Jones, vice-chairman of the International Accounting Standards Board (IASB), came after U.S. standard-setters unilaterally decided to dilute the controversial accounting rule earlier this month.

In an interview with the Financial Post, Mr. Jones warned of "a loss of credibility" and said the rationale for watering down so-called fair-value accounting is "crazy." He also cited concerns about political interference that could undermine the independence of accounting rule-setters.

These fears were echoed by other senior accountants, who urged Canadian authorities to resist pressure from big banks to follow the U.S. lead.

In early April, the U.S. Financial Accounting Standards Board pledged to backtrack on fair-value accounting under intense pressure from Wall Street and demands from Congress. U.S. lawmakers had even threatened to take the matter into their own hands rather than leave it to the accountants.

The resulting FASB rule changes allow banks to use judgment, rather than market prices, to value financial instruments.

Despite the urgings of Bay Street, the oversight council of Canada's standards board opted not to move to align itself with the United States when it met this month, though the organization will weigh the matter again after the international accounting board meets this week.

The Canadian stance has received significant backing from the accountancy profession.

Chris Clark, chief executive of Pricewater-houseCoopers Canada, said his firm does not support rushing to imitate the Americans, and urged authorities to "balance" the demands of banks with "the needs of the investor."

Nouriel Roubini, the New York University economist nicknamed "Dr. Doom" for his prescient forecast of the global economic downturn, yesterday called the U.S. rule changes "a big mistake" that has allowed Wall Street banks to "fudge" their latest set of quarterly accounts.

The changes circumvent capital rules set by bank regulators and would, if adopted, weaken Canada's banking system, said Wayne Landsman, a professor at the University of North Carolina who will speak on the topic at the Rotman School of Management in Toronto on Thursday.

Proponents of fair-value, or mark-to-market, accounting say it is the most accurate and independent way to price assets.

But bankers say fair-value accounting has exacerbated the current financial crisis by unfairly forcing them to take huge writedowns. They say illiquid markets for certain securities have led to fire-sale prices that do not represent appropriate valuations, and they have lobbied to be allowed to value certain troubled securities based on their own estimates.

The idea that banks have been forced to write down assets beyond any rational level is "actually crazy," said IASB's Mr. Jones. The market price for troubled financial instruments has probably not even hit the bottom yet, he added.

Mr. Jones insisted there are better answers to the current problems in the banking sector than tinkering with fair-value rules.

One possibility would be to change the amount of capital banks are required to set aside by bank regulators, he said.

Politicians and lobbyists in the United States seeking to further weaken fair value are having the effect of pressuring global standard-setters to follow FASB's lead, Mr. Jones said. European finance ministers, for instance, have already called standard setters outside the United States to "level the playing field" on fair value accounting.

The IASB has reacted by urgently cutting short a consultation period on changes to its rules on financial instruments.

The London-based IASB uses a different rule book than the FASB.

In recent years, most countries, outside of the United States, have adopted or pledged to adopt the IASB rules. At a meeting in the U. K. this month, G20 leaders called for significant progress toward a single set of global accounting standards. Some observers say a single set of rules would make it easier for investors around the world to make informed decisions.

Mr. Jones said the integration plans have not been derailed by the United States' decision to back away from fair-value accounting. Full adoption of IASB standards by the United States seems unlikely, but some form of convergence is expected in the long term.

"We are going to try to ensure the difference isn't as great as it seems," he added. Mr. Jones noted that IASB rules on fair value also allow companies to exercise judgment in some cases, like the amended U. S. rules.

Separately, members of a joint committee formed by the two accounting organizations to deal with the financial crisis also complained about political interference in their work.

At a London meeting of the Financial Crisis Advisory Group that was broadcast on the Internet, senior industry experts expressed concern about the politicization of the process of revising accounting standards.

Harvey Goldschmid, the group's joint chairman, who is a former commissioner of the Securities and Exchange Commission, and Sir David Tweedie, IASB chairman, were among those who warned of the dangers of political pressure that could weaken the independence of accounting standard-setters

Source: *Financial Post*, 21 April 2009 (www.financialpost.com/story.html?id=1516597&p=2). Material reprinted with the express permission of *The National Post Company*, a Canwest Partnership.

Q **In your own words explain what it means to show assets on the statement of financial position at fair value?**

Another aspect of asset valuation that has undergone much debate relates to the category of intangible assets, since they too appear under the heading of non-current assets in the statement of financial position. The debate on how these are to be valued has been ongoing and is a major consideration when companies are considering or more likely trying to defend themselves from a potential takeover bid. Some examples of tangible and intangible non-current assets are given below.

Tangible non-current assets	Intangible non-current assets
Land	Goodwill
Buildings	Brand names
Plant and machinery	Research and development

It is important that the value of assets provides a relevant reflection of what they can produce in terms of future cash flows. Companies will be keen to show their non-current assets at their most attractive value, as this has implications for the calculation of key accounting ratios and thus company performance. This will be discussed further in Chapter 9. Below is an article that demonstrates how the value of the assets can help companies protect themselves from potential takeover bids. The higher the asset value of the company, the stronger the statement of financial position appears.

Kingfisher, the owner of B&Q, yesterday sought to defend a grim performance and deter possible predators as it revalued its property portfolio at £3 billion.

Its shares rose 5p to 248p to reflect the £600 million increase in the value of the group's property. The rise came despite a 64.2 per cent slump in pre-tax profits to £231.8 million after £215.4 million of exceptional items, in line with expectations.

The profit slump was led by a poor performance at B&Q in the UK, where total sales fell 3.7 per cent to £3.9 billion and profits slid 52 per cent. Margins fell 5 per cent as a result of price cuts, a 4 per cent rise in fixed costs and the impact of a 7.8 per cent underlying sales decline.

Analysts said that the property revaluation had boosted Kingfisher's share price above the 240p a share that was likely to be the most a private equity firm would pay for the group.

Shares in Kingfisher have risen 10.5 per cent since early last month on hopes that a private equity firm or trade buyer such as the American DIY giants Home Depot or Lowe's would attempt a takeover.

One analyst said: "I know several private equity firms have taken a look, but they just can't make the maths stand up."

He said that it was unlikely that the American firms would make a move for Kingfisher in the near future as they could find better returns on investment in Asia.

Another analyst suggested that private equity firms could help to fund a bid for Kingfisher by selling off the property assets, which are worth about half the market value of the group, and other "crown jewels" such as the fast-growing Chinese B&Q chain.

Gerry Murphy, chief executive, declined to comment on whether the group had held talks with interested parties. He said that the management team was focusing on the turnaround of B&Q and expansion overseas.

The group plans a sale and leaseback programme of between £200 million and £300 million a year to fund property acquisitions abroad.

Stores in Poland, Italy, the Republic of Ireland, China and Taiwan are expected to double in the next five years, while Kingfisher is also investing in new ventures in Turkey, Spain, South Korea and Russia.

Fewer than 20 new B&Q stores are planned in the UK over the next five years as Kingfisher focuses on refurbishing its current portfolio.

Plans to attract customers back to B&Q also include new ways of organising staff to improve service in stores and adding 3,000 new products.

Mr Murphy said that these changes were unlikely to show any impact on the business until the six months to the end of next January.

Margins are expected to continue to come under pressure from fixed-costs rises of about 4 per cent and also to be affected by further price cuts.

Mr Murphy said that B&Q had trimmed its stock commitments by £100 million this year in anticipation of another tough trading period and this was likely to limit the level of discounting compared with last year.

Source: *The Times*, 22 March 2006. Reported by Sarah Butler © The Times 2006/nisyndication.com

Q   How might a revaluation of assets affect key accounting ratios?

As mentioned earlier in this chapter, non-current assets can be shown using alternative valuation methods after initially being recognized at cost. This is to derive a more realistic value of the non-current assets. However, this also means that one company may choose to revalue its assets to fair value whereas another may choose not to. This inconsistency can make it difficult to undertake a meaningful comparison between two companies. In fact if a company does not adopt a consistent valuation policy, then comparison of the same company's performance over time may become distorted, if not meaningless. For this reason, if companies choose to provide an alternative valuation of their non-current assets, certain rules need to be followed.

We now need to focus on how the financial statements need to be adjusted to allow for changes in asset values. The traditional historical cost method of valuing assets must be looked at with depreciation in mind. This results in bringing assets onto the statement of financial position at their net book value rather than at historical cost. We will therefore now focus on depreciation: how it impacts on the asset value and what impact it has on the financial statements.

> **Reflective Question**
> 1 | What are the various values at which a non-current asset can be recorded in the statement of financial position?

 ## 7.3 Depreciation

> **Depreciation** is the measure of the fall in the value of a non-current asset, due to wear and tear, that occurs over a period of time.

KEY TERM

Depreciation relates to tangible assets such as buildings, vehicles, machinery, etc. – those assets that are going to be used within the company and thus undergo some physical wear and tear. Depreciation is nothing more than a monetary indication of a particular asset's wear and tear each year. As such, depreciation is based on the underlying economic concept of consumption, that being the reduction of value over time. It is a measure of consumption, i.e. a reduction in the asset's useful economic life. This reduction in the asset's useful economic life may be due to factors such as:

- the passing of time
- physical obsolescence
- changes in technology
- changes in the marketplace.

Therefore, it follows that the amount by which an asset depreciates will affect the value of the asset. By recognizing this depreciation, an asset in subsequent years can be shown at its net book value, rather than at original cost.

It is important to recognize that the depreciation charge calculated and then charged to each accounting period is not actually a physical movement of cash. It is merely a means of allocating the asset's initial capital expenditure over the asset's useful economic life. If the asset is recorded in the statement of financial position at cost or at a revalued amount, then the depreciation accumulated to date will reduce the value of that asset in the statement of financial position to show it at its net book value, i.e. the value of the asset at cost after deducting depreciation.

Depreciation gives rise to yet another adjustment and thus a calculation needs to happen so that the financial statements adhere to the accruals/matching concept.

> **Reflective Question**
> 2 | What is meant by the accruals/matching concept?

By looking at depreciation we are matching the one-off capital expenditure cost incurred when purchasing a non-current asset with the revenue that will be generated by that asset. This revenue may potentially last for several years.

Aside from satisfying the matching/accruals principle, recognition of depreciation enables the organization to carry on trading at the end of the asset's useful economic life. By charging depreciation as an expense in the income statement we are effectively recognizing that operating capacity has to be maintained. In theory, the company is maintaining enough funds so that when the asset needs replacing they have the funds to do so. However, any changes in price or other relevant changes in the environment are not taken into account, in which case the theory relating to the provision of depreciation is perhaps not sufficient to maintain operating capacity at some future point when the asset may need replacing.

Let's now look at the following worked example which illustrates what happens if we do not account for depreciation and instead make the assumption that everything else remains constant.

Worked Example

Ruby sets up her own business by converting her double garage into a beauty salon. She spends £10,000 on equipment, which has a five-year life span, so that the salon is set up and ready to go. £2,000 cash is put into the business for subsequent purchases of inventory items, such as lotions, wax, towels, polishes, sheets and oils.

The cash flows per year over the next five years are shown below:

Cash from sales	£12,000
Operating expenses	£9,000
Net cash flow from sales	**£3,000**

(Assuming that all inventory had been used in generating a cash sale, total cash comes to £2,000 + £3,000 = £5,000.)

Given the above figures, Ruby decides to take out £3,000 from the business as she feels this leaves the business no worse off than its starting position i.e. £2,000 cash and the salon equipment at £10,000.

Based on the above, extracts from the financial statements will look like this:

Income statement extracts over five years

	Year 1	Year 2	Year 3	Year 4	Year 5
Sales	12,000	12,000	12,000	12,000	12,000
Cost of sales	(9,000)	(9,000)	(9,000)	(9,000)	(9,000)
Profit	3,000	3,000	3,000	3,000	3,000
Drawings	(3,000)	(3,000)	(3,000)	(3,000)	(3,000)
Profit for the year	0	0	0	0	0

Statement of Financial Position extracts over 5 years

	Year 1	Year 2	Year 3	Year 4	Year 5
Non-current assets:					
Equipment	10,000	10,000	10,000	10,000	0
Current assets:					
Cash	2,000	2,000	2,000	2,000	2,000
	12,000	12,000	12,000	12,000	2,000
Owner's equity					
Capital	12,000	12,000	12,000	12,000	2,000

The above suggests that at the end of the assets' life its value will be zero and the business does not have sufficient funds to carry on trading since it does not have the funds to replace the equipment.

If, however, we consider the impact of charging for depreciation, the position of the financial statements changes somewhat:

Income statement extracts over five years

	Year 1	Year 2	Year 3	Year 4	Year 5
Sales	12,000	12,000	12,000	12,000	12,000
Cost of sales	(9,000)	(9,000)	(9,000)	(9,000)	(9,000)
Gross Profit	3,000	3,000	3,000	3,000	3,000
Depreciation	(2,000)	(2,000)	(2,000)	(2,000)	(2,000)
Net profit	1,000	1,000	1,000	1,000	1,000
Drawings	(1,000)	(1,000)	(1,000)	(1,000)	(1,000)
Profit for the year	0	0	0	0	0

Under such circumstances the profit is reduced to £1,000 because of the depreciation charge and Ruby can now only take out £1,000 as drawings.

Statement of Financial Position extracts over five years

	Year 1	Year 2	Year 3	Year 4	Year 5
Non-current assets:					
Equipment	10,000	10,000	10,000	10,000	10,000
Depreciation	(2,000)	(4,000)	(6,000)	(8,000)	(10,000)
NBV	8,000	6,000	4,000	2,000	0

	Year 1	Year 2	Year 3	Year 4	Year 5
Current assets:					
Cash	4,000	6,000	8,000	10,000	12,000
	12,000	12,000	12,000	12,000	12,000
Owner's equity					
Capital	12,000	12,000	12,000	12,000	12,000

From the above it can be seen that by charging depreciation the yearly profit has fallen, which in turn has led to a reduced amount being withdrawn. As such, cash balances will go up by £2,000 each year up to year 5 – the end of the assets' life. At this point cash will equate to the original value of the asset and therefore the theory suggests that enough liquid funds are available to maintain the business, since there are sufficient funds to purchase more salon equipment to replace the equipment that has just reached the end of its life.

Of course, the above example makes an assumption that there have been no changes in the market. However, this is unlikely, so the above example serves only to highlight the theory behind depreciation as a way of maintaining a company's future existence.

Reflective Questions

3 | Assets are valued using depreciation methods. What is the underlying economic concept of depreciation?

4 | How is depreciation categorized in the financial statements and which financial statement is it included in?

7.4 Calculating depreciation

Having established the need to reflect non-current assets net of depreciation, it is necessary to know how to calculate a depreciation charge. Now that we understand what depreciation is measuring, namely a reduction in an asset's value due to wear and tear, and reflecting, namely what the asset is worth each year, it follows that in order to calculate depreciation there are certain factors that need to be identified:

- original cost of the asset
- useful economic life of the asset
- residual value of the asset
- depreciation method.

KEY TERM

Residual value is an estimate of the amount that an asset can eventually be sold for or scrapped for at the end of its useful economic life; to some extent, it represents a recovery of part of the asset's original cost.

There are two well-known methods that are used to determine a depreciation rate/charge: the **straight line method** and the **reducing balance method**. We shall now consider these methods in turn and then determine where these charges should appear in the financial statements.

The straight line method

> Straight line method is where depreciation is calculated by taking the cost of the non-current asset less any residual value that the asset may bring and dividing it by the asset's useful economic life (the latter is expressed by the number of years the asset is expected to serve the company).

The formula for calculating depreciation using the straight line method is as follows:

$$\text{Depreciation} = \frac{\text{Cost of asset} - \text{residual value}}{\text{Estimated useful life of the asset (in years)}}$$

The numerator in this equation represents the total depreciation value of the asset over its whole life. In other words, the total amount by which the asset has depreciated. In order to satisfy the accrual/matching concept we need to determine an annual depreciation charge. We can determine this by applying the denominator in the above formula, i.e. spreading the total depreciation charge over the number of years. Under this method the depreciation charge each year is constant.

By so doing we are matching the revenue earned in the period with a part of the cost incurred to earn it.

Consider the following example which illustrates the calculation of depreciation using the straight line method.

The Bun Factory Ltd purchases a new dough making machine for £32,000. It is estimated to have a useful economic life of ten years, after which the machine can be sold for £2,000.

The depreciation charge each year using the straight line method will be:

$$\text{Depreciation} = \frac{\text{Cost of asset} - \text{residual value}}{\text{Estimated useful life of the asset (in years)}}$$

$$\text{Depreciation} = \frac{£32,000 - £2,000}{10 \text{ years}}$$

Depreciation = £3,000 per year

Effect of the straight line method on the financial statements

Looking again at the example above, the annual depreciation charge of £3,000 will be charged each year to the income statement. In published financial statements this will be grouped under the heading 'administration and distribution expenses', for example.

The £3,000 will also appear in the statement of financial position. It will reduce the non-current asset that it relates to by the depreciation to date. Staying with the example of Bun Factory Ltd, below is an extract from their statements of financial position over the next ten years of the asset's life.

Statement of Financial Position as at 31 Dec 20X9 for the Bun Factory Ltd

	Cost	Depreciation	Net book value
Non-current assets:	£	£	£
Tangible: machinery			
Year 1	32,000	3,000	29,000
Year 2	32,000	6,000	26,000
Year 3	32,000	9,000	23,000
Year 4	32,000	12,000	20,000
Year 5	32,000	15,000	17,000
Year 6	32,000	18,000	14,000
Year 7	32,000	21,000	11,000
Year 8	32,000	24,000	8,000
Year 9	32,000	27,000	5,000
Year 10	32,000	30,000	2,000

Note: The £2,000 net book value at the end of year 10 will be exactly offset by the £2,000 that will be received when this asset is disposed, as indicated by the residual value.

Reducing balance method

KEY TERM

Reducing balance method is where depreciation is calculated by applying a fixed percentage each year to the asset's net book value.

When using the reducing balance method, note that the fixed percentage is **not** applied to the cost of the asset. As such, the depreciation charge each year will not be constant; instead the depreciation charge will be lower and lower as the asset progresses further and further towards the end of its useful economic life.

The fixed percentage used in the reducing balance method in effect reflects the rate required to bring the asset from cost to its residual value, as reflected at the end of its useful economic life. This can be estimated using the following formula:

$$\text{Depreciation rate (\%)} = 1 - \sqrt[\text{life}]{\frac{\text{residual value}}{\text{original cost}}}$$

Let us return to our earlier example of the Bun Factory Ltd.

The Bun Factory Ltd purchases a new dough making machine for £32,000. It is estimated to have a useful economic life of 10 years, after which the machine can be sold for £2,000.

Assume a depreciation rate of 21%.

The depreciation charge for the first three years will be calculated as follows:

	£	
Cost of asset	32,000	
Depreciation		
Charge (32,000 × 21%)	(6,720)	(for year 1)
Net book value	**25,280**	(at end of year 1)
Depreciation		
Charge (22,400 × 21%)	(5,309)	(for year 2)
Net book value	**19,971**	(at end of year 2)
Depreciation		
Charge (15,680 × 21%)	(4,194)	(for year 3)
Net book value	**15,777**	(at end of year 3)

And so on…

The point to note here is that the depreciation rate expressed as a percentage is charged to the asset's reduced net book value each year, and not just to the asset's original cost at the start of its life.

Effect of the reducing balance method on the financial statements

The depreciation charge will be recorded in the financial statements in the same way as the straight line method depreciation was recorded. The charge for the income statement will be different each year but will reflect that year only, whereas the charge for the statement of financial position will be cumulative.

Staying with the example of the Bun Factory Ltd, below is an extract from the statements of financial position over the next ten years of the asset's life.

Statement of Financial Position as at 31 December 20X9 for the Bun Factory Ltd

	Cost	Depreciation	Net book value
Non-current assets:	£	£	£
Tangible: machinery			
Year 1	32,000	6,720	25,280
Year 2	32,000	5,309	19,971
Year 3	32,000	4,194	15,777
Year 4	32,000	3,313	12,464
Year 5	32,000	2,617	9,846
Year 6	32,000	2,068	7,778
Year 7	32,000	1,633	6,145
Year 8	32,000	1,290	4,855
Year 9	32,000	1,019	3,386
Year 10	32,000	805	2,581

Note: The £2,581 net book value at the end of year 10 will be offset by the £2,000 that will be received when this asset is disposed of, as indicated by the residual value. (The difference is due to rounding of the depreciation rate.)

We will now look at the depreciation and adjustments question to look at the impact of depreciation on the income statement and statement of financial position.

Worked Example

From the following trial balance and footnotes, we will prepare an income statement and a statement of financial position:

Trial balance as at 31 December 2011

	£	£
Receivables	34,600	
Payables		20,900
Vehicle at cost	7,000	
Provision for depreciation on vehicle		1,400
Fixtures at cost	12,800	
Provision for depreciation on fixtures		2,560
Purchases	94,500	
Revenue		166,100
Insurance	3,500	
Salaries	29,600	
Bank	8,200	
Rates	3,600	
Electricity	4,960	
Land	60,000	
Drawings	18,200	
Sundry expenses	1,200	
Opening inventory	19,800	
Capital		107,000
	297,960	297,960

Notes:

1 Closing inventory £20,500
2 £250 of the rates for next year has been paid in advance.
3 £150 is owing for electricity.
4 The vehicle is to be depreciated at 20% per year using the reducing balance method.
5 Fixtures are to be depreciated at 10% per year using the straight line method.

Solution:
Income statement for the year ended 31st December 2011

	£	£
Revenue		166,100
Opening inventory	19,800	
Purchases	94,500	
	114,300	
Closing inventory	−20,500	
Cost of sales		93,800
Gross profit		72,300

	£	£
Expenses		
Insurance	3,500	
Salaries	29,600	
Rates	3,350	
Electricity	5,110	
Sundry expenses	1,200	
Depreciation :		
Vehicle 20% × (7000 − 1400)	1,120	
Fixtures (10% × 12,800)	1,280	
		45,160
Net Profit		**27,140**

Statement of Financial Position for the year ended 31st December 2011

	£	£
Assets		
Non-current assets		
Land	60,000	
Vehicles (7000 − 1400−1,120)	4,480	
Fixtures (12,800 − 2,560−1,280)	8,960	
		73,440
Current assets		
Inventory	20,500	
Receivables	34,600	
Bank	8,200	
Prepayments	250	
		63,550
Total assets		**136,990**
Capital		107,000
Drawings		−18,200
Net profit		27,140
		115,940
Current liabillities		
Payables	20,900	
Accruals	150	
		21,050
		136,990

ACTIVITY

4 | (a) Name the two most common methods of depreciating assets.

(b) Explain what impact depreciation will have on the bottom line profit figure in the income statement.

(c) Explain how depreciation affects the value of the assets as they are shown in the statement of financial position.

When should each method of depreciation be used?

Although there are many other methods available for the calculation of depreciation, the two methods described above are the most common. In order to satisfy the accruals/matching concept, organizations should select the depreciation method that best enables the revenue generated by the asset to be matched with the cost incurred in earning it. To determine this it may be necessary for organizations to consider looking at the pattern of revenues (i.e. benefits) that are being generated by the asset. If it appears that the revenues flow pretty evenly over the course of the asset's life, then it would make sense to apply the straight line method. This method spreads the cost of the asset evenly over the asset's life. If, however, the asset is used very heavily in its early years and is thus generating greater revenues (benefits) earlier on, then it is better to use the reducing balance method. This method results in a greater part of the asset's cost being charged to the early years, thereby matching the greater revenues flowing to the organization in the early years.

Whichever approach is chosen, it should be selected on the basis of appropriateness in relation to the asset and how it is used in the business. It should not be selected so as to manipulate the bottom line profit figure in the income statement. Nor should assets be inflated by charging low depreciation or upward re-valuations simply to fight off a potential takeover bid. The case study below shows how important asset valuation can be if a company is in danger of being taken over. An increase in the value of the asset has been pursued as a defence tactic against an unwanted takeover.

CASE STUDY Mitchells & Butler

Mitchells & Butler (M&B), the pub and restaurant group facing a possible £4 billion-plus takeover from Robert Tchenguiz, is expected to revalue its assets and return cash to shareholders as part of its bid defence.

The group, which owns chains such as All Bar One and Harvester, is tipped to lift its net debt from £1.6 billion to £2 billion, allowing it to return the proceeds to shareholders through share buybacks or a special dividend. Since it was demerged from Six Continents three years ago, M&B has returned — or committed to return — £700 million.

The company is considering appointing property consultants to revalue its estate for the first time since 1999. Analysts believe that such an exercise could add £1 billion to the £3.5 billion value put on its assets in 1999. A partial revaluation in 2003, conducted as part of a securitisation, valued its assets at closer to £3.9 billion.

Any bid defence from M&B is also likely to focus on its strong trading record since the demerger, with strong like-for-like sales growth allowing it to make big market share gains. It has also won plaudits for its ability to offset increases in energy and regulatory costs through purchasing and efficiency improvements.

M&B has refused to comment on last week's announcement from Mr Tchenguiz's R20 investment vehicle that it was considering making a bid. R20 is understood to have secured debt funding from a consortium of banks led by Barclays Capital and Goldman Sachs. HBOS, Goldman and a private equity firm — possibly Apax Partners — are thought to be supplying equity alongside Tchenguiz family trusts.

It is understood that Royal Bank of Scotland has withdrawn from the consortium after it became clear that its banking relationship with M&B could be put at risk.

R20 is tipped to make a formal approach next week at a price of about 525p a share, which would value M&B at £2.57 billion, or about £4.2 billion including debt. Shares in M&B fell 8¼p to 474p.

However, Mr Tchenguiz may face competition for the group. Bob Ivell, chairman of Regent Inns and former head of Scottish & Newcastle's restaurant arm, said yesterday that he had been approached about becoming involved with a possible bid. "These talks are at a very early stage at the moment," he said.

Source: *The Times*, 21 March 2006. Reported by Dominic Walsh
© The Times 2006/nisyndication.com

Q   How can an asset revaluation potentially protect a company from being taken over?

ACTIVITY

5 | The straight line method of depreciation is the most commonly used. Using straight line formula, calculate the annual straight line depreciation charge or yearly depreciation amount of a car using the following information:

Cost of the asset = £45,000

Residual value of the asset = £4,000

Useful economic life of the asset = 10 years

Reflective Question

5 | (a) Which depreciation method is considered an accelerated method?

(b) If you use an accelerated depreciation method, when is the majority of your asset 'written off'?

7.5 Accounting for the sale of a non-current asset

The financial statements also need to be adjusted to account for and reflect the company's position following the sale of a non-current asset. The implication of a sale is twofold. First, the asset is no longer owned by the company and so reduces the company's asset base, as reflected in the statement of financial position. Second, any gain or loss made as a consequence of the sale of an asset needs to be recorded in the income statement.

Calculating the gain or loss on the sale of a non-current asset

It is unlikely that the net book value of the non-current asset as shown in the statement of financial position will be representative of the non-current asset's market value. This therefore creates a difference between the sale price of the asset and the price at which it is recorded in the statement of financial position. It follows therefore that:

- if the sales price exceeds the asset's statement of financial position value then there is a gain on disposal of the asset; and
- if the sales price is less than the asset's statement of financial position value then there is a loss on disposal of the asset.

Returning again to the example of the Bun Factory Ltd, let us assume that the dough making machine is sold at the end of year 3 for a value of £15,000. The gain or loss on disposal will depend on the method of depreciation used.

1 | Under the straight line method, the disposal would generate a loss of £8,000. This being net book value at year 3 (£23,000) minus the sale price (£15,000).

2 | Under the reducing balance method, the disposal would generate a *loss* of £777. This being net book value at year 3 (£15,777) minus the sale price (£15,000).

3 | The asset and its associated depreciation are removed from the statement of financial position.

4 | The gain or loss is shown in the income statement. Note this is only a paper gain or loss.

5 | The actual cash received for the sale is shown in the cash flow statement.

ACTIVITY

6 | State which financial statements are affected by the sale of an asset and describe how they are affected.

The following information relater to a company that has just sold one of its non-current assets.

KEY THEMES Selling a fixed asset

When a fixed asset or plant asset is sold, the asset's depreciation expense must be recorded up to the date of the sale. Next:

1. The asset's cost and accumulated depreciation is removed,
2. The amount received is recorded, and
3. Any difference is reported as a gain or loss.

Here's an example.

The asset is a machine, which originally cost the company £54,000 with an expected useful life of nine years. The company sells this asset on 31 Jan 2012 for £5,000; at this date the accumulated depreciation amounted to £42,000.

The last time depreciation was recorded was on 31 December 2011. Depreciation expense is £500 per month, (54,000 divided by 9 years = 6,000 per year; divide by 12 months to get a monthly charge of £500 per month).

On 31 January the company will debit depreciation expense in the income statement for £500 and will credit accumulated depreciation for £500 in order to record the depreciation during January.

In its next entry on 31 January, the company will:

- debit cash for £5,000 (this is the amount received on the assets sale);
- debit accumulated depreciation for £42,000 (the balance at 31 January);
- debit loss on disposal of asset £6,500; and
- credit machines for £54,000.

Let's step back and review the disposal of the machine.

As of 31 January, the machine's book value is £11,500 (cost of £54,000 minus its accumulated depreciation of £42,500). Since the asset has been sold, the £11,500 of book value or carrying value is removed from the accounts.

In its place, the company received and records the cash of £5,000. However, because the company received £6,500 less than the amount it removed, it will report a loss of £6,500.

If the company had received more cash than the asset's book value, it would report the difference as a credit to gain on disposal of asset.

Q   What entry is made when selling a fixed asset?

Relating depreciation to real company accounts

Although this chapter has looked in detail at asset valuation and depreciation and how each should be accounted for, it is perhaps useful to look at some real company accounts to actually see how assets appear. You will find that in most accounts the asset will be shown at historical cost and depreciation will either have its own column in the statement of financial position or, more typically, will be included in a note to the accounts. In order to obtain more detail on depreciation and which assets it applies to, you will usually have to read the note against this category and the accounting policy adopted by the company.

Reflective Question

6   Visit the accounts of Vodafone plc at **www.vodafone.com/context/ annualreport/annual_report10/financials/consolidated_balance_sheet_at_31_ March.html** and take a look at the Annual Report. Look at how the assets and corresponding depreciation are shown there.

 **7.6 Summary**

Key ideas

Asset valuation methods

- at cost – calculated on the purchase price of the asset
- at net book value – calculated using cost minus depreciation to date
  at fair value – calculated using market value.

Straight line method of depreciation

- calculated by cost of asset less the residual value divided by the estimated useful life of the asset (in years)
- the impact on the income statement is that a constant amount is charged to the income statement each year
- the impact on the statement of financial position is that the cost of the asset is reduced by the cumulative depreciation amount
- the impact on the cash flow statement is that it is added back to the operating profit to reflect the non-cash movement.

Reducing balance method of depreciation

- is calculated by the following method:

$$\text{Depreciation rate (\%)} = 1 - \frac{\sqrt[\text{life}]{\text{residual value}}}{\text{original cost}}$$

- this is applied to the asset's cost initially and then to the NBV
- the impact on the income statement is that a varying (reduced amount) is charged to the income statement each year
- the impact on the statement of financial position is that initially the cost of the asset is reduced by the depreciation charge to derive a net book value. In subsequent years the NBV of the asset is reduced by the depreciation amount each year
- the impact on the cash flow statement is that it is added back to operating profit to reflect the non-cash movement.

Review questions

1. Assets are categorized into two main categories on the statement of financial position: current and non-current. Explain the difference between these categories.

2. Assets are further broken down on the statement of financial position into tangible and intangible. Explain the difference between tangible (non-current) assets and intangible assets and provide two examples of each type.

3. Square plc purchases a cutting machine for £60,000 on 1 March 2010. The machine is estimated to have a useful economic life of 10 years, after which it can be sold for £8,000.

    (a) Assuming Square plc uses the straight line depreciation method what would be the depreciation charge in the income statement for the year ending 30th April 2011?

    (b) What would be the NBV of the machine at the end of year 6?

    (c) Assume a new machine comes onto the market. As a result Square plc decides to sell the original cutting machine at the end of February 2014 for £40,000. What is the gain or loss on disposal?

    (d) How is the disposal reported in each of the financial statements?

4. Circle plc purchases car wheels at a cost of £6,000 on 1 March 2011. Circle plc applies a depreciation rate of 40%. Show the depreciation charge to the income statement for the next three years and determine the NBV at this time.

5. Triangle plc has the following trial balance for the year ending 30 September 2010.

	£	£
Capital		12,000
Cash	800	
Payables		11,800
Receivables	10,000	
Plant at cost	16,000	
Expenses	28,000	
Insurance	4,000	
Purchases	42,000	
Revenue		80,000
Electricity	3,000	
	103,800	**103,800**

The notes below refer to the period after the trial balance and are therefore not included in the above figures.

- inventory at 30 September 2011 is £6,000
- plant is depreciated at a rate of 15% on cost
- at 30 September insurance was prepaid by £400 and £1,000 was due for electricity.

Prepare the income statement and statement of financial position for Triangle plc for the year ending 30 September 2011.

Recommended reading

Berry, A. and Jarvis, R. (2006) *Accounting in a Business Context*, London: Thomson Learning.

Black, G. (2009) *Introduction to Accounting and Finance*, Harlow: FT Prentice-Hall.

Brockington, R. (1993) *Dictionary of Accounting and Finance*, London: Pitman Publishing.

Davies, T. and Boczko, T. (2005) *Financial Accounting: An Introduction*, Maidenhead: McGraw-Hill.

Useful websites

http://universityforbusiness.wordpress.com/2009/09/19/how-can-depreciation-help-me/ – American blog on accounting issues for entrepreneurs

Cash flow statements 8

*'In the **business** world, everyone is paid in two coins: **cash** and experience. Take the experience first; the cash will come later'.* (HAROLD S. GENEEN)

CHAPTER OUTLINE

8.1 Introduction

8.2 The importance of cash

8.3 Cash versus profit

8.4 Purpose of the cash flow statement

8.5 Presentation of the cash flow statement

8.6 Interpreting cash flow statements

8.7 Cash flow budgets

8.8 Summary

CHAPTER OBJECTIVES

After carefully reading the text and completing the tasks and activities provided in this chapter you should have a better understanding and knowledge of:

- the difference between cash and profit
- the layout and structure of the cash flow statement
- how to identify the cash inflow and cash outflow items that make up the cash flow statement
- the preparation of a basic cash flow statement
- how a cash flow statement can be used to aid decision making
- the ways in which a cash budget differs from a cash flow statement.

8.1 Introduction

The cash flow statement is the third key financial statement that companies quoted on the stock exchange are required to produce, the other two being the statement of financial position and the income statement, which you looked at in Chapters 3 and 4.

This chapter seeks to focus on the cash inflows and cash outflows that make up the cash flow statement. It is evident from both television and newspaper reports just how important a role cash plays in a company. At the time of writing (September 2011), the economic climate of the last three years has resulted in companies collapsing at an alarming rate. The reason for these collapses is quite simple – the companies concerned did not have sufficient cash to carry on trading. Before we continue we need to define what we mean by **cash**.

> **Cash** comprises money available to hand (i.e. not tied up in assets) and bank deposits that can be withdrawn on demand.

KEY TERM

> **Cash equivalents** are short-term, highly liquid investments that are readily convertible to known amounts of cash and which are subject to an insignificant risk of changes in value (BPP, 2009).

KEY TERM

8.2 The importance of cash

It is important to note from the above definitions that cash is not just pounds and pence, but also those assets that can be converted into pounds and pence very quickly. The emphasis on cash is twofold: First, companies need to have cash to survive, and second, companies need to be able to access cash in order to survive. If a company lacks cash, the end result will always be no cash to carry on or no cash to meet liabilities that have been built up.

Looking back at the UK recession that occurred in the late 1980s and early 1990s, many organizations such as BCCI and Polly Peck suffered initially because their profits had been boosted by fraudulent means. This led to the collapse of each company because of a lack of cash. The article below on BCCI is an interesting read that adequately illustrates this point.

CASE STUDY Timeline: BCCI

n 1972 Pakistani banker Agha Hasan Abedi founds the Bank of Credit and Commerce International, incorporated in Luxembourg with headquarters in London

Mid-1980s BCCI earns a reputation as a banker to drugs cartels, arms smugglers and dictators

July 5 1991 BCCI is found to be riddled with fraud and collapses with liabilities of $14bn. The

Bank of England declares that it may never have been profitable in its history. The size of the debts is later reduced to $10bn

Late 1991 Deloitte begins the process of trying to recover money for creditors. The first agreement is reached in February 1992 but creditors have to wait until December 1996 for their first dividend after legal wranglings in courts in Luxembourg

Spring–Summer 1992 During the spring and summer of 1992 Abu Dhabi, a major shareholder in the bank, offers compensation to give creditors 30–40% of their money back

October 1992 The Bank of England's supervision of BCCI is severely criticised in the report of Lord Justice Bingham's independent inquiry

May 24 1993 The liquidators issue the writ against the Bank of England for malicious recklessness against 22 Bank officials who oversaw the supervision of BCCI

April 1997 Abbas Gokal, whose Gulf Group was a major borrower from BCCI, is found guilty of false accounting and conspiracy to default. He is sentenced to 14 years' imprisonment and must serve a further three years because he has not paid £3m to the liquidators

May 2003 The liquidators admit that the search for cash, which has spanned 70 countries and affects more than 70,000 creditors, has run up costs of $1.2bn

January 2004 The case against the Bank of England begins.

November 2005 The case against the Bank of England ends after lasting 255 days and having won a place in legal history books thanks to the Bank's QC Nicholas Stadlen's record-breaking 119-day opening address.

Source: Extract from *The Guardian*, 3 November 2005 (www.guardian.co.uk/business/2005/nov/03/bcci.money2). Copyright Guardian News & Media Ltd 2005.

Q   Imagine that you are a bank manager. You have been approached by a medium-sized company for a bank loan. Before you reach your decision, what questions would you ask and what information would you like to see?

More recently, the collapse of Lehmen Brothers in September 2008 occurred because the bank's net worth fell below its total liabilities. This meant it simply did not have the liquid funds to meet its liabilities, nor could it access any further cash as lenders were not willing to lend. This again illustrates the simple notion that without cash or the means to quickly access cash a company cannot survive. The article below again illustrates how important cash is for an organization.

KEY THEMES Cash flow

The global financial crisis and resultant economic turbulence has dealt a double blow to companies. They are finding it more difficult to secure outside funding, just when cash flows are harder than ever to generate. Though not as battered by bankruptcies as corporate America, many companies in India Inc are experiencing severe cash flow problems.

Airlines in India are prominent examples with Air India, Kingfisher and Jet Airways facing heavy operating losses due to the slowdown and, as a result, are seeking government assistance such as reduced taxes on fuel.

Whether in India or elsewhere, the bottom line is that senior executives can no longer regard managing cash flow and liquidity as tactical and mundane. In today's brutally unforgiving environment, cash management has become strategic. Companies that manage cash and liquidity aggressively, and use the perspective and the data that come with it to gain forward visibility, have a big advantage in facing headwinds.

Wal-Mart, for instance, is aggressively managing resources to take advantage of others' weaknesses. The company cut capital expenditures, halted a stock buyback programme and trimmed inventories. It shifted cash from opening new stores to remodelling existing ones. That has allowed Wal-Mart to keep cutting prices and maintain a stable business amid the recession that has battered other retailers.

In India, Pantaloon Retail, the country's largest listed retailer, kept its ears to the ground early last year and prepared itself for a change in the business climate. It did so by cutting costs, redeploying existing staff to new stores and outsourcing its IT function, among other steps. It called its programme: "Say with pride we are stingy." When the slowdown did hit later that year, Pantaloon was ready. And its "stinginess" paid.

The retailer's EBITDA surged over 43% in the tough October–December 2008 quarter to Rs 1.57 billion year-on-year as it cut staff costs and rationalised administrative and selling costs, while its competitors struggled. Pantaloon managed this while continuing to expand, albeit at a slower pace.

In turbulence, scenario plans built from cash flow and liquidity measures can show management teams how much cash they need to preserve and protect the business under different conditions. But the immediate opportunity is to use cash and capital resources more efficiently.

The idea is to capture real-time information on what is flowing into and out of each business segment on a weekly and monthly basis, and then compare those flows with budgeted amounts. Big variances raise red flags in product lines, routes to the customers and <u>vendor</u> relations that can be addressed before it is too late.

The data helps companies spot patterns and understand how big changes in liquidity flow through to the profit-and-loss statement. By running similar analyses on the cash flows of competitors, customers, and vendors, companies can learn which rivals are vulnerable, which customers are strongest, and which vendors might not survive.

With enough reliable data, companies can make better predictions and manage effectively through even a sustained period of turbulence.

The visibility gained this way can be powerful. One large high-tech industrial group in Europe discovered that <u>payment</u> cycles in several older industrial equipment businesses had been stretched out as sales slowed and customers struggled with payments. That tied up cash in mature parts of the business and prevented the company from investing in a major competitive opportunity in power from renewable sources.

Managers tackled the problem by first examining the company's net working capital requirements by business line and function. They determined how long cash was locked up, from raw materials acquisition to the last customer payment. By comparing those cash cycles against the competition, they discovered rivals were collecting faster and aggressively managing <u>inventories</u>.

Closing that gap released more than $350 million in cash, providing money to fortify the mature businesses against the downturn and capital to invest in the promising solar business. The moves were not radical: cracking down on receivables collection, enhancing <u>account payables</u> terms with suppliers and managing inventories better. The key was focusing managers' attention on careful cash management.

Many companies have discovered in the downturn that their reliance on free-flowing, cheap capital during good times covered up a host of problems. At one major cosmetics company, high-, medium-, or low-volume <u>accounts</u> were all treated the same, and incentives encouraged orders, not sell-through.

When business slowed, the cash cycle lengthened, exposing the highly leveraged company to a liquidity squeeze. An analysis of all the inputs determined the company was spending $1.86 for each dollar of sales. Investing more intelligently by focusing on the cost of sell-through promised as much as $800 million in freed-up capital.

Source: Extract from Singh, A. and Sweig, D. 'Cash is not only king, it's strategic'. *The Economic Times*, 23 September 2009 (http://economictimes.indiatimes.com/Opinion/Editorial/Cash-is-not-only-king-its-strategic/articleshow/5044636.cms?curpg=1)

Q   Identify at least three ways in which companies in this case study have managed their cash.

It should be obvious from these articles that while companies may find ways to adjust their bottom-line profit figures, through the creative use of accounting, it is not yet possible for a company to 'create cash'. The need for a cash flow statement is therefore clear, since profits are not an adequate reflection of the liquid state of a company and profits do not equal cash.

8.3 Cash versus profit

The following factors will result in a company's profit figure being different from its cash figure:

- timing differences
- depreciation
- accounting transactions that bypass the income statement
- changes in the working capital requirements.

Timing differences

The point at which the cash is paid and/or received is often different from when the cash is shown in the income statement. This difference is a result of the accruals concept (see Chapter 1). In the income statement we show the effect of transactions as soon as they have taken place. This means that any income earned or cost incurred is shown in the income statement immediately. However, we do not show the effect of any income earned or cost incurred in the cash flow statement until the cash has *actually* been paid or received. The example below illustrates the effect of timing differences.

Worked Example

The Cloth Company landed an order worth £20m on 1 March 2010. The order is due to be completed by 31 March 2010. The cost of the order is estimated at £16m.

Let us assume that:

- this is the only work the Cloth Company has undertaken for March, and
- the customer will pay three months after delivery of the order.

What will the operating profit look like for the month ending 31 March 2010 under an accruals-based approach and then under a cash-based approach?

Solution:
The difference in the accounts is as follows:

	Accruals basis	Cash basis
	£m	£m
Revenue	20	0
Expenses	(16)	(16)
Operating profit	4	(16)

As can be seen, the Cloth Company would show a profit of £4m if their accounts are based on an accruals basis, but a negative cash flow of £16m if the accounts are shown on a cash basis. A simple difference in timing can present the accounts in a completely different way.

Depreciation

Depreciation will appear in the income statement, but it is not a cash movement so will not appear in the cash flow statement. Depreciation is merely an accounting transaction that has no impact on the physical movement of cash.

Accounting transactions that bypass the income statement

Any cash transaction that takes place will pass through the cash flow statement. However, not all transactions pass through the income statement. This is because the income statement only gives a picture of the company's activities for any given year. As such it focuses on revenue income and expenditure types – those that arise and are incurred in order to support the day-to-day running of the company. The income statement does not reflect capital expenditure, which is predominately concerned with a longer term benefit. For example, expenditure on capital items is a drain on the cash flow but leaves the income statement unchanged, because this expenditure is not specific to the revenue generated in that year only.

Changes in the working capital requirements

Any movement in inventory, receivables and payables will have an impact on cash flow and as such should be recorded in the cash flow statement under operating activities.

Reflective question

1| Consider what is meant by the 'accruals/matching concept'.

8.4 The purpose of the cash flow statement

As you saw in Chapter 4, the purpose of the income statement is to give an idea of how a company has performed for a given financial year. The reliability of the income statement for providing such an assessment was touched on in Section 8.2, with reference to fraudulent trading, creative accounting and boosting of the bottom-line profit figure. The assessment of a company's financial performance will be addressed in more detail in Chapter 9. With this in mind, the assessment of a company's performance can be enhanced by the provision of some additional information that may not be explicitly obvious in the income statement. In the previous section we looked at some reasons why profit does not match cash, thus allowing the income statement to disguise the true cash position of a company. For this reason a cash flow statement is needed, so that a reconciliation between the company's profit for the year and its cash can be presented. This reconciliation demonstrates by how much cash has gone up or down for a given financial period.

In the past, the income statement and the statement of financial position were considered to be sufficient for financial reporting purposes. However, the Accounting Standards Board has now recognized the importance of the cash flow statement and the need for companies to publish this information.

The cash flow statement provides users of accounts with information on cash receipts and cash payments for a given period, i.e. the financial year in question. The provision of such information gives a picture of the cash inflows and cash outflows of the company. The importance of this information is evident when we consider that a company must have cash in order to survive.

Cash is required to:

- pay for assets (albeit after a potential credit period)
- settle debts against the company

- pay employees
- pay out dividends to shareholders
- take advantage of potential investment opportunities.

We cannot access the true **liquidity** position of a company just by looking at the income statement; instead we refer to the cash flow statement in order to gain a picture of how liquid a company is. This picture enables users to form a view on the survival of the company. As the case studies mentioned earlier in this chapter and the case study below illustrate, no cash usually leads to no company.

KEY THEMES Cash is king: collect with passion

It's easy to forget the state of your bank balance in the cut and thrust of business life. But losing sight of your cash situation can be disastrous.

Cash is crucial to success for any commercial enterprise — if you're out of cash and out of credit you're out of business. A company can fail because of shortage of cash even while profitable. And the current scarcity of credit makes this even truer. In the words of Caroline Theobald, managing director of Bridge Club: "In this difficult environment you need to keep eyes like a hawk on cash."

Of course, cash isn't the only factor in business success. As Theobald says: "It's still important to invest in people and training, but every penny has to count. There's no room for complacency or casual spending." One service she has found particularly useful is the text message her bank sends every morning saying how much is in her account. "It's not very nice waking up to it on the mobile phone, but it makes you focused on your bank balance and it's very easy to see whether you are in the red or black."

Gut feelings are not enough when dealing with cash flow — good solid paperwork takes the guessing out of running a business and in the long run saves time and anxiety. It is also a legal requirement: limited companies must submit annual audited records to Companies House or face a £5,000 fine.

To monitor your cash situation you need records covering income and expenses as well as assets and liabilities. This will help prepare financial statements and forecasts such as the statement of financial position, profit and loss statement and cash flow projection, ideally looking three years ahead.

Paperwork is boring and easily slips down the priority list, but it can't be avoided. So if you hate it, delegate the task to a book-keeper. New businesses can tackle accounts manually, but it makes sense to use a computer. Spreadsheets and financial accounting packages such as Microsoft Excel and Sage start from a few hundred pounds.

Having your cash flow on a computer lets you predict trends, calculate how much you need to save, and schedule investment. You can also model "what if?" scenarios, work out measures such as internal rates of return and net present value, and discover whether you are charging enough. A practical suggestion from Theobald is to have a separate bank account into which you place all payments you owe for VAT and PAYE, so there are funds there to pay when they are due.

One factor that can seriously damage your cash flow is the present tendency for businesses to hold onto their money longer and pay late. "These late payments are having a ripple effect through the SME community," says entrepreneur and contributor to VentureNavigator Doug Richard. "Receivables will trend up, and some of your customers may become troubled as well. Don't keep extending credit." If certain customers consistently pay late, try issuing them with invoices earlier.

The trouble is that you may be more focused on winning the next sale than collecting payment for the last one. Theobald admits having got it wrong in the past and been lax about the need to invoice promptly. If your clients are public sector, they should pay within 10 days, she says. "If you're not paid on time you should be on the phone asking for the money."

Female entrepreneurs are particularly reticent about this, perhaps because they are embarrassed or worried they will seem rude and pushy, says Theobald. "You've supplied the goods or services, you have a right to insist on being paid."

Another factor that can affect cash flow is seasonal variation. If you sell T-shirts you are likely to do more business in summer, whereas a focus on ski gear will bring most of your sales in the winter months. You need some financial reserves to cover the barren times and unforeseen expenses.

There may be more cash in the business than you realized. Alan Leighton, who transformed Asda from a £500m company to one sold to Wal-Mart for £6.2bn, recommends going through a "cash marathon" to review the opportunities. "Cash has always been king – now it is more than king," he says. "If you have £1m in cash today it will buy you what £5m would have done a year ago. I call it the power of five. If you have cash, its power has gone up fivefold."

Leighton recently put the nine companies on whose boards he sits through a cash review, including Royal Mail, Selfridges and BSkyB. "They have been coming back to me and saying they found more cash in the business than they thought they would," he says. "You may be amazed at the results if you take these measures."

Ways to find more cash include improving productivity i.e. doing more for less, bargaining hard with suppliers, and setting tougher targets when you invest in new equipment to shorten the return on investment. Aim to get your money back in four years rather than five or six.

eBay flourished at a time when other dotcoms went bust thanks to its strong cash position. The company made a commission on each sale, its costs were minimal with few staff and no distribution or manufacturing, and marketing was largely by word of mouth. Cash was not tied up in working capital or inventory, waiting for customers to pay, or having to pay suppliers.

Similarly, Tesco online was successful in the UK because it didn't need expensive infrastructure — groceries were picked and packed in the company's largest stores. Given Tesco's broad market presence, expensive marketing was unnecessary, and online shoppers tended to pick products with higher margins. Their orders were also typically larger than in the shops, making the delivery expense worthwhile. By contrast, Webvan, a dedicated online grocery service in the US, failed, despite a $1.2bn investment. Margins were thinner (2 to 3 per cent as opposed to 6 to 8 per cent in the UK), the cost of acquiring each customer was high, delivering the orders was expensive, it lacked the buying power of large grocery chains, and people didn't spend enough.

Webvan's sums simply didn't add up. If it costs you too much to do what you want to do, however innovative you are, the business will die. That's why you need the cash-flow model and the forecasts.

In the end, it's quite simple. To quote Charles Dickens' Mr Micawber addressing his wife in David Copperfield: "Annual income twenty pounds, annual expenditure nineteen nineteen six, result happiness. Annual income twenty pounds, annual expenditure twenty pounds ought and six, result misery."

Source: University of Essex (www.venturenavigator.co.uk/content/593)

Q   It is evident that cash flow impacts everyone, you don't have to be running a company. Everyone has to manage their own personal finances too. Take some time out to see what methods you could use to ensure that you are fully aware of your personal cash position.
You may want to start with a basic spreadsheet.

8.5 Presentation of the cash flow statement

Let us now turn to the actual format of the cash flow statement. In order to be able to understand what the cash flow statement is telling us, we first need to be able to construct one. Initially we shall focus on a basic cash flow statement that may be put together for a sole trader. The chapter will then proceed to introduce the cash flow statement as it would appear in published accounts. The latter is probably a format students are most likely to come across when researching companies' published financial information.

IAS 7 states there are two methods of preparing cash flows; the **direct** method and the **indirect** method.

The direct method of reporting cash flows from operating activities re-states the income in terms of cash receipts and cash payments only. IAS 7 encourages this approach as it provides additional information to the users of financial statements which would not otherwise be available. In contrast, the indirect method starts with the net profit for the year and adjusts it for non-cash items (e.g. depreciation), items shown elsewhere in the statement of cash flows (e.g. investment income and interest received) and for changes in working capital (e.g. inventory, trade receivables, trade payables). The majority of businesses use the indirect method, since it is quicker and easier, and can be prepared directly from the statement of financial position and statement of comprehensive income with little additional information.

You can see from the cash flow statement shown below that it is concerned with three main activities that involve cash:

1 | Operating activities.
2 | Investing activities.
3 | Financing activities.

A typical cash flow statement:

Cash flow statement for the year ending 31st Dec 2011

	£000
Cash flows from operating activities	X
Interest paid	(X)
Tax paid	(X)
Net cash flow from operating activities	X
Cash flows from investing activities	
Purchase of non-current assets	X
Proceeds from the sale of non-current assets	X
Net cash used in investing activities	X
Cash flow from financing activities	
Proceeds from issue of shares	X
Dividends paid	(X)
Repayment of loan	(X)
	X
Net cash flow from financing activities	
Net (decrease)/increase in cash & cash equivalents	(X)/X
Cash & cash equivalents at the start of the period	(X)/X
Cash & cash equivalents at the end of the period	(X)/X

The above is simply an illustration of what type of transactions may appear under the three key headings of operating, investing and financing. It is worth spending some time looking at what items are likely to appear under each heading and how we can derive these values.

Cash flows from operating activities

This section of the cash flow statement starts with the profit before tax. Operating activities should include all amounts received and paid as a result of the company's trading activities. This means adjusting the operating profit before tax so that it reflects the cash effect of the company's trading/operating activities only. Most of the adjustments involve comparing the SoFPs for the last two years to determine the adjustments. Adjustment is made by following the stages in the flow diagram in Figure 8.1. The net operating cash flow is often the hardest figure to arrive at in the cash flow statement, so it is worth working through the basic example that appears after Figure 8.1.

Worked Example

Extracts from the accounts of Planet plc are given below.

	2011 £m
Turnover	95.16
Cost of sales*	(21.96)
Net operating profit	73.20

*Cost of sales includes depreciation of £20.4m

	2011 £m	2010 £m
Inventory	10.2	9
Receivables	12.6	14.4
Payables	11.4	10.8

The cash flow from operating activities is determined as follows:

	£m
Net operating profit	73.2
Add back depreciation	20.4
	93.6
Increase in inventory	(1.2)
Decrease in receivables	1.8
Increase in payables	0.6
Net cash flow from operating activities	**94.8**

This tells us that the net inflow from operations was £93.6m, of which £1.2m was used to purchase inventory. Planet plc received cash from its customers and paid out less to its suppliers, thus the overall impact is a net cash inflow of £94.8m.

FIGURE 8.1 Deriving net operating cash flows

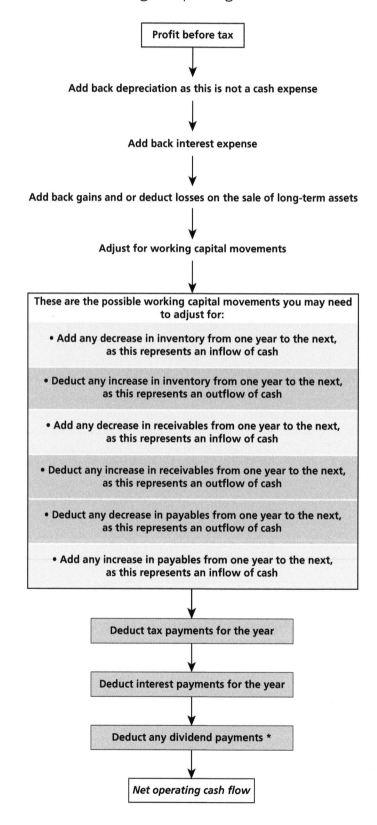

Think about working capital movements. Working capital typically reflects the company's current assets minus current liabilities. When considering the cash impact of changes in working capital we need to consider movements in the following:

- inventory
- receivables
- payables.

These need to be considered in the light of their impact on cash. For example, if inventory goes up from one year to the next it means the company has spent money on more inventory, thus a cash outflow is indicated. Likewise, if payables have gone down from one year to the next it means the company has paid off suppliers, thus a cash outflow is indicated. Had payables gone up between the two years then cash would have been retained in the business and thus a cash inflow indicated.

Work through the table below to ensure that the flow of cash is correctly determined and thus recorded in the cash flow statement.

TABLE 8. 1 The impact of working capital on cash

Working capital	Increase/ decrease	Impact on cash
Inventory	Increase	Cash outflow as inventory has been bought, so cash goes down
	Decrease	Cash inflow as inventory has been sold, so cash goes up
Receivables	Increase	Cash goes down as money has not been received
	Decrease	Cash goes up as money has been received
Payables	Increase	Cash goes up as payments have not been made
	Decrease	Cash goes down as payments owing have been made

ACTIVITY

1 Below are extracts from the accounts of Sun plc.

	2011 £m
Turnover	150.15
Cost of sales*	(34.65)
Net operating profit	115.50

*Cost of sales includes depreciation of £28.7m

	2011 £m	2010 £m
Inventory	16.1	15.4
Receivables	14.7	12.6
Payables	11.9	10.5

Calculate the figure in the cash flow statement for cash flows from operating activities.

Cash flows from investing activities

In this section of the cash flow statement the focus is on how the statement of financial position amounts change in relation to non-current asset accounts from one year to the next. Non-current asset accounts include:

- long-term investments
- land
- buildings
- equipment
- furniture and fixtures
- vehicles.

The emphasis here is on cash flows arising due to the purchase and/or disposal of *non-current assets*. In Chapter 7 you will have seen that such activities would affect all three financial statements (the statement of financial position, income statement and cash flow statement). In this chapter we focus on how these activities are reflected in the cash flow statement. The point to remember here is that only the cash flow element of a disposal or purchase is to be recorded in the cash flow statement so we are looking only at the cash that has been paid for an asset and/or the amount of cash that has been received for an asset. Note the latter is different from a loss or gain made on the sale of an asset.

Worked Example

Consider the following information relating to the purchase and disposal activity during a year for Jupiter Ltd:

Plant with a net book value of £12,000 (cost £23,500) was sold during the year for £7,800. The loss on sale has been included in the profit before interest and tax.

KEY TERM

Net book value (NBV) is the value of an asset at cost after deducting depreciation.

The following are extracts from the statement of financial position of Jupiter Ltd.

Statement of Financial Position at 31 March 2009

	£	£
Non-current tangible assets:		
Plant at cost		70,000
Plant accumulated depreciation		22,500
Investments		16,900

Statement of Financial Position at 31 March 2010

	£	£
Non-current tangible assets:		
Plant at cost		84,600
Plant accumulated		
Depreciation		37,600

From the above extracts we can calculate the cash effect of this transaction, by looking at the movement in non-current assets from one year to the next.

Plant cost

Plant b/d	70,000	Disposal	23,500
Additions (balance)	38,100	Plant c/d 84,600	4,600
	108,100		**108,100**

The cash amount that has been spent on non-current assets is £38,100 and this should be shown in the cash flow statement under the heading 'Cash flows from investing activities' as a cash outflow. Equally the cash received for the disposal during the year amounting to £7,800 should be shown as a cash inflow under the same heading.

> **Reflective question**
>
> 2| What does NBV stand for?

ACTIVITY

> 2 | Using the data for Jupiter Ltd in the example above calculate the gain or loss on the disposal of the plant.
>
> 3 | The following information is available for Sun plc's non-current assets:
>
> | | 2010
£m | 2011
£m |
> |---|---|---|
> | Property, plant and equipment at NBV | 50 | 125 |
>
> - During the year there was a £10m depreciation charge.
> - A revaluation surplus of £30m existed.
> - Assets with a net book value of £7.5m were disposed of.
> - £15m worth of non-current assets were acquired.
>
>   (a) How much cash was spent on non-current assets in the year?
>   (b) In which financial statement will this amount appear and under what heading?

Cash flows from financing activities

This section of the cash flow statement reports on cash flows arising from the way in which the company finances itself. The cash flows therefore are typically associated with a share issue or purchase and/or a long-term loan or repayment of this loan.

In short, financing activities involve the issue and/or repurchase of a company's own debt or shares. Dividend payments can also be reported in this section.

> **Reflective question**
>
> 3| What are the three main headings of a cash flow statement?

To obtain a better understanding of how this may help managers make decisions, work through the example for Mercury plc below.

Worked Example

The worked example below shows the accounts for Mercury plc. From this information, a cash flow statement has been prepared, enabling us to draw out some useful information about the current position of Mercury plc.

The accounts of Mercury plc as at 31 January are shown below.

	2010		2011	
	£000	£000	£000	£000
Non-current assets				
Land		300		350
Current assets				
Inventory	50		60	
Payables	100		125	
Cash	3		5	
		153		190
		453		540
Equity and reserves				
Ordinary shares £1		350		400
Income statement		13		30
		363		430
Current liabilities				
Receivables		90		110
		453		540

From the above we can prepare the cash flow statement and form a view about the current position of Mercury plc.

Solution:
Cash flow statement for the period ending 31 Jan 2011

	£000
Net cash flow from operating activities (W1)	2
Cash flow from investing activities	
Purchase of non-current assets	(50)
Cash flow from financing activities	
Issue of ordinary shares	50
Net increase in cash (W1)	2

	£000
Operating profit (30–13)	17
Increase in inventory	(10)
Increase in payables	(25)
Increase in receivables	20
Cash flow from operating activities	2

What does this tell us about Mercury plc? We can see that:

- Mercury generated £2,000 cash for the period from its operating activities alone.
- Mercury increased its cash by £2,000 for the period.
- Some investments amounting to £50,000 were made during the year.
- It appears that the investments have been financed by monies raised through a share issue.

On closer examination, it appears that the cash from the operating activities has been reduced due to poor management of the working capital. Inventory is not selling and customers are not paying. As a consequence of this, Mercury appears to be not paying its suppliers. If this continues and operating activities do not start generating more cash, the company could find itself running into cash flow problems.

The need for an analysis of the company's cash position should by now be clearer to you. It is perfectly feasible for a company to report a profit and then for that same company to go bankrupt. The reason for this is that the company has simply run out of cash. The various case studies in this chapter highlight exactly this point. If we consider a smaller organization, the issue of the importance of cash is perhaps even more paramount. Smaller companies not listed on the stock exchange have less access to finance, and as such management of their cash position is crucial to their survival.

As mentioned, a profitable company can end up out of business. With smaller companies, this is often because they are trying to grow too quickly with an insufficient working capital base. This is referred to as **overtrading**. The company is taking on too many orders, selling to customers on credit, buying from suppliers on credit, selling more on credit and buying more to meet the increasing sales demand. Notice there has as yet been no mention of payment for the goods or payment to the suppliers. Eventually the goodwill of the suppliers will diminish and the company struggles to meet orders, because there is simply not enough cash with which to buy materials. This leads to the company not being able to carry on, even though the sales figures in the income statement are high and display an overall profit. Note this is paper profit only. Such a situation can be highlighted by looking at the company's cash flow and liquidity position.

The issue of overtrading is perhaps most relevant for smaller companies and/or new companies trying to start up.

It is probably a good idea to remind ourselves of what a cash flow statement, as we would see it in a set of published accounts, would look like. Look at the pro-forma below before working through the cash flow statement of the retailers Morrisons plc.

Cash flow statement (indirect method)

	£
Cash flows from operating activities	
Operating profit	X
Adjustments for:	
Depreciation	X
Foreign exchange loss	X
Investment income	(x)
Interest expense	X
	X
Increase/decrease in trade and other receivables	(x)/x
Increase/decrease in inventories	(x)/x
Increase/decrease in trade payables	x/(x)
Cash generated from operations	X
Interest paid	(x)
Income taxes paid	(x)
Net cash from operating activities	**X/(X)**
Cash flows from investing activities	
Acquisition of subsidiary X	(x)
Purchase of property, plant and equipment	(x)
Proceeds from sale of equipment	X
Interest received	X
Dividends received	X
Net cash used in investing activities	**X/(X)**
Cash flows from financing activities	
Proceeds from issue of share capital	X
Proceeds from long-term borrowings	X
Payment of finance lease liabilities	(x)
Dividends paid*	(x)
Net cash used in financing activities	**X/(X)**
Net increase/(decrease) in cash and cash equivalents	X/(X)
Cash and cash equivalents at beginning of period (from the Statement of Financial Position)	X
Cash and cash equivalents at end of Period (from the Statement of Financial Position)	X

* This could also be shown as an operating cash flow.

We will now look at the cash flow statement of a real-life company, Morrisons plc.

Morrisons: Consolidated Cash Flow Statement
52 weeks ended 1 February 2009

	Note	2009 £m	2008 £m
Cash flows from operating activities			
Cash generated from operations		964	756
Interest paid		(70)	(70)
Taxation paid		(104)	(107)
Net cash inflow from operating activities		790	579
Cash flows from investing activities			
Interest received		29	50
Proceeds from sale of property, plant and equipment		22	94
Purchase of property, plant and equipment and investment property		(678)	(402)
Net cash outflow from investing activities		(627)	(258)
Cash flows from financing activities			
Proceeds from issue of ordinary shares		3	17
Shares repurchased for cancellation		(146)	–
Finance lease principal payments		(2)	(3)
New borrowings		250	–
Repayment of borrowings		(2)	(266)
Decrease/(increase) in long-term cash on deposit		74	(74)
Dividends paid to equity shareholders		(131)	(108)
Net cash inflow/(outflow) from financing activities		46	(434)
Net increase/(decrease) in cash and cash equivalents		209	(113)
Cash and cash equivalents at start of period		118	231
Cash and cash equivalents at end of period		**327**	**118**

Cash flow from operating activities	2009 £m	2008 £m
Profit for the period	460	554
Adjustments for:		
Taxation	195	58
Depreciation and amortization	290	289
Profit on disposal of property, plant and equipment	(2)	(32)
Net finance cost	16	–
Other non-cash changes	17	6
Excess of contributions over pension service cost	(103)	(148)
Increase in stocks	(52)	(74)
Increase in debtors	(44)	(60)
Increase in creditors	214	169
Decrease in provisions	(27)	(6)
Cash generated from operations	**964**	**756**

By looking at Morrisons' cash flow above we can determine that an operating profit of £964m has been arrived at.

Morrisons have clearly been investing during the year, resulting in a huge cash outflow of £627m. As can be seen, this is largely associated with the purchase of property, plant and equipment.

Morrisons have also used cash to claw back some equity and pay off some debt, although this seems to have been financed through taking out more debt. It is possible that the company is seeking to increase its equity control at the expense of higher gearing (gearing measures how much of the company's finance has been raised through borrowing). Analysis of the statement of financial position would help confirm this.

Overall, Morrisons has a healthy net cash inflow of £209m for the period.

Reflective question

4 | (a) What are the two methods that can be used to prepare a cash flow statement?
  | (b) Which is the most widely used of these two methods?

8.6 Interpreting cash flow statements

Having established the information that goes into the cash flow statement we are now able to determine what the cash flow statement is saying about a company's cash position. Almost instantly the cash flow statement can show the movement of cash in the year, by looking at the net increase/decrease in cash and cash equivalents towards the end of the cash flow statement. An increase in profits cannot be translated as a positive cash balance. This has been illustrated by the collapse of many profitable companies over the years.

By separating out cash flows under the various headings (cash flows from operating activities; cash flows from investing activities and cash flows from financing activities) it is possible to determine by how much each activity type has been responsible for the cash increase or decrease, and thus the solvency position of the company.

This enables an analysis of further issues such as:

- Is the company able to pay a dividend?
- What is the level of spending on non-current assets?
- Has the company raised new finance?
- Why is the company showing a negative cash flow from operating activities?

Is the company able to pay a dividend?

Typically, most organizations in the UK prefer to pay a dividend as there is a school of thought that suggests that this can send out a positive signal to existing and potential shareholders about the ability and performance of the company. However, when the economy is depressed, many companies may find they do not have the cash available to pay the dividend. The cash flow statement can help determine what the company's overall cash position is and how it will be affected by a dividend payout. The article below provides a real-life example of this.

The New York Times Company has suspended its first quarter dividend in order to pay off its debt and conserve cash.

The New York Times board of directors voted to suspend dividends for its Class A and Class B common shares, extending the action they took in the fourth quarter of 2008, when they cut the dividend from $0.23 per share to $0.06.

The board follows several other US publishers who have recently cut dividends, including McClatchy, EW Scripps and CBS.

The Ochs-Sulzberger family own about a fifth of the publicly traded Class A shares and nearly 90% of Class B shares, which dictate control over the company.

Struggling under $1.1bn in debt amid bleak economic times, the suspension is the latest move by the company to ensure its survival.

Source: Media Week, 20 February 2009 (www.mediaweek. co.uk/news/882980/New-York-Times-Company-abandons-dividend-save-cash/). Reproduced from *MediaWeek* magazine with the permission of the copyright owner, Haymarket Business Publications Limited.

Q **Start reviewing the *Financial Times* to monitor what companies are doing to manage their cash positions. Are there any companies using dividends to retain cash in the company?**

What is the level of spending on non-current assets?

This can be ascertained from the cash flow statement and by analysing the pattern of expenditure. Again, there is a cash flow implication involved here, and if times are hard it may be the case that such expenditure has to be postponed. Equally, if assets need replacing then this cash outflow needs to be planned for. This highlights the link between the strategic and financial decisions companies are so often faced with. A company cannot make such decisions without considering the state of the economy and the nature of its business.

Has the company raised new finance?

A company may have to raise more cash to avoid future potential cash shortages that have been identified. The cash flow statement can identify where and how much cash has come from which source over the last few years. This can help formulate a future financing strategy.

Although the above points highlight some of the questions that a cash flow statement can help address, it must be noted that the impact of activities that both generate and utilize cash cannot be determined by the cash flow statement alone. There is a need to understand the nature of the company's business and its strategic direction.

Why is the company showing a negative cash flow from operating activities?

By grouping cash flows by activity it is possible to see which areas of the company need to be focused on. If cash flows from operating activities are negative then possible causes for this may be that management of the working capital is inadequate, or that the company is expanding and has therefore had to spend more on building up its inventory, etc.

8.7 Cash flow budgets

A **cash flow budget** differs from a cash flow statement in that the latter focuses on events that have taken place, whereas a cash flow budget focuses very much on the future. The whole purpose of a cash flow budget is to analyse what future cash flows are anticipated to occur. This will involve some mapping of future expected revenues and future anticipated costs. The budget will also need to pay attention to what cash funds may be needed to service future planned investments. Unlike a cash flow statement, a cash flow budget has no set pro forma that needs to be followed. Its layout is determined by the needs of the managers within the company. This may typically be a cash budget produced on a monthly basis for a given year. Managers can use this tool to provide useful information for decision making. For example, by estimating future cash flows and then comparing them with the actual cash flows for that same period, managers can undergo a useful variance analysis exercise. Finally, the cash flow budget is likely to be a crucial part of a proposed business plan. Think about the BBC TV programme 'Dragon's Den' and how one of the main considerations is the amount of cash the idea is expected to generate and over what time period.

KEY TERM

> **Cash flow budget** a forecast of the *future* cash inflows and *future* cash outflows for a given period.

The cash flow budget serves a different purpose to the cash flow statement. The cash flow budget provides managers with a forecast of future cash expenses and revenues, enabling them to look at the short-term financial needs of, and opportunities for, the company. In such cases the cash budget is developed on a monthly basis, allowing managers to establish what cash is available (or not). The focus of the cash flow budget is on planning and the future, whereas for the cash flow statement the data is derived from the historical-based statement of financial position.

Below is an example of a typical cash flow budget.

Worked Example

Star Ltd has estimated receipts and payments for the 6 months from January to June as shown below.

- **Sales (£):** Dec 1440, Jan 1800, Feb 2160, March 1620, April 2520, May 2700, June 2250.
- **Materials (£):** Dec 1000, Jan 1250, Feb 1500, March 1100, Apr 1750, May 1850, June 1500.
- **Labour (£):** Dec 496, Jan 620, Feb 744, Mar 558, Apr 868, May 930, June 744
- **Rent (£):** 200 per month
- **Overheads (£):** Dec 360, Jan 400, Feb 460, March 380, April 520, May 560, June 470.
- **Bank loan (£):** Receivable March 6,000.
- **Machinery purchase (£):** Feb 600, May 1400.

Notes:

- Opening cash balance: £4,600.
- One month's credit given on sales and material purchases paid for one month later.
- All other payments made in month incurred.

Required: Prepare a six-month cash budget for January to June.

Solution

Star Ltd

Cash flow forecast – 6 months

	Jan	Feb	Mar	Apr	May	Jun
	£	£	£	£	£	£
Sales	1440	1800	2160	1620	2520	2700
Bank loan			6000			
Total inflows	**1440**	**1800**	**8160**	**1620**	**2520**	**2700**
Materials	1000	1250	1500	1100	1750	1850
Labour	620	744	558	868	930	744
Rent	200	200	200	200	200	200
Overheads	400	460	380	520	560	470
Machine purchase		600			1400	
Total outflows	**2220**	**3254**	**2638**	**2688**	**4840**	**3264**
Opening cash balance	4600	1910	1183	3944	3410	2250
Total cash inflows	1440	1800	8160	1620	2520	2700
Less total cash outflows	(2220)	(3254)	(2638)	(2688)	(4840)	(3264)
Closing balance	**3820**	**2366**	**7888**	**6820**	**4500**	**3936**

FIGURE 8.2 Example of a cash flow budget

Month:	Pre-Start	1	2	3	4	5	6	7	8	9	10	11	12	Totals
Receipts														
Cash sales			12	16	22	34	46	54	58	44	42			328.00
Collections from credit sales														0
New equity inflow														0
Loans received														0
Other														0
Total Receipts	0	0	12	16	22	34	46	54	58	44	42	0	0	328.00
Payments														
Cash purchases		25		25	25	25	25							120.00
Payments to creditors														0.00
Salaries and wages														0
Employee benefits														0
Payroll taxes														0
Rent														0
Utilities														0
Repairs and maintenance														0
Insurance														0
Travel														0
Telephone														0
Postage														0
Office supplies														0
Advertising														0
Marketing/promotion			20											20
Professional fees														0
Training and development														0
Bank charges														0
Miscellaneous														0
Owner's drawings														0
Loan repayments														0
Tax repayments														0
Capital purchases	68													68
Other														0
Total payments	68	25	20	25	25	25	25	0	0	0	0	0	0	212.50
Cashflow surplus/deficit (–)	–68	–25	–8	–9	–3	9	21	54	58	44	42	0	0	115.50
Opening cash balance	0	–68	–93	–101	–110	–113	–104	–83	–29	30	74	116	116	
Closing cash balance	–68	–93	–101	–110	–113	–104	–83	–29	30	74	116	116	116	

Cash How Forecast–12 Months (£)

8.8 Summary

Key ideas

Income statement

- the profit statement is prepared on an accruals basis
- it shows the profit for a given period

- the users of a profit statement will be external to the company
- it is a document that is prepared using historical data, so can be said to be 'backward looking' there is a legal requirement for companies to publish their profit statement.

Cash flow statement

- the cash flow statement is prepared on a cash basis
- its purpose is to determine the amount of cash a company has
- the users of the cash flow statement will be external to the company
- again, it is a document that is prepared using historical data, so is 'backward looking'
- there is a legal requirement for companies to publish their cash flow statement.

Cash budget statement

- the cash budget statement is prepared on the basis of forecasting
- its purpose is to aid management decision making
- the users of the cash budget statement will be internal
- it is a document that focuses on the future and is forward looking
- there is no legal requirement for companies to publish their cash budget.

Review questions

1. What will be the impact (increase or decrease) of the following transactions on a company's cash in its cash flow statement?
   (a) The company pays its suppliers early.
   (b) Inventory is purchased in bulk.
   (c) Shares are issued successfully to existing shareholders.
   (d) The long-term loan has been repaid.
   (e) Non-current assets are depreciated.

2. Can you remember how to account for the sale of a non-current asset in the statement of financial position and the income statement?

3. What are the main reasons that result in profit not being the same as cash?

4. Moon plc's income statement for the year ended 31 December 2011 and the statements of financial postion for the years ending 31 December 2010 and 2011 are shown on page 152:

   Prepare the cash flow statement for Moon plc for 2011. Also provide a brief analysis on what this tells us about Moon plc.

Income statement

	£m	£m
Revenue		312
Cost of sales		(177)
Gross profit		135
Distribution costs	36	
Administrative costs	15	(51)
		84
Other investment income		7
		91
Interest receivable		7
		98
Interest payable		(13)
		85
Taxation		(18)
Profit after tax		67
Retained profit brought forward		27
		94

SoFP

	£m	£m
	2010	2011
Non-current assets:		
Intangible: Patents	19	16
Tangible:		
Land and buildings	155	155
Plant and machinery	144	141
	318	312
Current assets:		
Inventory	21	17
Receivables	70	73
Cash	1	3
	410	405
Equity and reserves:		
Ordinary shares £1	100	150
Share premium account	20	–
Reserves	70	39
Income statement	52	94
	242	283
Non-current liabilities:		
Loans	125	75
Current liabilities:		
Overdraft	4	17
Payables	27	21
Tax	12	9
	410	405

Notes:

(i) During the year £34m was spent on purchasing additional plant and machinery. No other non-current assets were purchased or disposed of.

(ii) The movement in reserves of £26m includes a dividend payment.

(iii) There was no share issue for cash.

5   Extracts from the consolidated financial statements of Court plc are given below

Consolidated Statement of Financial Position as at 31 March

	2011		2010	
	£000	£000	£000	£000
Non-current assets:				
Property, plant and equipment	11,630		10,180	
		11,630		10,180
Current assets:				
Inventories	70		55	
Receivables	280		270	
Short-term deposits	10		–	
		360		325
		11,990		10,505
Equity:				
Share capital	3,000		3,000	
Share premium	1,000		1,000	
Retained earnings	5,105		4,755	
		9,105		8,755
Non-current liabilities:				
Interest-bearing borrowings	1,440		1,200	
Deferred tax	160		150	
		1,600		1,350
Current liabilities:				
Trade payables	165		130	
Bank overdraft	890		80	
Income tax	230		190	
		1,285		400
		11,990		10,505

Consolidated Income Statement for the year ended 31 March 2011

	£000
Revenue	1,515
Cost of sales	(454)
Gross profit	1,061
Other operating expenses	(320)
Profit from operations	741
Finance cost	(60)
Gain on sale of asset	94
Other income	90
Profit before tax	865
Tax	(200)
Profit after tax	**665**

Notes:

Property, plant and equipment

The following transactions took place during the year:

- During the year depreciation of £95,000 was charged in the income statement.
- A property was disposed of during the year for £400,000 cash. It had a carrying value of £340,000 at the date of disposal. The gain on disposal has been included within cost of sales.

Sale of asset

On 1 January 2011 Court plc disposed of a non-current asset for £485,000 in cash. The asset had the following net book value at the date of disposal:

Asset at NBV £391,000

Prepare the cash flows from operating activities extract of the consolidated cash flow statement for Court plc for the year ended 31 March 2011 in the form required by IAS 7 Cash Flow Statements. Show your workings clearly.

6. The accounts of Judge plc as at 31 January are shown below.

	£000	2010 £000	£000	2011 £000
Non-current assets:				
Machinery at cost		600		600
Less depreciation		(160)		(200)
		440		400
Investments		–		200
Current assets:				
Inventory	320		380	
Payables	440		220	
Cash	–		20	
		760		620
		1,200		1,220
Equity & reserves:				
Ordinary shares £1		600		600
Share premium		100		100
Income statement		60		80
		760		780
Non-current liabilities:				
Loans		–		120
Current liabilities:				
Receivables	400		320	
Overdraft	40		–	
		440		320
		1,200		1,220

There were no other purchases or disposals of non-current assets during the year.

You are required to:

(a) Prepare the cash flow statement for Judge plc for the year ended 31 January 2011.

(b) Analyse the cash flow and form a view as to what it tells you about Judge plc.

7. Complete the table below by filling in the blank boxes with the appropriate text.

Working capital	Increase/decrease	Impact on cash
Inventory	Increase	?
	?	Cash inflow as inventory has been sold, so cash goes up
?	Increase	Cash goes down as money has not been received
	Decrease	?
Payables	?	Cash goes up as payments have not been made
		Cash goes down as payments owing have been made

8. (a) Name three items from the statement of financial position that may affect a company's cash flow.

   (b) State what impact they would have on the cash flow of the company.

9. What are the main headings that appear in a cash flow statement under IAS 7?

10. Under what heading in the cash flow statement will the cash impact of the following transactions appear?

   (a) Purchase of a new machine

   (b) Repurchase of equity shares

   (c) Interest paid on the loan

   (d) Dividends paid out to shareholders

   (e) Monies received from customers

   (f) A new bank loan

   (g) Gain on the sale of building

Recommended reading

Berry, A. and Jarvis, R. (2006) *Accounting in a Business Context*, London: Thomson Learning.

Black, G. (2009) *Introduction to Accounting and Finance*, Harlow: FT Prentice-Hall.

Brockington, R. (1993) *Dictionary of Accounting and Finance*, London: Pitman Publishing.

CIMA study text, (2009) Management Paper F2 Financial Management, BPP.

Interpretation of accounts 9

*'As with most things in life, the **objective** dictates the **activity**.'* (PARMINDER JOHAL, 2009)

CHAPTER OUTLINE

9.1 Introduction

9.2 Users of financial statements

9.3 The interpretation process

9.4 Ratio analysis

9.5 Interpreting published financial statements

9.6 Other analytical measures

9.7 Limitations of ratio analysis

9.8 Summary

CHAPTER OBJECTIVES

After carefully reading the text and completing the tasks and activities provided in this chapter you should have a better understanding and knowledge of:

- the importance of ratio analysis

- who needs to interpret financial statements and why

- the process of interpreting accounts

- how to calculate the important ratios

- how to analyse the important ratios

- the limitations of ratio analysis.

 ## 9.1 Introduction

All users of financial statements need to be able to interpret accounting data and information to help them make decisions. An initial look at an income statement and statement of financial position will provide you with some interesting data, but the accounts will require some interpretation in order to fully understand the data and convert it into meaningful information. One of the first things you need to do when interpreting accounts is to calculate the relevant ratios. Accounting ratios are mathematical comparisons used to highlight the relationships that exist between different figures on the income statement and statement of financial position. Once you have calculated the ratios you either need to compare them to previous ratios of the same business in order to establish trends, or compare them to the ratios of other organizations to see how the business is performing, in comparison to its competitors.

 ## 9.2 Users of financial statements

There are many users of financial statements and each group has different information needs. The Accounting Standards Board (ASB) has divided these users into seven user groups:

User groups:

1	Shareholders
2	Loan creditors
3	Employees
4	Analyst-advisers
5	Business contacts
6	The government
7	The public

Both current and potential shareholders may wish to interpret a set of financial statements. They will be particularly interested in the business's profitability and the impact of this on the shareholders' dividend payment. In addition, shareholders will be interested in the future prospects of the company to determine whether to make or retain an investment in a particular business.

Loan creditors will incorporate both current and potential creditors as they will primarily wish to establish whether or not the business will be in a position to repay its debts both today and in the future. Consequently, loan creditors are interested in both the liquidity and the profitability of a business.

Employees may wish to analyse the information in financial statements to determine the likelihood of a pay increase or bonus and the future security of their employment. Consequently, they will be interested in the profitability and liquidity of the business. If they have the opportunity to invest in some shares they will also be interested in the investment ratios.

The analyst-adviser group includes investment analysts, trade union representatives and credit rating agencies. They will need to identify and extract data to look at trends and carry out comparisons with other businesses in the same sector or against industry norms.

The business contact group includes customers, suppliers and competitors. Customers will be interested in forecasts as one of their main interests will be in the security of future supplies and the continuing opportunity to obtain parts or service advice for a product they have purchased. Suppliers, like creditors, will want to know if they are likely to get paid, whether the business is expanding (giving rise to the possibility of increased sales) or whether the business is declining and is therefore considered to be an unacceptable risk. Competitors will utilize companies in the same business sector as themselves in order to benchmark their progress.

The government will analyse financial statements to help plan economic policy, design fiscal policy, assess taxation liabilities and provide support for business sectors in need.

Finally, the public are becoming increasingly concerned about the global environment and sustainability and will therefore be interested in the policies of an organization and how these affect the environment, as well as potential employment opportunities.

FIGURE 9.1 Simple charts showing Tesco's financial position

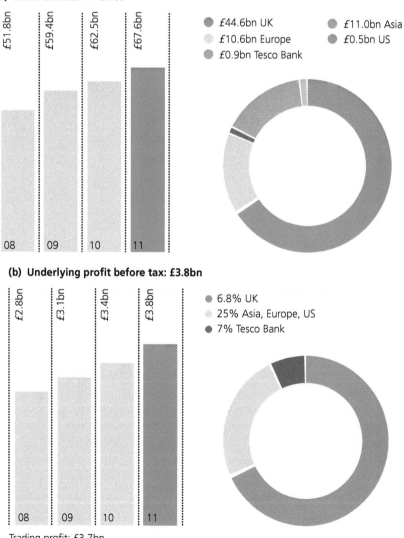

Source: Tesco (2011) Annual Report and Financial Statements

9.3 The interpretation process

The interpretation process consists of six stages:

1 | **Identify:** the users and their information needs.
2 | **Review:** the accounts under consideration.
3 | **Select:** the most relevant ratios.
4 | **Calculate:** the chosen ratios.
5 | **Interpret:** by examining, comparing and considering other information.
6 | **Evaluate:** the findings and form an opinion.

The first stage of the interpretation process is to decide who requires the information and for what purpose (see Section 9.2 above). It is important to get a general impression of the financial statements to be investigated by looking at the income statement and statement of financial position to determine the size of the business, its profitability and the value of its assets. The person carrying out the investigation can then decide on the most appropriate ratios to use and determine the benchmark for comparison purposes. Formulae are then used to calculate the relevant ratios and the findings are compared to the chosen benchmark in order to investigate the trends or variations. The ratios that show significant changes or variations should undergo further analysis by assessing any additional information available. Once all the information has been collected an opinion should be formed on the financial statements.

 ## 9.4 Ratio analysis

The focus of this chapter is the calculation and interpretation of ratios. In accounting, the term ratio is used to express a comparison between two or more figures, usually found in the financial statements. These comparative relationships can be expressed in a variety of forms as follows:

● | as a percentage (%)
● | in pence (p)
● | as times (x times)
● | in days (x days)
● | as a ratio (x:1)

For simplicity, all the relationships are referred to as ratios. Calculating the ratios does not involve complicated mathematics as it simply requires one number to be divided by another. The hardest part of calculating ratios is to identify the numbers that are used in the calculations. To improve the presentation of the solutions it is best to calculate the figures to the same number of decimal places. The examples in this chapter will be calculated to two decimal places.

There are numerous ratios that can be calculated but the four most commonly used groups are shown below.

1 | Profitability
2 | Liquidity

| 3 | Efficiency |
| 4 | Investment. |

Most ratios can be calculated for any form of business: sole traders, partnerships or companies. To introduce the calculations we will begin by considering the accounts of a sole trader, Simon.

Simon: Income statement for the year ended 30 June 20X8

	£	£
Revenue		236,135
Cost of sales		141,681
Gross profit		94,454
Expenses		
Business rates	17,921	
Salaries and wages	35,685	
Telephone	810	
Motor expenses	9,505	
Advertising	2,530	
Administration expenses	6,750	
		73,201
Net profit		**21,253**

Simon: Statement of Financial Position as at 30 June 20X8

	£	£
Assets		
Non-current assets		
Premises	158,000	
Motor vehicles	65,700	
Fixtures	8,880	
		232,580
Current assets		
Inventory	11,200	
Accounts receivable	6,805	
Cash at bank	5,490	23,495
		256,075
Capital		39,160
Non-current liabilities		
Bank loan	210,000	
Current liabilities		
Accounts payable	6,915	
		216,915
		256,075

We are now going to calculate some of the main ratios for Simon. To do this we need to know the formula and which financial statement the figures will come from. We will start by considering four profitability ratios. Table 9.1 shows the formulae and which statement the numerator and denominator come from.

TABLE 9.1 Profitability ratios

Ratio	Formula (Numerator / Denominator)	Which financial statement do we get the numerator from?	Which financial statement do we get the denominator from?
Gross profit %	$\dfrac{\text{Gross Profit}}{\text{Revenue}} \times 100$	Income statement	Income statement
Net profit %	$\dfrac{\text{Net Profit}}{\text{Revenue}} \times 100$	Income statement	Income statement
Expense %	$\dfrac{\text{Expense}}{\text{Revenue}} \times 100$	Income statement	Income statement
Return on capital employed (ROCE)	$\dfrac{\text{Profit}}{\text{Capital employed}} \times 100$	Income statement	SoFP

To calculate the **gross profit percentage** we look in the income statement to find both the gross profit figure and the revenue figure and then divide the gross profit by the revenue and multiply by 100 to give the answer in the form of a percentage, as follows:

$$\text{Gross profit \%} \quad \frac{\text{gross profit}}{\text{revenue}} \times 100 \quad \frac{94{,}454}{236{,}135} \times 100 \quad 40.00\%$$

We carry out a similar exercise to calculate the **net profit percentage**:

$$\text{Net profit \%} \quad \frac{\text{net profit}}{\text{revenue}} \times 100 \quad \frac{21{,}253}{236{,}135} \times 100 \quad 9.00\%$$

A ratio can be calculated for any of the expenses using the formula shown in Table 9.1 above. For Simon, we are going to calculate the salaries and wages as a percentage of revenue as follows:

$$\text{Salaries and wages \%} \quad \frac{\text{salaries \& wages}}{\text{revenue}} \times 100 \quad \frac{35{,}685}{236{,}135} \times 100 \quad 15.11\%$$

The return on **capital employed** can be calculated to show the return on the investment in the business. This ratio is calculated using figures from both the income statement and the statement of financial position as follows:

$$\text{ROCE} \quad \frac{\text{net profit}}{\text{capital employed*}} \times 100 \quad \frac{21{,}253}{249{,}160} \times 100 \quad 8.53\%$$

(*capital employed = capital + borrowings: 39,160 + 210,000 = 249,160)

We will now consider two liquidity ratios for Simon. Table 9.2 provides the formulae and shows where the numerator and denominator come from.

TABLE 9.2 Liquidity ratios

Ratio	Formula (Numerator / Denominator)	Which financial statement do we get the numerator from?	Which financial statement do we get the denominator from?
Current ratio	$\dfrac{\text{Current assets}}{\text{Current liabilities}} : 1$	Statement of financial position	Statement of financial position
Quick ratio (acid test)	$\dfrac{\text{Current assets} - \text{closing inventory}}{\text{Current liability}} : 1$	Statement of financial position	Statement of financial position

These liquidity ratios are expressed in the form of a simple ratio – X:1. The figures for both ratios are found in the statement of financial position. You will notice that the **quick ratio** may alternatively be referred to as the **acid test**.

Current ratio	$\dfrac{\text{Currents assets}}{\text{Current liabilities}}$	$\dfrac{23{,}495}{6{,}915}$	3.40:1
Quick ratio	$\dfrac{\text{Currents assets} - \text{inventory}}{\text{Current liabilities}}$	$\dfrac{23{,}495 - 11{,}200}{6{,}915}$	1.78:1

ACTIVITY

Hazel is a sole trader who makes picture frames. Her income statement and statement of financial position for the year ended 30 September 20X8 are as follows:

Income statement for the year ended 30 June September 20X8

	£	£
Revenue		125,020
Cost of sales		77,513
Gross profit		47,507
Expenses		
Rent and rates	6,821	
Remuneration	14,785	
Light and heat	710	
Motor expenses	3,605	
Professional fees	1,630	
Administration expenses	5,650	
		33,201
Net profit		**14,306**

Hazel

Statement of Financial Position as at 30 September 20X8

	£	£
Assets		
Non-current assets		
Machinery	58,000	
Motor vehicles	15,700	
Fixtures	8,880	
		82,580
Current assets		
Inventory	10,200	
Accounts receivable	5,805	
Cash at bank	4,490	20,495
		103,075
Capital		36,150
Non-current liabilities		
Bank loan	60,000	
Current liabilities		
Accounts payable	6,925	
		66,925
		103,075

You are required to calculate the following ratios for 20X8:

(a) Gross profit %
(b) Net profit %
(c) Remuneration as a % of revenue
(d) Administration expenses as a % of revenue

(e) ROCE
(f) Current ratio
(g) Quick ratio

Once the ratios have been calculated they need to be interpreted. For the interpretation to be meaningful the ratios need to be compared to a previous year or compared to a similar business operating in a similar environment over a similar period of time.

To introduce basic interpretation the following 20X7 and 20X8 ratios for Hazel have been tabulated as follows:

	20X7	20X8
Gross profit %	37.10%	38.00%
Net profit %	13.36%	11.44%
Remuneration/Revenue %	10.40%	11.83%
Administration	4.50%	4.52%
ROCE	16.25%	14.88%
Current ratio	2.43:1	2.96:1
Quick ratio	1.46:1	1.49:1

The interpretation begins with a brief review of the income statement and statement of financial position to get an overview of the size of the business. Hazel has revenue of £125,020, a net profit of £14,306 and non-current assets of £82,580. The ratios for the two years can be compared by considering whether or not the ratio has improved from one year to the next and then by considering the possible reasons for any changes. The ratios above show that Hazel's business was profitable in both 20X7 and 20X8. The gross profit percentage is relatively consistent but shows a slight improvement over the two years, moving from 37.10 per cent in 20X7 to 38.00 per cent in 20X8. The net profit percentage has declined from 13.36 per cent to 11.44 per cent over the two years, which is a considerable decline and requires further investigation. From the information we have been provided with, we can see that one of the reasons for the decline is the increase in remuneration as a percentage of revenue, which has gone up from 10.40 per cent in 20X7 to 11.83 per cent in 20X8. There is also a decline in the **return on capital employed** of 1.37% (14.88 − 16.25).

The ratios show that Hazel has a sound liquidity position, which has improved slightly over the two years under consideration, with the **current ratio** moving from 2.43:1 to 2.96:1. When considering the liquidity ratios, textbooks often argue that the current assets should exceed the current liabilities to ensure that the current liabilities can easily be paid off when they fall due. Some authors suggest that the current ratio should be at least 2:1 and the quick ratio should be at least 1:1.

This may be useful as a very general guide but different businesses operating in different sectors will operate successfully on ratios below these general guidelines. For example, a company such as Marks and Spencer plc, operating in the retail sector, will have few amounts owing to them (trade receivables) as their customers pay by cash (or their own credit card) but they will have substantial amounts owing to their suppliers (trade payables) and will therefore operate successfully on ratios below the suggested standards. We can see that Hazel can quite easily pay off all of her current liabilities as they fall due, by considering the quick ratio, which stands at 1.49:1 in 20X8.

9.5 Interpreting published financial statements

Now we have considered the basics of interpreting financial statements we can consider a more in-depth example, using the financial statements of a public limited company, to lead us through the main ratios used by analysts in interpreting the income statement and statement of financial position. The following financial statements for Sandhaven plc, which operates a sea-sport equipment business, will be used to show examples of the ratio calculations throughout the rest of this chapter.

Sandhaven plc
Income Statement for the year ended 31 December 20X1

	20X0	20X1
	£000	£000
Sales revenue	2000	2080
Cost of sales	1530	1590
Gross profit	**470**	490
Operating costs	250	400
Net profit before interest and taxation	**220**	90
Finance costs (interest)	(30)	(50)
Profit before taxation	190	40
Taxation	50	30
Profit for the financial year	**140**	**10**

Statement of Financial Position as at 31 December 20X1

	20X0	20X1
	£000	£000
Non-current assets		
Property, plant and equipment	490	620
Current assets		
Inventories	280	310
Trade receivables	210	230
Cash	20	–
	510	540
Total assets	**1,000**	**1,160**
Equity		
£1 ordinary shares	200	200
Share premium	50	50
Retained earnings	150	120
	400	370
Non-current liabilities		
10% debentures	300	400
Deferred tax	20	10
	320	410
Current liabilities		
Trade payables	220	290
Dividends payable	30	30
Taxes payable	30	10
Bank overdraft	–	50
	(280)	(380)
	1,000	**1,160**

Notes to the accounts

1. At 1 January 20X0 the equity stood at £390,000 and the 10% debentures stood at £300,000.
2. Assume all purchases and sales are made on credit.
3. The market value of the £1 ordinary shares at 31 December were:

	20X0	20X1
	£10.20	£0.30

4. The total dividend for both 20X0 and 20X1 was £30,000.

Profitability ratios

- gross profit percentage
- net profit percentage
- return on capital employed (ROCE).

Gross profit percentage (GP%)

Most users of accounts are interested in the profitability of a business. The following formula can be used to calculate the gross profit percentage.

$$\frac{\text{Gross profit} \times 100}{\text{Sales revenue (turnover)}}$$

> **Gross profit (GP)** is the money made by the company once stock has been sold and after the cost of sales has been deducted; Gross profit equals the sales revenue minus the cost of sales.

KEY TERM

The ratio shows gross profit as a percentage of sales and consequently highlights the efficiency in production or buying and has a fundamental impact on the overall profitability of a business. The gross profit percentage shows how much gross profit is made per £1 of sales revenue. This ratio will vary considerably between different business sectors, for example a supermarket will operate on a low gross profit percentage whereas a manufacturing company is likely to operate on a higher gross profit percentage.

The gross profit percentage for Sandhaven plc can be calculated as follows:

20X0	**20X1**
$\frac{470}{2000} \times 100$	$\frac{490}{2080} \times 100$
= 23.50%	= 23.56%

You can see there has been very little change in the gross profit percentage between 20X0 and 20X1. This could be compared to other similar businesses to determine if it highlights the buying is being carried out as efficiently as possible.

Net (operating) profit percentage (NP%)

The following formula can be used to calculate the net profit percentage.

$$\frac{\text{Net profit}}{\text{Sales revenue}} \times 100 \quad \text{or} \quad \frac{\text{Profit before interest and taxation (PBIT)}}{\text{Sales revenue}} \times 100$$

When analysing the accounts of a sole trader or partnership the net profit version should be used and when analysing the accounts of a company the PBIT (operating profit version should be used.

> **KEY TERM**
>
> **Net profit/operating profit** is the profit made after deducting expenses.

This ratio highlights the net profit the business has made and the extent to which expenses affect profitability. It also shows the amount of net profit made per £1 of sales revenue. Just like the gross profit percentage the net profit percentage will vary from business to business. Again, supermarkets are likely to operate on lower margins than manufacturing companies.

The net profit percentage for Sandhaven plc can be calculated as follows:

20X0	20X1
$\frac{220}{2000} \times 100$	$\frac{90}{2080} \times 100$
= 11.00%	= 4.33%

You can see there has been a considerable decline in the operating profit percentage between 20X0 and 20X1. The business should look carefully at how it can control its costs. It would therefore be useful, if the figures were available, to look at the individual expenses to investigate the reasons for the decline.

> **KEY TERM**
>
> **Capital Employed (CE)** can be defined as all of the money invested in a business, in which case it equals the share capital (money that has come from shareholders), plus reserves (money that belongs to the shareholders), plus long-term loans (money that has come from borrowing).

Return on capital employed (ROCE)

The following formula can be used to calculate the return on capital employed:

$$\frac{\text{Profit}}{\text{Capital Employed}} \times 100$$

> **KEY TERM**
>
> **Return on Capital Employed (ROCE)** is a useful ratio that highlights the performance of the business, showing how much profit is made in comparison to the capital invested. However, there are various ways in which the ratio can be calculated so it is important to make sure the profit and capital employed are comparable.

The formula for the total return on total capital employed can be written as follows:

$$\frac{\text{Profit before interest and tax}}{\text{Share capital} + \text{reserves} + \text{long-term borrowings}} \times 100$$

If the ratio is being calculated on behalf of the shareholders it may be more appropriate to calculate the return on equity only and exclude the long-term borrowings. In this case the relevant profit figure can either be the profit before taxation or the profit after taxation. Therefore it can be re-written as:

$$\frac{\text{Profit before tax}}{\text{Share capital} + \text{reserves}} \times 100$$

or

$$\frac{\text{Profit after tax}}{\text{Share capital} + \text{reserves}} \times 100$$

There is no best method of calculating the ROCE. You should decide on which you feel is more appropriate for the analysis you are carrying out. To improve the accuracy of the ratio an average figure can be used for the capital employed if the information is available, by taking an average of the opening and closing capital employed figures.

Since the equity plus long-term borrowings equals total assets minus current liabilities minus other long-term liabilities – which are referred to as net assets (look at the statement of financial position of Sandhaven plc on page 164 to check your understanding) – the ratio may also be referred to as the return on net assets and be written as:

$$\frac{\text{Profit after tax}}{\text{Net assets}}$$

$$\text{Net assets} = \text{equity} + \frac{\text{long term}}{\text{borrowings}} = \text{total assets} - \frac{\text{current}}{\text{liabilities}} - \frac{\text{other long-term}}{\text{liabilities}}$$

The ROCE percentage can be compared to the Bank of England lending rate. If the return is less than the Bank of England lending rate then it would have been more advantageous for the investors to invest their money in the bank.

The total return on total capital employed for Sandhaven plc can be calculated as follows:

20X0	20X1
$\dfrac{220}{\frac{1}{2}(690 + 700)} \times 100$	$\dfrac{90}{\frac{1}{2}(700 + 770)} \times 100$
$\dfrac{220}{695} \times 100$	$\dfrac{90}{735} \times 100$
$= 31.65\%$	$= 12.24\%$

The denominator figures for 20X0 are made up of the equity plus the long-term loans at the beginning and end of the year:

$$(390 + 300 = 690) \qquad (400 + 300 = 700)$$

You can see the ROCE has declined substantially over the two years and this should be investigated further. The main reason for this is the decline in the net profit of £130,000 (£220,000 – £90,000). However, the return on the investment in the business for 20X1, at

12%, remains higher than a return that could be gained from investing the money in a bank.

Liquidity ratios

Liquidity is of prime concern to a business for it is essential that a business can pay its liabilities as these fall due or it will run the risk of being closed down. The current assets are all part of the cash operating cycle and the time period between paying for purchases from suppliers and receiving cash from customers can have a significant impact on a business' liquidity

- current ratio
- quick ratio.

KEY TERM

Liquidity refers to the ability of a business to quickly turn current assets into the most liquid asset of cash. It is essential that a business can pay its liabilities as they fall due or the company will run the risk of being closed down.

Current ratio

The following formula can be used to calculate the current ratio:

$$\frac{\text{Current assets}}{\text{Current liabilities}}$$

The current ratio is usually expressed in the form of X:1. It measures how many times the current assets cover the current liabilities and therefore highlights the business's ability to meet its short-term liabilities out of the current assets. The term 'current' can be taken to mean twelve months and therefore the current liabilities figure from the published accounts can be used. Although some textbooks may suggest a ratio of 2:1 is ideal, it should be remembered that different business sectors will operate effectively on different ratios. Supermarkets may operate on a comparatively low ratio as they trade in fast-moving, often perishable goods that are usually sold for cash, whereas manufacturing businesses hold stocks of raw materials, work-in-progress and finished goods that get converted into trade receivables before generating cash, thus creating a higher current ratio.

The current ratio for Sandhaven plc can be calculated as follows:

20X0	20X1
510	540
280	380
1.82:1	1.42:1

You can see the liquidity of Sandhaven has declined between 20X0 and 20X1. Although the industry may operate efficiently on a ratio of less than 2:1, a year on year decline is a source of concern. It can be seen that current assets have increased by £30,000 while current liabilities have increased by £100,000, mainly due to an increase in the trade payables and the bank overdraft.

Quick ratio

The following formula can be used to calculate the quick ratio:

$$\frac{\text{Current assets} - \text{inventory}}{\text{Current liabilities}}$$

This is sometimes referred to as the acid test ratio and again is usually expressed as a ratio in the form X:1. It is a variation of the current ratio that excludes inventories as most businesses cannot immediately convert their inventories into cash. This is a more stringent test of liquidity. Textbooks sometimes quote an ideal ratio of 1:1 but for the reasons outlined above, there are variations between industries and some businesses can operate with no liquidity worries on a ratio of less than 1:1.

The quick ratio for Sandhaven plc can be calculated as follows:

20X0	20X1
$\dfrac{510 - 280}{280}$	$\dfrac{540 - 310}{380}$
0.82:1	0.61:1

You can see this ratio also shows a declining trend.

Efficiency ratios

- asset turnover
- inventory turnover period
- trade receivables turnover period
- trade payables turnover period.

Efficiency ratios may also be referred to as activity ratios.

Asset turnover

The following formula can be used to calculate the **asset turnover**:

$$\frac{\text{Sales revenue}}{\text{Capital employed}} = \frac{\text{Sales revenue}}{\text{Net assets}}$$

The asset turnover shows how efficient the company's assets are in generating sales.

The asset turnover for Sandhaven plc can be calculated as follows:

20X0	20X1
$\dfrac{2,000}{\frac{1}{2}(690 + 700)}$	$\dfrac{2,080}{\frac{1}{2}(690 + 700)}$
$\dfrac{2,000}{695}$	$\dfrac{2,080}{735}$
2.88 times	2.83 times

You can see that the asset turnover of Sandhaven plc has declined slightly. The ratio shows the company has managed to generate a small increase in sales through its additional investment in net assets.

The asset turnover ratio together with the profit ratios feed into the return on capital employed.

$$\text{ROCE} = \frac{\text{profit}}{\text{capital employed}} = \frac{\text{profit}}{\text{revenue}} \times \frac{\text{revenue}}{\text{net assets}}$$

(capital employed = net assets)

We can now calculate the ROCE for Sandhaven in 20X0

ROCE = profit % × asset turnover

$$\frac{220}{695} = \frac{220}{2000} \times \frac{2000}{695}$$

31.7% ≠ 11% × 2.88 times

When analysing the ROCE any interesting changes can be traced by looking at both the gross profit percentage and the operating profit percentage along with the asset turnover.

Inventory turnover period

The following formula can be used to calculate the **inventory turnover period**:

$$\frac{\text{Average inventory}}{\text{Cost of sales}} \times 365$$

This ratio highlights the average number of days between purchasing goods and selling them. The average inventory figure is calculated by taking an average of the opening and closing inventory figures. If the opening inventory figure is not available the ratio can be calculated by using just the closing inventory. When comparing ratios it is important they are calculated on the same basis for each year or each company. Businesses generally strive to reduce their inventory turnover period, to reduce their investment, while remaining conscious of the implications of being out of stock.

The inventory turnover period for Sandhaven plc can be calculated as follows:

20X0	**20X1**
$\frac{280}{1530} \times 365$	$\frac{310}{1590} \times 365$
67 days	72 days

(These figures have been calculated using the closing inventory figures as the opening inventory is not available for 20X0.)

You can see that the inventory turnover period has increased by five days, showing a reduction in efficiency as more money will be invested in the inventory. This may indicate the company should tighten up its inventory control.

Trade receivables turnover period

The following formula can be used to calculate the **trade receivables turnover period**:

$$\frac{\text{Average trade receivables}}{\text{Credit sales}} \times 365$$

This ratio highlights the average number of days between making a credit sale and receiving the cash from the customer. The average trade receivables figure is calculated by taking an average of the opening and closing trade receivables, but if the opening figure is not available, the year end figure can be used. Businesses generally strive to keep the trade receivables turnover period to a minimum and are conscious that the length of time taken by customers to pay can have a significant impact on the cash flow of a business.

The trade receivables turnover period for Sandhaven plc can be calculated as follows:

20X0

$$\frac{210}{2000} \times 365$$

39 days

20X1

$$\frac{230}{2080} \times 365$$

41 days

You can see the trade receivables collection period has marginally increased, showing a reduction in efficiency. The business should pay attention to this area to ensure the trade receivables do not take advantage of a lack of control by Sandhaven plc.

Trade payables turnover period

The following formula can be used to calculate the **trade payables turnover period**:

$$\frac{\text{Average trade payables}}{\text{Credit purchases}} \times 365$$

This ratio highlights the average number of days between purchasing an item on credit and making a payment to the supplier. Again, the average trade payables figure is calculated by taking an average of the opening and closing trade payables, but if the opening figure is not available, the year end figure can be used. Alternatively, the cost of sales figure can be used instead of purchases.

The trade payables turnover period for Sandhaven plc can be calculated as follows:

20X0

$$\frac{220}{1530} \times 365$$

53 days

20X1

$$\frac{290}{1590} \times 365$$

67 days

(These ratios have been calculated using the cost of sales figure.)

You can see the trade payables period has increased considerably, by 14 days. Ultimately this could have a significant impact on the business as suppliers may refuse to deal with Sandhaven plc in the future or require them to pay cash in advance if they fail to pay within a suitable time period. It can be seen from the statement of financial position that Sandhaven plc is struggling for cash as they have gone from having cash in the bank of £20,000 in 20X0 to an overdraft of £50,000 in 20X1.

Reflective question

1. The return on capital employed (ROCE) is one of the most important ratios. What does it highlight? What is the general ROCE formula (for the total return on the total capital employed)? What can the ROCE percentage be compared to and what can this comparison tell us?

Investment ratios

- earnings per share
- dividend cover
- price/earnings ratio.

There are a number of investment ratios that can be calculated to assist investors in assessing the performance of their investment. This section will concentrate on three of the most commonly used ratios.

Earnings per share (EPS)

The following formula can be used to calculate the earnings per share:

$$\frac{\text{Earnings available to ordinary shareholders}}{\text{Number of ordinary shares in issue}}$$

Earnings available to ordinary shareholders is the profit after taxation less any preference dividend that may be deducted.

Earnings available to ordinary shareholders is useful as an aid to monitor the changes within a business over time, but is less useful as a comparison to other businesses as no two businesses are sufficiently alike, especially regarding their share structure, to provide meaningful comparisons. This is the most fundamental measure of share performance.

The earnings per share for Sandhaven plc can be calculated as follows:

20X0	20X1
140	10
200	200
70p	5p

You can see the earnings per share have declined dramatically due to declining profitability.

Dividend cover

The following formula can be used to calculate the **dividend cover**:

$$\frac{\text{Earnings available to ordinary shareholders}}{\text{Dividend for the year}}$$

This highlights how many times the earnings cover the dividend paid. The dividend includes both the interim and final dividends. A high dividend cover shows a business is retaining a considerable proportion of its profits for reinvestment and can easily pay the dividend, whereas a low dividend cover shows a business may be struggling to maintain its level of dividend.

The dividend cover for Sandhaven plc can be calculated as follows:

	20X0	20X1
	140	10
	30	30
	4.67 times	0.33 times

The dividend payment would be considered excessive in 20X1 as you can see the dividend exceeds the profit for the financial year. This situation cannot continue and unless profitability improves the shareholders can expect a considerably reduced dividend in the following year.

Price/earnings ratio (P/E ratio)

The following formula can be used to calculate the **price/earnings ratio**:

$$\frac{\text{Market value per share}}{\text{Earnings per share}}$$

P/E ratio is the ratio of price to earnings.

The P/E ratio highlights the relationship between the earnings and the market value of a business. It provides a useful guide to market confidence in the future performance of the company. The higher the P/E ratio, the greater the confidence the market has in the future earning potential of the business. With this, an informative comparison can be made with other businesses.

The price/earnings ratio for Sandhaven plc can be calculated as follows:

	20X0	20X1
	10.2	0.30
	0.70	0.05
	14.57	6

(The earnings figures have been taken from the previous EPS calculation.)

You can see that the P/E ratio of Sandhaven plc has declined, indicating the market's reduced confidence in the business.

Market capitalization

The following formula can be used to calculate a company's market capitalization:

$$\text{share price} \times \text{number of shares in issue}$$

The market capitalization is not a ratio but is a useful piece of information for investors and analysts as it gives an indication of the market's opinion on the total value of a company.

The market capitalization for Sandhaven Plc can be calculated as follows:

	20X0	20X1
	$200,000 \times 10.20$	$200,000 \times 0.30$
	£2,040,000	£60,000

You can see that the market capitalization has declined significantly, showing a decline in the market's opinion of the company.

FIGURE 9.2 Marks & Spencer plc Summary Ratios

		2011 **52 weeks**	2010 53 weeks	2009 52 weeks	2008 52 weeks	2007 52 weeks
Net margin	Operating profit/revenue	**8.6%**	8.9%	9.6%	13.4%	12.2%
Basic earnings per share	Basic earnings/ Weighted average ordinary shares in issue	**38.8p**	33.5p	32.3p	49.2p	39.1p
Dividend per share		**17.0p**	15.0p	17.8p	22.5p	18.3p
Dividend cover	Profit attributable to shareholders/ Dividend payable	**2.3x**	2.2x	1.8x	2.3x	2.1x

Source: Marks & Spencer Annual Report 2009

Published accounts contain a significant amount of information. The income statement, statement of financial position and notes to the accounts will provide detailed financial data that can be utilized in calculating ratios. However, a great deal of information can also be found in the chairman's statement and director's report, providing a broader insight into an organization. Additional financial data can be found in the cash flow statement and the auditors' report will confirm whether the accounts show a true and fair view or if there are any reservations regarding the accounts.

 ## 9.6 Other analytical measures

You can gain some useful information just by considering the difference between two figures. This can be referred to as **horizontal analysis** and if figures for a number of years are used it is possible to carry out **trend analysis.** Financial statements generally provide five-year summaries of key figures that can be used for trend analysis. This type of analysis can be applied to any figures in the financial statements but it is more commonly applied to sales revenue, gross profit, net profit and non-current assets.

$$\text{Percentage change in profit} = \frac{\text{current year's profit} - \text{previous year's profit}}{\text{previous year's profit}} \times 100$$

If a business makes £20,000 profit in year 1 and £28,000 profit in year 2, what is the percentage change in profit?

$$\frac{28{,}000 - 20{,}000}{20{,}000} \times 100 = 40\%$$

If a business makes a £15,000 profit in year 2 and a £12,000 profit in year 3, what is the percentage change in profit?

$$\frac{12{,}000 - 15{,}000}{15{,}000} \times 100 = -20\% \text{ (a decrease in profit of 20\%)}$$

The structure of the formula can be applied to other figures in the accounts such as sales revenue:

The percentage change in the sales revenue of Sandhurst plc (see page 164) can be calculated as follows:

$$\frac{2{,}080 - 2{,}000}{2{,}000} \times 100 = 4\%$$

CASE STUDY Sainsbury's plc

Sainsbury's has revealed its convenience stores are now a £1bn business, following good sales and profit performance for 52 weeks to 19 March 2011.

Total sales (including VAT) were up 7.1% to £22.9bn, with total sales (including VAT, ex fuel) up 4.9% with like-for-like sales (including VAT, ex fuel) up 2.3%.

The supermarket outperformed the market in a "challenging environment", increasing market share, with weekly customer transactions now 21 million, up one million on last year, and over 6,000 jobs created through store investment.

Sainsbury's has also opened six new food colleges to train over 10,000 colleagues each year, plus it had a successful re-launch of its £1bn 'Taste the Difference' brand.

Justin King, chief executive, said: "Sainsbury's has continued to perform well. Customer numbers are at an all-time high of 21 million transactions every week, which is up one million on last year, a clear indication of our growing universal customer appeal across all channels.

"We have added gross space of 1.5 million sq ft to our store estate, creating over 6,000 new jobs with Sainsbury's. Strong sales growth, combined with productivity savings and tight control on operating costs, have helped to deliver good profit growth. Our colleagues continue to deliver great service, exceeding our stretching customer service targets, and we are delighted to be paying our colleagues a bonus of around £60m.

"We expect the economic environment to remain uncertain over the coming year. We remain confident that our strategy, alongside continued strong operational performance, will enable the business to make further good progress."

Source: Sainsbury's, 11 May 2011

Q What would the total sales (including VAT) have been in the previous year?

9.7 Limitations of ratio analysis

Although ratio analysis is a useful technique, users must be aware of its limitations. Ratios are only as good as the information on which they are based. Consequently if accounting information has been manipulated through 'window dressing', the ratios will be unreliable. It must also be remembered that the statement of financial position is only a snapshot of a business on a particular day; it may not be representative of the business's year-round position, for example, a retail outlet selling surfing equipment is likely to have a far higher inventory at the end of June than at the end of December.

Since ratios are a relative measure, which ignore the actual values, the underlying figures should always be considered to put the ratios into context. A large business with sales of £10,000,000 and a net profit of £700,000 will show a net profit percentage of 7 per cent, but likewise a small business with sales of £30,000 and a net profit of £2,100 would also have a net profit percentage of 7 per cent.

The financial statements used for ratio analysis are based upon historical data. In order to carry out a full analysis of a business, information is required about its future aims and objectives, its product development and budgeted cash flows. Some of this information is likely to be found in the chairman's statement or director's report.

If ratios are being compared to those of other businesses it must be remembered that companies can choose their own accounting policies, such as the method of depreciation and the rate, and these variations may distort the comparison. In addition, no two businesses are identical in terms of structure or activities so like-for-like comparisons are difficult to make.

When carrying out trend analysis it is important to consider the impact the economic climate will have on the data. In times of high inflation comparisons of sales revenue, profit figures and asset values will be distorted. New accounting standards and changes in the business activities will also reduce the usefulness of year-on-year comparisons.

FIGURE 9.3 Diagrammatic representation of Sainsbury's profitability

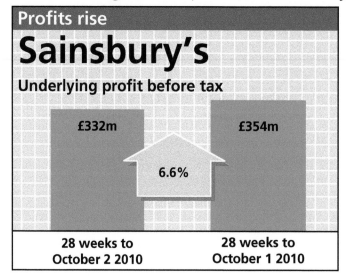

Source: Sainsbury's plc.

9.8 Summary

Key ideas

Financial statements

- there are seven main user groups that analyse financial statements:
  - shareholders
  - loan creditors
  - employees
  - analyst-investors
  - business contacts
  - the government
  - the public.

Ratio analysis

- a useful technique used to assist in the interpretation of accounts
- mathematical comparisons are used to highlight the relationships that exist between different figures on the income statement and statement of financial position.
- once ratios are calculated they need to be compared
- comparisons can be made with previous ratios of the same business to establish trends or to the ratios of other organizations to measure how the business is performing against its competitors.

Accounting ratios

- four main categories: profitability, liquidity, efficiency and investment.

Profitability ratios

- gross profit %
- net profit %
- return on capital employed (ROCE).

Liquidity ratios

- current ratio
- quick ratio.

Efficiency ratios

- asset turnover
- inventory turnover period
- trades receivables turnover period
- trade payables turnover period

Investment ratios

- earnings per share
- dividend cover
- price/earnings ratio.

Limitations of ratio analysis

- users must be aware of the limitations of ratio analysis when using it as the basis for decision making
- ratios are only as good as the information on which they are based
- the underlying figures should always be considered to put the ratios into context
- the financial statements used for ratio analysis are based upon historical data

- the statement of financial position is only a snapshot of a business on a particular day and may not be representative of the year-round position
- different accounting policies distort comparisons
- when carrying out trend analysis it is important to consider the impact of the economic climate.

Review questions

1. Justin is a sole trader who prepares accounts to 31 December each year. For the year ended 31 December 20X3 his income statement and statement of financial position are as follows:

Income Statement for the year ended 31 December 20X3

	£	£
Revenue		293,350
Cost of sales		181,950
Gross profit		111,400
Less expenses		
Rent and rates	9,470	
Light and heat	2,860	
Wages and salaries	30,400	
Motor expenses	4,950	
Professional fees	1,250	
Sundry expenses	2,620	51,550
Net profit		**59,850**

Statement of Financial Position as at 31 December 20X3

	£	£
Non-current assets		
Factory	148,000	
Motor vans	31,180	
		179,180
Current assets		
Inventory	28,700	
Accounts receivable	29,480	58,180
Total assets		**237,360**
Capital		159,660
Non-current liabilities		
Loan	50,000	
Current liabilities		
Bank overdraft	5,400	
Accounts payable	22,300	
		77,700
		237,360

You are required to calculate the following ratios:
(a) Gross profit %
(b) Net profit %
(c) Wages and salaries as a % of revenue
(d) Rent and rates as a % of revenue
(e) ROCE
(f) Current ratio
(g) Quick ratio

2. Liquidity comparison
Elizabeth runs a small business called Data Services (DS) and her brother runs a small business called Engineering Services (ES). In the year ended 31 March 20X3 they both generated sales of £160,000 and both made a gross profit of £52,500. Their statements of financial position as at 31 March 20X3 were as follows:

		DS		ES	
	£	£	£	£
Non-current assets		52,270		91,160
Current assets				
Inventory	36,480		37,200	
Accounts receivable	42,140		2,520	
Bank balance	10,420	89,040	2,300	42,020
Total assets		141,310		133,180
Capital		111,830		111,830
Current liabilities				
Accounts payable	29,480		16,580	
Bank overdraft	0	29,480	4,770	21,350
		141,310		133,180

You are required to assess the liquidity of the two businesses by:
(a) calculating the relevant ratios
(b) analysing the ratios.

3. Lisa

Income statements for the years ended 30 April

		20X4		20X5
	£	£	£	£
Revenue		78,750		88,590
Opening inventory	3,540		4,140	
Purchases	38,280		39,940	
	41,820		44,080	
Closing inventory	4,140		4,330	
Cost of sales		37,680		39,750
Gross profit		41,070		48,840

| | | 20X4 | | | 20X5 |
	£	£	£	£
Less expenses					
Business rates	6,490		6,570		
Light and heat	1,480		1,560		
Motor expenses	1,110		1,480		
Stationery	430		210		
Training	100		100		
Wages	10,380	19,990	13,690	23,610
Net profit		21,080		25,230

Lisa
Statement of Financial Position as at 30 April

| | | 20X4 | | | 20X5 |
	£	£	£	£
Non-current assets					
Property		82,800		82,800
Motor vehicles		7,900		7,110
Office furniture		1,570		1,250
		92,270		91,160
Current assets					
Inventory	4,140		4,330	
Trade receivables	8,420		12,150	
Bank balance	2,000	14,560	340	16,820
Total assets		106,830		107,980
Capital					
Opening balance		31,270		37,350
Add profit for the year		21,080		25,230
		52,350		62,580
Less drawings		15,000		21,180
		37,350		41,400
Non-current liabilities					
Business loan	60,000		55,000	
Current liabilities		69,480		66,580
Accounts payable	9,480		11,580	
		106,830		107,980

You are required to:

(a) Calculate the following ratios: gross profit percentage, net profit percentage, wages as a percentage of revenue, return on capital employed, current ratio, quick ratio, asset turnover, inventory turnover, trade receivables turnover and trade payables turnover.

(b) Write a short report (maximum 200 words) analysing the changes that have taken place between 20X4 and 20X5.

4. The following is an extract from the financial statements of Halwyn plc:

Income Statement for the year ended 31 March 20X9

	£'000
Revenue	6,923
Cost of sales	4,222
Gross profit	2,701
Distribution costs	(630)
Administration expenses	(847)
Operating profit	1,224
Finance costs (debenture interest)	140
Profit before taxation	1,084
Taxation	320
Profit for the year	764

Statement of Financial Position extract as at 31 March 20X9

Equity	
Ordinary share capital	1,500
Retained earnings	1,632
Other components of equity	821
Non-current liabilities	
10% debentures	200

(a) You are required to calculate the following profitability ratios:
  - Gross profit percentage
  - Operating profit percentage
  - Return on capital employed
  - Pre-tax return on equity

(b) Halwyn's revenue for the year ended 31 March 20X8 was £6,482,000. Calculate the percentage increase in the revenue.

5. Pentire plc is listed on the London Stock Exchange. The company's issued share capital is comprised of 2,000,000 ordinary shares of 50p each. On 31 December 20X8 the share price was £2.93 per share. The following data has been extracted from Pentire's financial statements for the year ended 31 December 20X8:

	£
Profit after taxation	366,000
Dividends	120,000
Retained profit for the year	246,000

You are required to calculate the investment ratios shown below and determine the market capitalization:
  - earnings per share
  - dividend cover
  - price/earnings ratio.

6. Budgisons and Morrens both operate in the retail environment.

Income statements for the year ended 30 November 20X8

	Budgisons plc		Morrens plc	
	£000	£000	£000	£000
Revenue		187,500		86,890
Opening inventory	27,800		10,140	
Purchases	107,560		56,130	
	135,360		66,270	
Closing inventory	24,140		11,520	
Cost of sales		111,220		54,750
Gross profit		76,280		32,140
Less				
Distribution expenses	27,890		13,620	
Administration expenses	18,000		8,470	
		45,890	22,090	
Operating profit		30,390		10,050
Finance costs		1,900		1,300
Profit before taxation		28,490		8,750
Taxation		4,200		1,420
Profit after taxation		**24,290**		**7,330**

Statement of Financial Position as at 30 November 20X8

	Budgisons plc		Morrens plc	
	£000	£000	£000	£000
Non-current assets				
Property		92,500		42,800
Motor vehicles		14,900		9,510
Office furniture		1,600		250
		109,000		52,560
Current assets				
Inventory	24,140		11,520	
Bank balance	1,040	25,180	12,300	23,820
		134,180		76,380
Equity				
Ordinary Shares of £1 each		5,000		2,000
Retained earnings		42,560		9,700
Other components of equity		5,630		100
		53,190		11,800

Non-current liabilities				
Business loan	60,000	80,990	50,000	64,580
Current liabilities				
Short-term borrowings	10,470		0	
Accounts payable	10,520		14,580	
		20,990		**14,580**
		134,180		**76,280**

(a) You are required to calculate the following ratios:
  ● gross profit %
  ● operating profit %
  ● return on capital employed
  ● current ratio
  ● quick ratio
  ● asset turnover
  ● inventory turnover
  ● earnings per share.
(b) Write a report comparing the two companies.

7. Write a short report to Mr X highlighting in bullet points five benefits and five limitations of ratio analysis.

8. (a) Analyse the financial statements of Tesco plc and calculate six key ratios from the information provided in the income statement and SoFP.
   (b) Write a confidential report to the CEO of Tesco plc commenting on the significance of the ratios (max. 400 words).

FIGURE 9.4 Tesco plc Income Statement and Statement of Financial Position

Group income statement			
		2009	2008*
53 weeks ended 28 February 2009	notes	**£m**	£m
Continuing operations			
Revenue (sales excluding VAT)	2	**54,327**	47,298
Cost of sales		**(50,109)**	(43,668)
Gross profit		**4,218**	3,630
Administrative expenses		**(1,248)**	(1,027)
Profit arising on property-related items	2/3	**236**	188
Operating profit	2	**3,206**	2,791
Share of post-tax profits of joint ventures and associates	13	**110**	75
Finance income	5	**116**	187
Finance costs	5	**(478)**	(250)
Profit before tax	3	**2,954**	2,803

Taxation	6	**(788)**	(673)
Profit for the year		**2,166**	2,130
Attributable to:			
Equity holder of the parent	30	**2,161**	2,124
Minority interests	30	**5**	6
		2,166	2,130
Earnings per share			
Basic	9	**27.50p**	26.95p
Diluted	9	**27.31p**	26.61p

Group balance sheet

28 February 2009	notes	2009 £m	2008* £m
Non-current assets			
Goodwill and other intangible assets	10	**4,027**	2,336
Property, plant and equipment	11	**23,152**	19,787
Investment property	12	**1,539**	1,112
Investments in joint ventures and associates	13	**62**	305
Other investments	14	**259**	4
Loans and advances to customers	17	**1,470**	–
Derivative financial instruments	22	**1,478**	216
Defferred tax assets	6	**21**	104
		32,008	23,864
Current assets			
Inventories	15	**2,669**	2,430
Trade and other receivables	16	**1,798**	1,311
Loans and advances to customers	17	**1,918**	–
Loans and advances to banks and other financial assets	18	**2,129**	–
Derivative financial instruments	22	**382**	97
Current tax assets		**9**	6
Short-term investments		**1,233**	360
Cash and cash equivalents	19	**3,509**	1,788
		13,647	5,992
Non-current assets classified as held for sale	7	**398**	308
		14,045	6,300
Current liabilities			
Trade and other payables	20	**(8,522)**	(7,277)
Financial liabilities			
Borrowings	21	**(4,059)**	(2,084)
Derivative financial instruments and other liabilities	22	**(525)**	(443)

Customer deposits	24	**(4,538)**	–
Deposits by banks	25	**(24)**	–
Current tax liabilities		**(362)**	(455)
Provisions	26	**(10)**	(4)
Net current liabilities		**(3,995)**	(3,963)
Non-current liabilities			
Financial liabilities			
Borrowings	21	**(12,391)**	(5,972)
Derivative financial instruments and other liabilities	22	**(302)**	(322)
Post-employment benefit obligations	28	**(1,494)**	(838)
Other non-current payables	20	**(68)**	(42)
Defferred tax liabilities	6	**(696)**	(802)
Provisions	26	**(67)**	(23)
		(15,018)	(7,999)
Net assets		**12,995**	11,902
Equity			
Share capital	29/30	**395**	393
Share premium account	30	**4,638**	4,511
Other reserves	30	**40**	40
Retained earnings	30	**7,865**	6,871
Equity attributables to equity holders of the parent		**12,938**	11,815
Minority interests	30	**57**	87
Total equity		**12,995**	11,902

Source: Tesco plc Annual Report and Financial Statements 2009

References

Johal, P. (2009) *Ratio Analysis notes*. Derby University.
Atrill, P. and Mc Laney, E. (2004) *Accounting & Finance for Non Specialists*. Harlow, FT Prentice Hall.

Recommended reading

Mc Laney, E. and Atrill, P. (2005) *Accounting an Introduction,* 3rd edition. Harlow, Prentice Hall.
Melville, A. (1999) *Financial Accounting,* 2nd edition. Harlow, Prentice Hall.
Wood, F. and Sangster, A. (2011) *Business Accounting 1,* 12th edition. Harlow, FT Prentice Hall.

Useful websites

http://www.google.com/hostednews/ukpress/article/ALeqM5hizcAjHZ5LOn_-hjp
WiitUjRneSQ?docId=N0543641320824636918A
Online news report about Sainsbury's profits rising 6.6%

http://www.dailymail.co.uk/news/article-2059292/Sainsburys-defies-economic-
gloom-6-6-profits-surge.html#ixzz1db025Aau
Online news report about Sainsbury's defying economic gloom with 6.6% profit

http://ar2011.tescoplc.com/overview/financial-highlights.html
Tesco (2011) Annual Report and Financial Statements

http://shares.telegraph.co.uk/fundamentals/?epic=MKS
Online data from *The Daily Telegraph* about Marks & Spencer plc

http://annualreport.marksandspencer.com/financial-statements/key-performance-
measures.aspx
Annual Report from Marks & Spencer plc

GLOSSARY OF TERMS

Account a record of the financial transactions for each asset, liability, revenue and expense, e.g. the account that deals with telephone expenses

Accounting the process of recording, summarizing, communicating and analysing the financial transactions of a business

Accounting concepts generally accepted accounting rules used in the preparation of financial statements; going concern, accruals, consistency, prudence, substance over form, materiality

Accounting data all the data contained in the accounting records that underpins the preparation of the financial statements, e.g. the data contained in the ledgers and journals

Accounting information system a computer-based collection of accounting records maintained by a business; the collection, storage, processing and analysing of accounting data

Accounting standards the rules and regulations that surrounding the preparation of annual financial statements; The International Accounting Standards Board issues International Financial Reporting Standards and the Accounting Standards Board, in the UK, issues Financial Reporting Standards

Accounts receivable amounts owed to the business by customers

Accounts payable amounts owed by the business to suppliers

Acid-test ratio a liquidity ratio that compares the current assets, excluding inventory, to the current liabilities at a given point in time; may also be called the quick ratio

Accrual 'a liability in respect of goods and services provided to a business in the form of continuous supply, consumed up to an accounting date but not billed by that date' (R. Brockington, 1993)

Assets a resource of value, controlled by a business, that helps to generate revenue

Asset turnover an efficiency ratio that compares the sales revenue, over a given period, to the capital employed, at a given point in time

Audit an examination of accounting records and relevant documents, such as purchase and sales invoices, to ensure the accuracy of financial statements, carried out by a professionally qualified accountant, e.g. a member of the Institute of Chartered Accountants in England and Wales (ICAEW)

Bad debt when it becomes reasonably certain that a credit customer will never pay, the money owed is said to be a bad debt

Balance sheet statement showing the financial position of a business at a given point in time, made up of the business assets, liabilities and capital

Bank reconciliation the process of checking the information on the bank statement against the information on the nominal ledger account for the bank and identifying errors, omissions and timing differences

Bonus issue free additional shares given to existing shareholders, in proportion to their original holdings

Called up share capital the value of the share capital that has been issued but remains unpaid

Capital amounts invested in a business by the owner; the owner has a claim against the business for this amount

Capital employed the capital invested in a business to allow it to function

Capital expenditure the money spent by a business on non-current assets (previously referred to as fixed assets), that will be retained in the business for more than one year e.g. machinery, motor vehicles

Cash flow budget a forecast of the *future* cash inflows and *future* cash outflows for a given period

Corporation tax a tax charged on the profits of companies

Cost of sales the cost to the business of the goods sold to customers, during a period; the purchases figure is adjusted to take into account opening and closing inventory

Credit an accounting entry made on the right-hand-side of an account, in a double-entry bookkeeping system; results in a decrease in an asset or expense account or an increase in a liability or capital account

Current assets assets including inventory, accounts receivable and bank and cash that are used to fund the business on a day-to-day basis; the inventory is converted into accounts receivable on the sale of goods, which in turn is converted into cash on payment; note that there is an expectation that all current assets will change within a year

Current liabilities amounts owed by the business to other organizations or individuals that need to be paid within a year

Current ratio a liquidity ratio that compares the current assets to the current liabilities at a given point in time

Debenture an acknowledgement of a long-term loan that is unsecured

Debit an accounting entry made on the left-hand-side of an account, in a double-entry bookkeeping system; results in an increase in an asset or expense account or a decrease in a liability or capital account

Depreciation a non-cash expense that estimates the cost of a non-current asset, e.g. a machine, used in trading activities over a given period of time and reduces the net book value of the asset

Dividend an amount of money paid by a company to its shareholders out of its profits

Dividend cover an investment ratio that compares the earnings generated by a company, over a given period of time, available to ordinary shareholders, to the dividend for the period

Double-entry bookkeeping a system of recording financial transactions that records each transaction as both a debit and a credit

Drawings amounts withdrawn from a sole trader's business by the owner

Entity a business unit that has a separate identifiable existence e.g. a sole trader, partnership or company

Equity the owner's capital of a limited company, which is made up of the ordinary share capital and reserves

Expenses he costs incurred by a business in generating revenue, e.g. rent and rates, advertising and accountancy fees

Financial accounting the branch of accounting that deals with the financial record-keeping and the preparation of financial statements

Financial statements a collection of reports, including the income statement, statement of financial position (balance sheet) and cash flow statement of a business that together summarise the finances

General reserve an amount set aside out of the retained profits of a company for future, as yet unknown, purposes

Going concern: a business is capable of continuing to carry out its activities for the foreseeable future

Gross profit the amount a business makes by buying and selling goods or manufacturing and selling goods, before the deduction of expenses

Gross profit percentage a profitability ratio that compares the gross profit to the revenue for a given period

Income the amount of money received during a period

Income statement a financial statement that shows the income, expenses and profitability of a business over a period of time; used to be called a profit and loss account

Inventory goods purchased by the business for re-sale at a profit

Inventory turnover period an efficiency ratio that compares the average inventory to the cost of sales over a given period

Issued share capital the part of the share capital that has been sold to shareholders

Ledger an accounting 'book', made up of a collection of individual accounting records that is used to record the financial transactions of a business

Liabilities amounts owed by the business to other organisations or individuals

Limited company a business structure where the business organization is separate from its owners, who invest in the organization by buying shares; the liability of the shareholders is limited to what they have invested or guaranteed to invest

Limited liability where an individual's personal financial liability is restricted to a fixed maximum amount, e.g. to the amount of shares fully paid in a company

Liquidity a measure of the ability, of an individual or business, to turn an asset into cash quickly or meet their short-term debts

Loss the opposite of profit that arises from business activity and decreases the capital of the owners

Net profit the profit made by a business after all costs, involved, have been deducted from the revenue

Net profit percentage a profitability ratio that compares the net profit to the revenue for a given period

Net realisable value the price that the inventory is now expected to fetch, minus any costs needed to complete the sale

Nominal value the face value of a share, which is usually established by the owners when the shares are first issued. It may be referred to as the par value

Non-current assets an asset owned by a business that is expected to be used for at least a year, to help generate revenue, e.g. land and buildings, machinery and office equipment

Non-current liabilities amounts owed by a business to other organizations or individuals that are payable after more than one year, e.g. loans and debentures

Ordinary shares the most common type of share, whose owners are entitled to the rewards of trading, in the form of dividends and the ownership of retained reserves

Overtrading a situation that arises when a business is operating at an activity level that cannot be supported by the capital of the business, i.e. the business is inadequately financed

Preference shares shares that have a fixed rate of dividend and are entitled to the payment of that dividend in preference to the payment of a dividend to the ordinary shareholders; the holders of preference shares also have priority of repayment in the case of the company going into liquidation

Prepayments 'amounts already paid which will fall to be treated as expenses in a forthcoming period' (R Brockington, 1993)

Partnership a business structure where two or more individuals run the organization together, e.g. accountants, solicitors

Price/earnings ratio (P/E ratio) an investment ratio that compares the market value per share, at a given point, to the earnings per share, over a given period

Private limited company a company that does not trade its shares on a stock exchange; private companies are generally smaller, often family-run concerns that have fewer shareholders than a Public Limited Company; must form part of the company name with Limited or Ltd, e.g. Leicester Engineering Services Ltd

Profit the positive gain arising from business activity that increases the capital of the owners

Public limited company a company whose shares are traded on a stock exchange. Public Limited Company or plc must be part of the name, e.g. Marks and Spencer Group plc

Published Accounts the annual reports of a limited company, containing both financial and non-financial information, about the activities of the business over a given period, usually a year

Quick ratio a liquidity ratio that compares the current assets, excluding inventory, to the current liabilities at a given point in time. It may also be called the acid test ratio

Reducing balance method where depreciation is calculated by applying a fixed percentage each year to the asset's net book value – note that the fixed percentage is not applied to the cost of the asset

Reserves part of the retained earnings of a company set aside for future use and unavailable for distribution as a dividend, e.g. revaluation reserve and general reserve

Retained earnings (profits) profits earned by a company, which have been retained within the business, to finance future trading

Return on capital employed (ROCE) a profitability ratio that compares the net profit to the capital employed in the business, for a given period

Revaluation reserve part of the equity of a company that is created when assets, such as land and buildings are revalued at a surplus

Revenue the income received by a business from its normal trading activities

Rights issue new shares offered to existing shareholders, in proportion to their original holdings, for a stated, usually discounted, price

Sole trader a business structure where an individual runs the organization on their own; there are numerous sole traders, e.g. driving instructors, wedding photographers

Share a unit of ownership of a company, which represents an equal part of the company's total share capital

Share capital the total amount of money invested in a company by the shareholders; it may also be called equity capital

Share premium the amount paid over and above the nominal value of a share

Stakeholders are individuals or organizations that have an interest in a business

Trade payables the amount owed, by a business, to the suppliers of goods or services (creditors)

Trade payables turnover period an efficiency ratio that compares the average trade payables to the credit purchases over a given period

Trade receivables the amount due to a business, by customers, for goods or services bought on credit (debtors)

Trade receivables turnover period an efficiency ratio that compares the average trade receivables to the credit sales over a given period

Transaction a financial event carried out by a business; all transactions are recorded by both a debit and credit entry in the accounting records

Trial balance a summary of the double entry accounting system that is made up of a list of balances from all accounting records; it is prepared in two columns, one for the debits and one for the credits; when prepared accurately the total of the debits equals the total of the credits

ANSWERS TO QUESTIONS

Chapter 1

Reflective questions

1. You may have said that accounting's main objective is any one (or more) of the following:

   - to let people know if their business is making a profit or a loss
   - to let people know what their business is worth
   - to let people know what a transaction was worth to them
   - to let people know how much cash they have
   - to let people know how wealthy they are
   - to let people know how much they are owed
   - to let people know how much they owe to someone else
   - to enable people to keep a financial check on the things they do.

   The list could go on and on. You may have used 'organization' rather than 'people' and you could have used terms like 'surplus' and 'deficit' instead of 'profit' and 'loss'.

2. Input to the accounting information system means any entry of data made to it, and can refer to things going into and out of the organization. You might have thought of some of the following:

   - details of goods purchased for resale (e.g. price, quantity, date received)
   - goods purchased to be used in the organization (e.g. machinery and computer equipment)
   - details of cash received from customers (e.g. the amount received, date received)
   - details of cash paid for wages, purchases, rent, rates, telephones, electricity.

   The actual list is very much longer. Just about anything that can be quantified coming into an organization or going out of it will be recorded as an input to the accounting system.

3. You might have thought of some of the following:

   - reports showing the total cost of everything sold and the total revenue from their sale
   - reports showing the profit made on a sale and/or for all sales over a period of time
   - payslips, totals of the amount spent on wages, or the cost of all the equipment belonging to the organization.

Outputs can also include data or information sent from the accounting system to another of the organization's information systems. As with inputs to the accounting information system, the actual list of outputs is very long indeed.

Some of the output is organized in a commonly agreed format so that anyone looking at the output will understand it. Other output is presented in a way that suits an individual or group of people who will use the information to take decisions of one type or another.

4. Stakeholder categories:
   (a) The managing director is part of the management stakeholder group, but as managing director, if he is a competent and conscientious one, he will also be concerned to ensure that other stakeholders' needs are addressed.
   (b) Mr Taylor is a potential investor, so will fall into the investor group.
   (c) Mr Harris will be one of the employee stakeholders.

5. (b) investors

6. On the face of it, this looks like a partnership, as two persons (Mr and Mrs Smith) have both contributed capital and appear to be working together with a view to making profit. However, this need not be the case. Mrs Smith may not be taking an active role in the business (the information is that Mr Smith has opened the shop), and the £10,000 she put into the business may be a loan to her husband. If this is the case the business may then be a sole trader operated by Mr Smith. The point to note here is that you often need a great deal of information to decide what might be going on in a business and cannot make assumptions.

7. (b) effective mandatory statements of acceptable accounting practice

8. Quite simply, financial statements do not tell you everything about a business because it is impossible to put a financial value on everything. For example, although financial statements show the value of all the assets and liabilities of the business, they do not show:
   - whether the firm has good or bad managers
   - if there are serious problems with the workforce
   - if a rival product is about to take away many of its best customers
   - if the government is about to pass a law which will cost the business a lot of extra expense in the future.

Regardless of the end user, financial statements should be seen as just one of a series of items of information required before any serious decisions about the business can be taken.

Activity

1. In addition to owners and managers, your list could have contained any or all of the following:
   - employees
   - lenders
   - suppliers
   - customers
   - competitors

- analysts
- government
- the public.

2.

Type of entity	Advantage	Disadvantage
(a) Sole trader	The owner has total control of the business	It may be difficult to obtain sufficient finance
(b) Partnership	The management of the business is shared	If the business is unsuccessful the partners may go bankrupt
(c) Limited liability company	The liability of the owners is restricted	Certain financial information about the company has to be disclosed publicly

3. Going concern is a key accounting concept, which assumes that the business can continue to trade for the foreseeable future. If it did not apply then that would indicate that the business had a very uncertain future, with a real possibility of failure.

Review questions

1. The data would enable the business to know how much it had sold and how much it had purchased; how much cash it had received and paid; how much was owing to it and how much was owed by it; and whether it was making a profit or a loss over a particular time period. However, sometimes even these basic pieces of data are not recorded. Instead, the invoices (each of which shows the details of a transaction) and receipts (each of which confirms that a payment has been made) are kept and then given to an accountant to calculate the profit or loss of the business up to some point in time. The accountant will be someone who has learnt how to convert the financial transaction data (i.e. the data recorded on invoices and receipts) into accounting information. Quite often, it is the owner of the business who will perform all the accounting tasks. In other cases, an employee will be given the job of maintaining the accounting records.

2. The following stakeholders will be using audited financial statements:

- potential shareholders or investors
- lenders of capital
- employees in order to decide wage negotiations
- financial analysts and advisers
- customers and suppliers for credit rating purposes
- business advisers
- government agencies for tax purposes and other government departments for macro-economic planning and national statistics.

3. No! Internal audit work will need to be reviewed every year by the external auditor to determine whether adequate standards have been maintained.

Chapter 2

Reflective questions

1. The 'dual aspect' rule is a useful practical rule, although it simply reflects what is obvious. It is built around the fact that every time a transaction takes place there is always a twofold effect. If a business buys inventory for cash, then the cash account goes down and the purchases account goes up.

2. **(a)** An account <u>is a historic record of a particular type of transaction.</u>

   (b) A ledger of accounts <u>is a group of accounts.</u>

   (c) A debit is <u>an entry on the left side of the account.</u>

   (d) A credit is <u>an entry on the right side of the account.</u>

3. Mr Jones should prepare the accounts in an orderly, systematic and practical manner. The process of recording should reflect a logical sequence. The most important task is identifying and assigning each transaction in the appropriate manner. This requires judgement to decide which account should be debited or credited. Accounts he should keep:

   - Bank/cash account
   - Capital account
   - Purchases account
   - Sales account
   - Payables account
   - Receivables account
   - Drawings account.

4. The accounts to be debited and credited for each of the transactions are as follows:

   - Payment to a creditor

Dr	£	Cr	£
Creditors a/c		Cash a/c	

   - Purchase of office equipment on credit.

Dr	£	Cr	£
Office equipment a/c		Creditors a/c	

   - Purchase of motor vehicle paying by cheque.

Dr	£	Cr	£
Motor vehicle a/c		Bank a/c	

5. The following errors will offset a trial balance:

   (a) £765 has been entered in both ledger accounts instead of £675 – the totals of the debit balances should always equal the total of the credit balances.

   (b) £1,000 has been put in Cash account instead of Purchases account – entering amounts in the wrong accounts.

   (c) The debit column in the account has been overstated by £100 – making an error that offsets the effect of another error.

Activity

1. **(a)** The accounting equation is reflected by <u>Assets</u> = <u>Capital</u> + <u>Liabilities</u>.

   (b) Every transaction must be recorded <u>twice</u>.

2. **(a)** Ledger accounts:

   - Capital account
   - Cash account
   - Furniture account
   - Bank account
   - Computer account
   - Computing Equip Ltd

   (b)

Capital account

	£		£
		Cash	2,000
		Bank	500

Cash account

	£		£
Capital	2,000	Furniture	300
		Bank	500

Furniture account

	£		£
Cash	300		

Bank account

	£		£
Cash	500	Computer	200
Capital	500		

Computer account

	£		£
Bank	200	Computer	200
Computer Equip Ltd	100		

Computer Equip Ltd account

	£		£
		Computer	100

3. Peter Davidson T-accounts

Bank account

	£		£
01 Mar X5 Capital a/c	1,000	02 Mar X5 Purchases	450
05 Mar X5 Cash a/c	50	05 Mar X5 Balance c/d	600
	1,050		**1,050**
06 Mar X5 Cash a/c	600		

Capital account

	£		£
05 Mar X5 c/d	1,000	01 Mar X5 Bank a/c	1,000
		06 Mar X5 Balance b/d	1,000

Purchases account

	£		£
02 Mar X5 Bank a/c	450	05 Mar X5 Balance	450
06 Mar X5 Balance b/d	450		

Sales account

	£		£
05 Mar X5 Balance c/d	60	03 Mar X5 Cash	60
		06 Mar X5 Balance b/d	60

Cash account

	£		£
03 Mar X5 Sales a/c	60	04 Mar X5 Bank a/c	50
		05 Mar X5 Balance c/d	10
	60		60
06 Mar X5 Balance b/d	10		

Peter

Trial balance as at 6 March X5

	£	£
Bank account	600	
Capital account		1,000
Purchase account	450	
Sales account		60
Cash account	10	
	1,060	**1,060**

Review questions

1.

(a) Ledger accounts:

- Bank account
- Capital account
- Machinery account
- Purchases account
- Sales account
- Payables account
- Receivables account
- Drawings account
- Loan account.

(b) T-accounts

Bank account

Day		£	Day		£
1	Capital a/c	80,000	2	Machinery a/c	20,000
4	Sales a/c	10,000	5	Payables a/c	30,000
8	Loan a/c	100,000	7	Drawings a/c	3,000

Capital account

Day		£	Day		£
			1	Bank a/c	80,000

Machinery account

Day		£	Day		£
2	Bank a/c	20,000			

Purchases account

Day		£	Day		£
3	Creditors a/c	46,000			

Sales account

Day		£	Day		£
			4	Bank a/c	10,000
			6	Receivables a/c	10,500

Payables account

Day		£	Day		£
5	Bank a/c	30,000	3	Purchases a/c	46,000

Receivables account

Day		£	Day		£
6	Sales a/c	10,500			

Drawings account

Day		£	Day		£
7	Bank a/c	3,000			

Loan account

Day		£	Day		£
			8	Bank a/c	100,000

Note that drawings is a capital account. Whatever value the owner removes from the business is entered in the drawings account and then the balance on the drawings account is subtracted from the balance on the capital account to find the net value of the owner's investment in the business at that date. Note also that only sole traders and partners can take drawings out of their business. Owners of companies cannot.

2. Miss Samphire's T-accounts and outline trial balance:

Bank account

Day		£	Day		£
1	Capital a/c	300,000	2	Shop a/c	250,000
5	Sales a/c	500	4	Fittings a/c	20,000
9	Loan a/c	100,000	6	Creditors a/c	2,000
			8	Drawings a/c	5,000
			10	Creditors a/c	7,000
			10	Balance c/d	116,500
		400,500			400,500
11	Balance b/d	116,500			

Capital account

Day		£	Day		£
10	Balance c/d	300,000	1	Bank a/c	300,000
			11	Balance b/d	300,000

Shop account

Day		£	Day		£
2	Bank a/c	250,000	10	Balance c/d	250,000
11	Balance b/d	250,000			

Purchases account

Day		£	Day		£
3	Payables a/c	40,000		Balance c/d	40,000
11	Balance b/d	40,000			

Payables account

Day		£	Day		£
6	Bank a/c	2,000	3	Purchases a/c	40,000
10	Bank a/c	7,000			
10	Balance c/d	31,000			
		40,000			40,000
			11	Balance b/d	31,000

Fittings account

Day		£	Day		£
4	Bank a/c	20,000	10	Balance c/d	20,000
11	Balance b/d	20,000			

Receivables account

Day		£	Day		£
7	Sales a/c	1,500	10	Balance c/d	1,500
11	Balance b/d	1,500			

Drawings account

Day		£	Day		£
8	Bank a/c	5,000	10	Balance c/d	5,000
11	Balance b/d	5,000			

Bank loan account

Day		£	Day		£
10	Balance c/d	100,000	9	Bank a/c	100,000
			11	Balance b/d	100,000

Sales account

Day		£	Day		£
10	Balance c/d	2,000	5	Bank a/c	500
			7	Receivables a/c	1,500
		2,000			2,000
			11	Balance b/d	2,000

Note that the date used for the entry in each account of the balance brought down is the first day after the period ended. This is because this is the balance on each account that you will be starting with at the beginning of the next period. In this example, the new period starts on day 11.

Trial balance as at Day 10

	Debit £	Credit £
Bank	116,500	
Capital		300,000
Shop	250,000	
Purchases	40,000	
Payables		31,000
Fittings	20,000	
Receivables	1,500	
Drawings	5,000	
Bank loan		100,000
Sales		2,000
	433,000	**433,000**

3. (a)

		Dr	Cr
(i)	Goods sold to Mr Johnson incorrectly debited to Mr Smith		
	Mr Johnson account	£36,000	
	Mr Smith account		£36,000
(ii)	Mr Smith declared bankrupt		
	Bad debts accoun	£28,000	
	Mr Smith account		£28,000
(iii)	Purchase of stationery incorrectly debited to Office equipment account		
	Office expense account	£1,300	
	Office equipment account		£1,300
(iv)	Drawings made by Mr Williamson incorrectly debited to the Wages account		
	Drawings account	£50,000	
	Wages account		£50,000

Mr Smith account

	£		£
Balance	28,000	Mr Johnson	36,000
Sales	36,000	Bad debts	28,000

Mr Johnson account

	£		£
Balance	93,000		
Sales	29,000		
Mr Smith	36,000		

Office equipment account

	£		£
Balance	213,000	Office expenses	1,300
Cash	98,000		
Cash	13,000		

Office expenses account

	£		£
Balance	129,000		
Sales	9,000		
Office equipment	1,300		

Wages account

	£		£
Balance	100,000	Drawings	50,000
Sales	50,000		

Drawing account

	£		£
Wages	50,000		

Bad Debts account

	£		£
Mr Smith	28,000		

4. Correction to trial balance:

	Dr	Cr
(a)	0	+£20,000
(b)	+£180,000	−£180,000
(c)	+90,000	+90,000
(d)	0	+60,000
(e)	0	0
(f)	0	0
	+270,000	**−10,000**

Item (e) will involve only a switch between receivables – it will not affect the trial balance.
Item (f) will involve only a switch between two debit balances.

5. (a) Fatima's ledger accounts:

Bank account

Day		£	Day		£
01.01.20X1	Balance b/d	10,000	31.12.20X1	Jeremy	58,000
31.12.20X1	Michael	90,000	31.12.20X1	Delivery van	24,000
31.12.20X1	Cash	6,000	31.12.20X1	Balance c/d	24,000
		106,000			106,000
01.01.20X2	Balance b/d	24,000			

Capital account

Day		£	Day		£
			01.01.20X1	Balance b/d	40,000

Cash account

Day		£	Day		£
01.01.20X1	Balance b/d	2,000	31.12.20X1	Purchases	30,000
31.12.20X1	Sales	40,000	31.12.20X1	Office expenses	18,000
31.12.20X1	Michael	14,000	31.12.20X1	Bank	6,000
			31.12.20X1	Balance c/d	2,000
		56,000			56,000
1.01.20X2	Balance b/d	2,000			

Jeremy account

Day		£	Day		£
31.12.20X1	Bank	58,000	01.01.20X1	Balance b/d	4,000
31.12.20X1	Balance c/d	6,000	31.12.20X1	Purchases	60,000
		64,000			64,000
			01.01.20X2	Balance b/d	6,000

Michael account

Day		£	Day		£
01.01.20X1	Balance b/d	12,000	31.12.20X1	Banks	90,000
31.12.20X1	Sales	100,000	31.12.20X1	Cash	14,000
			31.12.20X1	Balance b/d	8,000
		112,000			112,000
01.01.20X2	Balance b/d	8,000			

Furniture account

Day		£	Day		£
01.01.20X1	Balance b/d	20,000			

Purchases account

Day		£	Day		£
01.01.20X1	Jeremy	60,000			
31.12.20X1	Cash	30,000	31.12.20X1	Balance c/d	90,000
		90,000			90,000
01.01.20X2	Balance b/d	90,000			

Sales account

Day		£	Day		£
			31.12.20X1	Cash	40,000
31.12.20X1	Balance b/d	140,000	31.12.20X1	Michael	100,000
		140,000			140,000
			01.01.20X2	Balance b/d	140,000

Office Expenses account

Day		£	Day	£
31.12.20X1	Cash	18,000		

Delivery Van account

Day		£	Day	£
31.12.20X1	Bank	24,000		

(b)

	Dr	Cr
	£	£
Bank	24,000	
Capital		40,000
Cash	2,000	
Jeremy		6,000
Michael	8,000	
Furniture	20,000	
Purchases	90,000	
Sales		140,000
Office expenses	18,000	
Delivery van	24,000	
	186,000	186,000

Chapter 3

Reflective questions

1. Inventory, fixtures and buildings.

2. Loan from E Smith and accounts payable.

3. The following are current assets: inventory, current account at Bank, Accounts Receivable, cash kept in a tin.

Activity

1. Alex

Statement of Financial Position

	£
Non-current assets	23,400
Current assets	13,800
	37,200
Capital	24,750
Current Liabilities	12,450
	37,200

Net assets are £37,000 − £12,450 = £24,750

2.

Assets − £2,000 = £10,000
Assets = £10,000 + £2,000
Assets = £12,000
The assets will be valued at £12,000.

3. Waltz Ltd

Statement of Financial Position

	£000's
Assets	
Non-current assets	19,900
Current assets	14,300
Total assets	34,200
Equity	
Ordinary Share Capital	10,000
Retained earnings	11,800
Revaluation surplus	1,000
	22,800
Non-current liabilities	5,000
Current liabilities	6,400
	34,200

Review questions
(pages 51-3)

1. Suggested definitions are:
   (a) **Non-current assets:** assets purchased with the intention of using them in the business over a period of years, to generate revenue, for example machinery. They are not purchased for resale.
   (b) **Current liabilities:** debts that the business must pay within the next twelve months, for example, taxation owing to the revenue.
   (c) **Accounts receivable:** the amount of money owed to the business, for example, an amount due from a customer.
   (d) **Accounts payable:** the amount of money owed by the business to suppliers or service providers, for example, an amount due to a trade supplier.

2. Jessica
   (a) VAT payable to HMRC: Current liabilities
   (b) loan from E Green (repayable in three years' time): Non-current liabilities
   (c) bank overdraft: Current liabilities
   (d) accounts receivable: Current assets
   (e) rent owing to landlord: Current liabilities.

3. Faye
   Total assets – total liabilities = capital
   40,000 – 18,400 = 21,600
   The total of Faye's capital will be £21,600.

4. James
   (a) Current assets: £1,700 (300 + 1,400)
   (b) Total assets: £22,700 (13,000 + 8,000 + 1,700)
   (c) Current liabilities: £11,200 (700 + 10,000 + 500)
   (d) Owner's capital: £11,500 (22,700 – 11,200).

5. Akil
   (a)

Capital		
Opening balance		18,200
Capital introduced		22,000
		40,200
Less loss for the year	2,600	
Drawings	11,300	(13,900)
Closing balance		**26,300**

   (b) You will know the closing balance on the capital account of £26,300 is correct because

   Assets = Capital + Liabilities.

6. David

Statement of Financial Position as at 31 March 20X1

	£	£
Assets		
Non-current assets		
Freehold premises	60,000	
Motor vehicles	7,000	
		67,000
Current assets		
Inventory	5,000	
Accounts receivable	3,000	
Cash at bank	1,000	9,000
Total assets		76,000
Capital		73,500
Current liabilities		
Accounts payable		2,500
		76,000

7. Amy

Statement of Financial Position as at 30 September 20X4

	£	£
Assets		
Non-current assets		
Freehold shop	68,000	
Equipment	22,000	
Motor vehicles	18,000	108,000
Current assets		
Inventory: stationery	1,400	
Accounts receivable	3,700	
Cash at bank	6,500	11,600
Total assets		119,600
Capital		
Opening balance		36,000
Capital introduced		5,600
		41,600
Add profit for the year		27,800
		69,400
Less drawings		26,800
		42,600

Current liabilities

Accounts payable	1,100	
Income tax	1,300	
Loan	4,600	
	7,000	

Non-current liabilities

Loan	70,000	77,000
		119,600

---

8. Cubert Ltd

Statement of Financial Position as at 31 October 20X5

	£	£
Assets		
Non-current assets		
Freehold land and buildings	168,000	
Plant and machinery	22,000	
Motor vehicles	18,000	208,000
Current assets		
Inventory	21,600	
Trade receivables	3,700	25,300
Total assets		**233,300**
Equity		
Ordinary shares of £1 each		6,000
Share premium		600
Retained earnings		127,800
		134,400
Current liabilities		
Accounts payable	1,100	
Short-term borrowings (6,500 + 4,600)	11,100	
Current tax payable	1,300	
Short-term provisions	5,400	
	18,900	
Non-current liabilities		
Long-term borrowings	80,000	
Total liabilities		(98,900)
		233,000

9. Trencreek Ltd

Statement of Financial Position as at 30 April 20X7	£	£
Assets		
Non-current assets		
Land and buildings	280,500	
Fixtures and fittings	60,800	
		341,300
Current assets		
Inventory	30,600	
Trade receivables	15,600	
Bank	–	
Total assets		46,200
		387,500
Equity		
Issued share capital: ordinary shares of £1 each		50,000
Share premium		5,000
Retained earnings		302,080
General reserve		10,000
		367,080
Non-current liabilities		
10% debentures		20,000
Current liabilities		
Trade payables	12,540	
Current tax payable	4,700	
Bank		
		17,240
		404,320

The balance sheet shows that Trencreek Ltd has a current asset of £16,820 (404,320 – 387,506) cash at bank.

The statement of financial position can be rewritten as follows:

Statement of Financial Position as at 30 April 20X7

	£	£
Assets		
Non-current assets		
Land and buildings	280,500	
Fixtures and fittings	60,800	
		341,300
Current assets		
Inventory	30,600	
Trade receivables	15,600	
Bank	16,820	63,020
Total assets		404,320
Equity		
Issued share capital: ordinary shares of £1 each		50,000
Share premium		5,000
Retained earnings		302,080
General reserve		10,000
		367,080
Non-current liabilities		
10% debentures		20,000
Current liabilities		
Trade payables	12,540	
Current tax payable	4,700	
		17,240
Total liabilities		(37,240)
		404,320

Chapter 4

Reflective questions

1. Eloise

Income statement

	£
Revenue	42,900
Less cost of sales	(31,800)
Gross profit	11,100
Less expenses	(3,200)
Net profit	7,900

2. Daniel

Trading account

	£	£
Revenue		36,420
Opening inventory	2,210	
Purchases	28,050	
	30,260	
Closing inventory	(2,860)	(27,400)
Gross profit		9,020

3. Jenny

Income statement for the year ended 31 May 20X5

	£	£
Revenue		28,780
Opening inventory	1,740	
Purchases	14,350	
	16,090	
Closing inventory	(1,870)	(14,220)
Gross profit		14,560
Less expenses		
Rent and rates	3,860	
Light and heat	490	
Motor expenses	840	
Repairs	210	
Professional fees	450	(5,850)
Net profit		8,710

4. Eve

Income statement for the year ended 31 December 20X2

	£	£
Revenue		38,760
Less expenses		
Office expenses	4,870	
Telephone	970	
Motor expenses	1,140	
Rent and rates	3,870	
Light and heat	1,320	(12,170)
Net profit		**26,590**

Activity

1. **Chris**

Income statement for the year ended 31 January 20X2

	£
Revenue	24,350
Less cost of sales	20,050
Gross profit	4,300
Less expenses	1,980
Net profit	2,320

2. Dee

Income statement for the year ended 31 March 20X3

	£
Revenue	19,800
Less cost of sales	8,400
Gross profit	11,400
Less expenses	(11,800)
Net loss	(400)

3. Fred

Income statement for the year ended 30 September 20X5

	£	£
Revenue		54,800
Opening inventory	3,740	
Purchases	46,500	
	50,240	
Closing inventory	(3,570)	(46,670)
Gross profit		8,130
Expenses		(11,620)
Net loss		**(3,490)**

4. Charlotte

Income statement for the year ended 31 May 20X8

	£	£
Consultancy income		32,400
Less expenses		
Office expenses	2,300	
Telephone and broadband	990	
Light and heat	1,020	
Use of house as office	3,800	(8,110)
Net profit		**24,290**

Review questions

1. Parag

Income statement for the year ended 31 August 20X2

	£	£
Revenue		102,800
Opening inventory	17,895	
Purchases	68,760	
	86,655	
Closing inventory	(11,230)	(75,425)
Gross profit		27,375
Less expenses		
Wages	10,980	
Cleaning	1,420	

Light and heat	1,380	
Rent and rates	9,640	
Van expenses	2,320	
Staff uniforms	840	
Office expenses	960	(27,540)
Net loss		**(165)**

2. Nagin

Income statement for the six months ended 30 June 20X9

	£	£
Revenue		68,470
Purchases	14,350	
Closing inventory	(1,470)	
		(12,880)
Gross profit		55,590
Less expenses		
Rent and rates	3,540	
Light and heat	1,130	
Staff wages	12,000	
Protective clothing	450	
Cleaning materials	345	
Bank charges	280	(17,745)
Net profit		**37,845**

The revenue minus the cost of sales minus the expenses is positive and therefore the business made a profit during the first six months.

3. Lee: Window Advertising

Income statement for the year ended 30 April 20X4

	£	£
Revenue		78,750
Opening inventory	3,540	
Purchases	38,280	
	41,820	
Closing inventory	(4,140)	
Cost of sales		(37,680)
Gross profit		41,070

Less expenses		
Business rates	6,490	
Light and heat	1,480	
Motor expenses	1,110	
Stationery	430	
Training	100	
Wages	10,380	(19,990)
Net profit		**21,080**

Lee: Window Advertising

Statement of Financial Position as at 30 April 20X4

	£	£
Non-current assets		
Property		82,800
Motor vehicles		7,900
Office furniture		1,570
		92,270
Current assets		
Inventory	4,140	
Bank balance	10,420	14,560
Total assets		106,830
Capital		
Opening balance		31,270
Add profit for the year		21,080
		52,350
Less drawings		(15,000)
		37,350
Non-current liabilities		
Business loan	60,000	
Current liabilities		
Accounts payable	9,480	
		69,480
		106,830

4. Justin

Income statement for the year ended 31 December 20X3

	£	£
Revenue		293,350
Opening inventory	24,600	
Purchases	186,050	
	210,650	
Closing inventory	(28,700)	(181,950)
Gross profit		111,400
Less expenses		
Rent and rates	9,470	
Light and heat	2,860	
Wages and salaries	30,400	
Motor expenses	4,950	
Professional fees	1,250	
Bank charges	1,110	
Insurance	230	
Sundry expenses	1,280	(51,550)
Net profit		59,850

Justin

Statement of Financial Position as at 31 December 20X3

	£	£
Non-current assets		
Factory	148,000	
Motor vans	14,870	
Equipment	16,310	179,180
Current assets		
Inventory	28,700	
Accounts receivable	29,480	58,180
Total assets		237,360
Capital		
Opening capital		35,810
Add profit for the year		59,850
		95,660
Less drawings		(36,000)
		59,660
Non-current liabilities		
Loan		150,000
Current liabilities		
Bank overdraft	5,400	
Accounts payable	22,300	
		27,700
		237,360

5. Trevone Ltd

Income statement extract for the year ended 30 April 20X9

	£	£
Profit for the year before taxation		77,540
Less corporation tax		13,400
Profit for the year after taxation		64,140
Add retained profits brought forward		221,800
		285,940
Less		
Transfer to general reserve	3,000	
Ordinary dividend	50,000	
		53,000
Retained profit carried forward		232,940

Trevone Ltd

Statement of Financial Position extract as at 30 April 20X9

	£	£
Non-current assets		640,800
Current assets		197,890
Total assets		838,690
Equity		
Ordinary shares of £1 each		500,000
Share Premium		5,000
Revaluation reserve		10,000
General reserve (12,000 + 3,000)		15,000
Retained profit		232,940
		762,940
Current liabilities		
Trade payables	12,350	
Corporation tax	13,400	
Dividends payable	50,000	
Total liabilities		75,750
		838,690

Chapter 5

Activity

1. The answer is (b) £600. The cost is £800, but the piano can only be sold for £1,100 after paying £500 to repair it. The net proceeds the piano can generate or 'realise' are, therefore, only:

   £1,100 − £500 = £600

   The net realizable value is lower than cost so the value must be valued at £600.

2. The £7,000 due from V Ltd appears to be doubtful, and a provision (or 'allowance') is required. The £15,000 from C Ltd is definitely bad and must be written-off.

   Extract from the income statement for Troy

	£
Income	
Sales (unaffected by bad debt adjustments)	900,000
Expenses	
Bad debts expense (£15k write-off plus £7k increase in provision)	22,000

   Extract from the current assets section of the statement of financial position

	£
Trade receivables (£80k receivables − £15k write-off)	65,000
Less provision for bad debts (£7k doubtful)	(7,000)
	58,000

3.

	£
Balance per bank statement 2	8,800
Less cheque payments not yet cleared	(13,000)
Add deposits not yet credited	6,000
Balance per nominal ledger 1	1,800

   1 £2,000 − £200 bank charges that should have been recorded

   2 This must be the balance on the bank statement; it is simply the figure that makes this bank reconciliation add up.

Review questions

1. (a) £106,000

2. (c) £2,000

3. (d) (ii) and (iv) only

4. **(c)** £12

5. **(b)** £113

6. **(d)** all of the above

7. **(d)** Sales £800,000; Receivables £130,000

8. **(c)** £60, 280

9. **(a)** £65,000 current asset

10. **(b)** £10,000

11. **(d)** a liability

12. **(c)** to ensure that the nominal ledger bank balance is exactly the same as the balance on the bank statement

13. **(a)** £1,900 current asset

14. **(b)** £4,000

15. Showroad Antiques Ltd

Income statement for the year ended 30 November 2009

	£	£
Sales		699,000
Cost of sales:		
Opening inventory	88,000	
Purchases	380,000	
Closing inventory		
(£77,000 – £1,700 guitar write–down)	(75,300)	
		392,700
Gross profit		306,300
Less expenses		
Wages and salaries	141,000	
Telephone	7,000	
Rent and rates	14,000	
Travel	68,000	
Bad debts *(£16k write–off + £2k*		
increase in provision)	18,000	

Insurance	5,000	
Interest payable	2,000	
	255,000	
Net profit	**51,300**	

Balance sheet as at 30 November 2009

		£
Non-current assets		NBV
Fixtures & fittings		11,000
Motor vehicles		30,000
		41,000
Current assets		
Inventory *(£77,000 – £1,700 guitar write-down)*		75,300
Receivables *(£66,000 – £16,000 write-off)*	50,000	
Less provision for Doubtful debts (10% of receivables)	(5,000)	
		45,000
Cash at bank		2,000
		122,300
		163,300
Non-current liabilities		
Bank loan		20,000
Current liabilities		
Trade payables		27,000
		163,300
Equity		
Share capital		28,000
Retained earnings		88,300
		116,300

Key Themes
Accounting policy for inventory
A reason is that using LIFO implies assuming that the most recent purchases have been old first. The inventory that remains is therefore valued at the 'oldest' cost. In a time of changing prices, this 'old' cost may bear little relationship to the recent, current cost. LIFO is therefore felt to result in inventory valuations appearing on the statement of financial position that are insufficiently up-to-date and relevant.

Case studies
RBS
Such money received would of course increase the company's asset of bank (a debit entry). But what about the credit side of the entry? Clearly, the money cannot be credited to Receivables, since the original debt has been written-off and no longer exists in the records. The answer is therefore to credit it directly to the income statement (typically showing it as a 'negative expense').

Chapter 6

Reflective questions

1. **(a)** The accounts payable shows the total value of any money owed by the business to suppliers or service providers, such as an outstanding electricity bill.

    (b) It appears in the statement of financial position.

2. True

3. True

Activity

1. It is necessary to add the £1,100 to the expense account for Ring Ltd, so debit expenses and show this in the income statement for the year ending 31 March 2010.

    The double entry to this would be to recognise that the £1,100 is yet to be paid, so credit an accrual and show this in the statement of financial position as a current liability, for the year ending 31 March 2010.

    The transaction will therefore affect both statements, thus satisfying the rules of double entry.

2. **(a)** Only the expenses that are relevant to the year ending 31 March 2010 need to be included in the income statement. This would exclude the £300 paid in March 2010 as it relates to a service which is to be consumed in the next financial year. So, credit expenses and show the new lower expenses figure of £900 in the income statement.

    (b) The double entry to this would be to recognise that the £300 has already been paid, so debit a prepayment and show this in the statement of financial position as a current asset.

    The transaction will therefore affect both statements, thus satisfying the rules of double entry.

3. Together the accounts above and the notes to them provide a better picture of what obligations and assets the company has for the financial year in question.

    It is important to note that in published accounts it is unlikely that you will see expenses broken down into individual categories of rent, rates, telephone bill, etc. In published accounts, the adjustments covered by this chapter such as telephone bill and electricity bill will affect the income statement by appearing in the category headed 'administrative expenses' or 'cost of goods sold', depending upon the company policy on where such costs are to appear. Likewise, we cannot see the prepayments or accruals in the statement of financial position – they actually appear under note 17 and note 25 respectively.

Review questions

1. **(c)** Profit

2. **(c)** Current asset

3. **(d)** Wages payable

4. True

5. **(d)** Income statement for 2009

6. **(b)** An expense of £7,000 will be shown in the income statement

7. **(a)** An expense of £1,300 will be shown in the Income statement

8. **(d)** Current liability in the statement of financial position

Chapter 7

Reflective questions

1. Historical cost, net book value and fair value.

2. To match the revenue earned in the period with the costs incurred to earn that revenue.

3. The concept of depreciation is based on the idea that assets wear out over time, due to consumption. The assets therefore lose value over time or use, or both time and use. The concept assumes that, ultimately, the asset completely wears out and has little or no value or worth.

4. Depreciation is categorized as an expense and is included on the income statement, often as part of administrative expenses or sometimes as part of cost of sales. It depends upon the company's cost allocation policy.

   Depreciation does not have a category in the statement of financial position but it is included either on the face or in the notes as a reduction of the asset value.

5. **(a)** The reducing balance method is considered an accelerated method.
   (b) If an accelerated method is used, more of the cost is written off in the asset's early years.

6. There is no answer necessary for this question.

Activity

1. Non-current assets and current assets.

2. An asset is 'a resource that is controlled by the business as a result of past events and from which future economic benefits are expected to flow'.

   There are three aspects to this definition. The first is about control, the second is about the event being in the past and the third is about a future economic benefit of some sort. To be deemed an asset, all three aspects need to be satisfied.

3.

Characteristic	Non-current assets	Current assets
Time period in the business	Greater than one year	Less than one year
Purpose of purchase	Utilise to generate a future economic benefit to the company	Purchase with the intention to resell
Liquidity	Not easily converted into cash	Easily converted into cash

4. **(a)** Straight line and reducing balance method.

   (b) Depreciation will reduce the profit as it is an expense in the income statement.

   (c) Depreciation will reduce the assets from cost to net book value in the statement of financial position.

5. $$\text{Depreciation} = \frac{\text{Cost} - \text{Residual value}}{\text{Number of years}}$$

   $$\text{Depreciation} = \frac{\$45,000 - \$4,000}{10 \text{ years}} = \frac{\$4,100}{\text{year}}$$

6. All three financial statements are affected, as follows:

   - statement of financial position – the asset is removed
   - income statement – the gain or loss is shown
   - cash flow statement – the cash proceeds are shown as a cash inflow.

Review questions

1.

Characteristic	Non-current assets	Current assets
Time period in the business	Greater than one year	Less than one year
Purpose of purchase	Utilise to generate a future economic benefit to the company	Purchase with the intention to resell.
Liquidity	Not easily converted into cash	Easily converted into cash

2. A tangible fixed asset is an asset which is intended to be of a permanent nature and is used in the normal course of business. It is an asset that you can see and touch or a hard asset. Examples include:

   - plant and machinery
   - property and equipment
   - land
   - buildings
   - motor vehicles
   - inventory.

   An intangible asset is a soft asset or an asset that you cannot necessarily see and touch but adds worth to the company. Examples include:

   - goodwill
   - patents
   - trademarks
   - brands
   - customer relationships
   - customer base
   - employees.

3. **(a)** $\dfrac{60,000 - 8,000}{10 \text{ years}} = £5,200$

   (b) $60,000 - (5,200 \times 6) = £28,800$ NBV

   (c) $60,000 - (5,200 \times 4 \text{ years}) = 39,200$
      $40,000 - 39,200 = £800$ gain on disposal

   (d) Income statement – show the gain as income in the income statement.

      Statement of financial position – reduce non-current asset (machinery) by £60,000.

      Cash flow statement – add back the gain on disposal to operating profit to determine the cash equivalent amount.

4. Circle plc

Cost		6,000	
Depreciation to 28 February 2011		(2,400)	40% × 6,000
		3,600	
Depreciation to 29 February 2012		(1,440)	40% × 3,600
		5,040	
Depreciation to 28 February 2013		(2,016)	40% × 5,040
	NBV	**3,024**	

Income statement

Depreciation	2011	£2,400
	2012	£1,440
	2013	£2,016

5.

Triangle plc Income statement for year ending 30 September 2011

	£	£
Revenue		80,000
Less cost of goods sold:		
Purchases	42,000	
Less closing stock	6,000	
		18,000
Gross profit		44,000
Less expenses:		
Depreciation		
(15% × 16,000)	2,400	
Expenses	28,000	
Insurance (4,000 – 400)	3,600	
Electricity (3000 + 1000)	4,000	38,000
Net profit		**6,000**

Triangle plc Statement of Financial Position for year ending 30 September 2011

Non-current assets		
Plant		16,000
Depreciation		2,400
		13,600
Current assets		
Inventory	6,000	
Payables	10,000	
Prepayments	400	
Cash	800	17,200
		30,800
Equity and reserves		
Capital		12,000
Net profit		6,000
Current liabilities		
Receivables	11,800	
Accruals	1,000	12,800
		30,800

Key Themes

Warning on Fair Value

This simply means reflecting the assets at their market rather than historical value.

Selling a fixed asset

Case Study

Kingfisher plc

It will increase the valuation of property in non-current assets and increase the value of issues and, therefore, the net worth of the company.

Mitchells & Butler

It is a defence tactic that pushes up the value of the company, making it unaffordable for the bidder.

Chapter 8

Reflective questions

1. The accruals/matching concept means to match the revenue earned in a period with the costs Incurred to earn that revenue.
2. Net book value.
3. Cash flows from operating activities, cash flows from investing activities, cash flows from financing activities.
4. (a) Direct and indirect method.
   (b) Indirect method

Activity

1. The cash flow from operating activities of Sun plc is determined as follows:

	£m
Net operating profit	115.5
Add back depreciation	28.7
	144.2
Increase in inventory	(0.7)
Increase in receivables	(2.1)
Increase in payables	1.4
Net cash flow from operating activities	**142.8**

2. Using the data for Jupiter Ltd provided, the loss on the disposal is NBV of the plant – the sale price of the plant, i.e. £12,000 – £7,800 = £4,200

   This loss will be shown in the income statement.

3. (a) £47.5m, calculated thus:

   Property, plant and equipment

Bal b/d	50	Depreciation	10
Revaluation	30	Disposal	7.5
Additions	15		
Cash (balance)	47.5		
		Bal c/d	125
	142.5		142.5

4. (b) The amount of £47.5m will appear in the cash flow statement under the heading 'cash from investing activities'.

Review questions

1. (a) Decrease
   (b) Decrease
   (c) Increase
   (d) Decrease
   (e) Not a cash item, therefore add back to operating profit.

2. In the statement of financial position, the asset is removed.
   In the income statement, the gain or loss is shown.

3. Profit is not the same as cash because of:
   - timing differences – the point at which the cash is paid and/or received is often different from when the cash is shown in the income statement; this difference is a result of the accruals concept
   - depreciation
   - some accounting transactions bypass the income statement
   - changes in the working capital requirements.

4.

Cash flow statement for Moon plc

	£m	£m
Operating profit		91
Add back depreciation:		
Patents (19 – 16)	3	
Plant and machinery (144 + 34 – 141)	37	
		40
		131
Less increase in receivables (70 – 73)	(3)	
Less decrease in payables (27 – 21)	(6)	
Add decrease in inventory (21 – 17)	4	(5)
Cash generated from operating activities		126
Interest paid	(13)	
Tax (12 + 18 – 9)	(21)	
Net cash flow from operating activities		(34)
		92
Cash flows from investing activities		
Purchase of property, plant and equipment	(34)	
Interest received	7	
Net cash used in investing activities		(27)
Cash flows from financing activities		
Dividend paid	(26)	
Payment of loans	(50)	
Net cash used in financing activities		(76)
Net increase/(decrease) in cash and cash equivalents		(11)
Cash and cash equivalents at beginning of period (from the statement of financial position)		(3)
Cash and cash equivalents at end of period (from the statement of financial position)		(14)

Analysis of cash balances above:

	2009	2010
Cash	1	3
Bank overdraft	(4)	(17)
	(3)	(14)

5. Court plc

Extract from cash flow statement for the year ended 31 March 2010

Cash flows from operating activities	$000
Profit before tax	865
Depreciation	95
Gain on disposal of property (400 – 340)	(60)
Gain on sale of asset	(94)
Finance costs	60
Operating profit before working capital changes	866
Increase in inventory (70 – 55)	(15)
Increase in receivables (280 – 270)	(10)
Increase in payables (165 – 130)	35
	876
Interest paid	(60)
Tax paid (W1)	(150)
Net cash flow from operating activities	**666**

Workings

Total: 1

(W1)

Tax			
Tax paid (bal. fig.)	150	Income tax b/f	190
Bal c/f – income tax	230	Deferred tax b/f	150
Bal c/f – deferred tax	160		
		Income statement	200
	540		540

6.

(a)

Judge plc: Cash flow statement for the period ending 31 Jan 2011

	£000
Net cash flow from operating activities (W1)	140
Cash flow from investing activities	
Purchase of investments	(200)

Cash flow from financing activities

Issue of loan	<u>120</u>
Net increase in cash	<u>60</u>
Cash and cash equivalents at beginning of period (from the Statement of Financial Position)	(40)
Cash and cash equivalents at end of period (from the Statement of Financial Position)	20

(b) Analysis of cash balances shown above:

	2009	2010
Cash	–	20
Bank overdraft	<u>(40)</u>	<u>–</u>
	(40)	20

(W1)

	£000
Operating profit (80 – 60)	20
Add back depreciation	40
Increase in inventory	(60)
Decrease in payables	(220)
Decrease in receivables	<u>(80)</u>
Cash flow from operating activities	<u>140</u>

The cash position has improved, going from a negative to a positive cash flow. This is largely due to operating activities generating £140,000 cash inflow, coupled with a cash amount from the loan of £120,000. Some of this cash was used to make investments amounting to £200,000. It is hoped that this investment will generate further cash flows for Judge plc, although it is difficult to form a view on this at the present time.

7.

Working capital	Increase/decrease	Impact on cash
Inventory	Increase	<u>Cash outflow as inventory has been bought, so cash goes down</u>
	Decrease	Cash inflow as inventory has been sold, so cash goes up
Receivables	Increase	Cash goes down as money has not been received
	Decrease	<u>Cash goes up as money has been received</u>
Payables	Increase	Cash goes up as payments have not been made
	Decrease	Cash goes down as payments owing have been made

8.

(a) Statement of Financial Position Item	(b) Impact on cash
Non-current assets	Sale of non-current assets would increase cash Purchase of non-current assets would decrease cash flow
Ordinary share capital	Issue of ordinary share capital would increase cash flow Repurchase of ordinary share capital would decrease cash flow
Loans	Issue of loans would increase cash flow Repayment of loans would decrease cash flow

9.
- Cash generated from operating activities
- Cash flows from investing activities
- Cash flows from financing activities
- Net increase/decrease in cash
- Cash at start of the year
- Cash at end of the year.

10.

Transaction	Heading in the cash flow statement
(a) Purchase of a new machine	Cash flow from financing activities
(b) Repurchase of equity shares	Cash flow from investing activities
(c) Interest paid on the loan	Cash flow from operating activities
(d) Dividends paid out to shareholders	Cash flow from financing activities *or* Cash flow from operating activities
(e) Monies received from customers	Cash flow from operating activities
(f) A new bank loan	Cash flow from financing activities
(g) Gain on the sale of a building	This does not appear in the cash flow statement. It would be shown in the income statement.

Key Themes
Cash flow
The following can be identified:

- cut capital expenditures, (e.g. shift cash from opening new stores to re-modelling existing ones)
- halt stock buyback
- reduce inventories
- keeping their ears to the ground so that they can be responsive to a change in the business climate

- cutting costs, (e.g. redeploying existing staff to new stores).
- outsourcing its IT function.
- better management of cash cycles.

Cash Is king: collect with passion

There is no definitive answer to this exercise, the aim is to encourage the student to think about managing money.

Case Study

Timeline: BCCI

The student should be considering the following:

- purpose of the loan
- amount of the loan
- repayment strategy
- time period for loan
- security provision.

The manager would ask for a business plan and the statement of financial position, IS and cash flow statement. This provides some insight into liquidity, profitability and asset base. It also provides information on the companies existing borrowings.

New York Times Company

This is a research exercise that is dependent on what the *FT* reports, so there is no definitive answer.

Chapter 9

Reflective questions

1. The ROCE highlights the performance of the business, showing how much profit is made in comparison to the amount invested in the business.

    The general formula is:

$$\frac{\text{Profit before interest \& tax}}{\text{Share capital} + \text{reserves} + \text{long-term liabilities}} \times 100$$

    The ROCE percentage can be compared to the Bank of England lending rate. If the ROCE is *less* than the Bank of England lending rate, it would be beneficial to invest the money in a bank rather than in the business. If the ROCE is *greater* than the Bank of England lending rate, it will be advantageous to continue to invest in the business.

Activities

1.

Gross profit %	$\dfrac{47,507}{125,020} \times 100$	38.00%
Net profit %	$\dfrac{14,306}{125,020} \times 100$	11.44%
$\dfrac{\text{Remuneration \%}}{\text{Revenue}}$	$\dfrac{14,785}{125,020} \times 100$	11.83%
$\dfrac{\text{Administration \%}}{\text{Revenue}}$	$\dfrac{5,650}{125,020} \times 100$	4.52%
ROCE	$\dfrac{14,306}{36,150 + 60,000} \times 100$	14.88%
Current ratio	20,495 : 6,925	2.96:1
Quick ratio	10,295 : 6,925	1.49:1

Review questions

1. Justin

(a) Gross profit %	$\dfrac{111,400}{293,350} \times 100$	37.98%
(b) Net profit %	$\dfrac{59,850}{293,350} \times 100$	20.40%
(c) Wages and salaries as a % of revenue	$\dfrac{30,400}{293,350} \times 100$	10.36%
(d) Rent and rates as a % of revenue	$\dfrac{9,470}{293,350} \times 100$	3.23%
(e) ROCE	$\dfrac{59,850}{209,660*} \times 100$	28.55%
(f) Current ratio	$\dfrac{58,180}{27,700}$	2.10:1
(g) Quick ratio	$\dfrac{29,480}{27,700}$	1.06:1

*(159,660 + 50,000 = 209,660)

2. Liquidity comparison

(a)

	DS	ES
Current ratio	$\dfrac{89{,}040}{29{,}480} : 1 = 3.02{:}1$	$\dfrac{42{,}020}{21{,}350} : 1 = 1.97{:}1$
Quick ratio	$\dfrac{52{,}560}{29{,}480} : 1 = 1.78{:}1$	$\dfrac{4{,}820}{21{,}350} : 1 = 0.23{:}1$

(b) It is obvious from the ratios that although the businesses are similar regarding revenue and profitability, they are considerably different regarding liquidity. The ratios show that DS appears to be sound from a liquidity perspective whereas ES appears to be experiencing liquidity problems. The quick ratio shows that ES cannot pay off its accounts payable and bank overdraft by using its accounts receivable and bank balance.

A profitable business may fail if it has insufficient funds to pay its current liabilities when they fall due. However, it should be remembered that businesses with high current and quick ratios may be operating inefficiently by having too many resources tied up in current assets.

3. Lisa

(a) ratios

	20X4		20X5	
Gross profit%	$\dfrac{41{,}070}{78{,}750} \times 100$	52.15%	$\dfrac{48{,}840}{88{,}590} \times 100$	55.13%
Net profit %	$\dfrac{21{,}080}{78{,}750} \times 100$	26.77%	$\dfrac{25{,}230}{88{,}590} \times 100$	28.48%
Wages/revenue %	$\dfrac{10{,}380}{78{,}750} \times 100$	13.18%	$\dfrac{13{,}690}{88{,}590} \times 100$	15.45%
Return on capital employed	$\dfrac{21{,}080}{97{,}350*} \times 100$	21.65%	$\dfrac{25{,}230}{96{,}400} \times 100$	26.17%
Current ratio	$\dfrac{14{,}560}{9{,}480}$	1.54:1	$\dfrac{16{,}820}{11{,}580}$	1.45:1
Quick ratio	$\dfrac{10{,}420}{9{,}480}$	1.10:1	$\dfrac{12{,}490}{11{,}580}$	1.08:1
Asset turnover	$\dfrac{78{,}750}{97{,}350}$	0.81 times	$\dfrac{88{,}590}{96{,}400}$	0.92 times
Inventory turnover	$\dfrac{4{,}140}{37{,}680} \times 365$	41 days	$\dfrac{4{,}330}{39{,}750} \times 365$	40 days
Trade receivables turnover	$\dfrac{8{,}420}{78{,}750} \times 365$	40 days	$\dfrac{12{,}150}{88{,}590} \times 365$	51 days
Trade payables turnover	$\dfrac{9{,}480}{38{,}280} \times 365$	91 days	$\dfrac{11{,}580}{39{,}940} \times 365$	106 days

* 20X4: 37,350 + 60,000 = 97,350
20X5: 41,400 + 55,000 = 96,400

(b) Report

> **To:** Lisa
> **From:** Mr Accountant
> **Re:** Ratio Analysis 20X4/20X5
>
> *The profitability of the business shows an increasing trend. The net profit has increased by £4,150 (25,230 – 21,080). The gross profit percentage has increased by 2.98 per cent and the net profit percentage has increased by 1.71 per cent. The improving gross profit percentage may be due to arranging improved discounts from suppliers or increasing the mark up on goods sold. The wages and salaries have increased as a percentage of revenue. This may be due to a wage increase. This increasing profitability is highlighted in the improved return on capital employed, which shows a high return on the investment in the business of 26.17 per cent in 20X5.*
>
> *The liquidity appears to be sound with both the current ratio and the quick ratio showing figures in excess of 1:1. However, both ratios show a declining trend which should be investigated to ensure it is due to improved efficiency rather than relaxed debt collection.*

4. Halwyn plc

Gross profit %	$\frac{2,701}{6,923} \times 100$	39.01%
Operating profit percentage	$\frac{1,224}{6,923} \times 100$	17.68%
Return on capital employed	$\frac{1,224}{4,153^*} \times 100$	29.47%
Pre-tax return on equity	$\frac{1,084}{3,953^{**}} \times 100$	27.42%
% increase in revenue	$\frac{6,923 - 6,482}{6,482} \times 100$	6.80%

(* Capital employed: 1,500 + 1,632 + 821 + 200 = 4,153)
(** Equity: 1,500 + 1,632 + 821 = 3,953)

5. Pentire plc

Earnings per share	$\frac{366,000}{2,000,000}$	18.3p per share
Dividend per share	$\frac{120,000}{2,000,000}$	6p per share
Dividend cover	$\frac{366,000}{120,000}$	3.05 times
Price/earnings ratio	$\frac{293}{18.3}$	16.01 times
Market capitalisation	2.93 × 2,000,000	£5,860,000

6. Budgisons plc and Morrens plc

(a) Ratios

	Budgisons			Morrens	
Gross profit%	$\dfrac{76,280}{187,500} \times 100$		40.68%	$\dfrac{32,140}{86,890} \times 100$	36.99%
Operating profit %	$\dfrac{30,390}{187,500} \times 100$		16.21%	$\dfrac{10,050}{86,890} \times 100$	11.57%
ROCE	$\dfrac{30,390}{53,190 + 60,000} \times 100$		26.85%	$\dfrac{10,050}{11,800 + 50,000} \times 100$	16.26%
Current ratio	$\dfrac{25,180}{20,990}$		1.20:1	$\dfrac{23,820}{14,580}$	1.63:1
Quick ratio	$\dfrac{1,040}{20,990}$		0.05:1	$\dfrac{12,300}{14,580}$	0.84:1
Asset turnover	$\dfrac{187,500}{113,190^*}$		1.66 times	$\dfrac{86,890}{61,800}$	1.41 times
Inventory turnover	$\dfrac{24,140}{111,220} \times 365$		80 days	$\dfrac{11,520}{54,750} \times 365$	77 days
EPS	$\dfrac{24,290}{5,000}$		486p	$\dfrac{7,330}{2,000}$	367p

(*Net assets: 134,180 – 20,990 = 113,190)

(b) Report

To: Mr X
From: A student
Re: Comparison of Budgisons plc and Morrisons plc

Budgisons (B) is a larger company, with revenue and non-current assets both being just over twice the figures of Morrens (M). B has a higher gross profit percentage, possibly due to being able to agree a higher discount with suppliers, due to the additional volume of purchases. B also has a higher net profit percentage, partially due to the higher gross profit percentage but also due to a slightly better control of its expenses. B's distribution expenses as a percentage of revenue are 14.87 per cent (27,890/187,500 × 100) compared to M's of 15.68 per cent (13,620/86,890 × 100) and B's administration expenses as a percentage of revenue are also slightly lower at 9.60 per cent (18,000/187,500 × 100) compared to M's of 9.75 per cent (8,470/86,890 × 100).

B's return on capital employed is over 10 per cent higher than M's. This is partially due to its higher profitability but is also due to a higher asset turnover. B is using its assets more efficiently than M. M's inventory turnover is slightly better than B's, but both appear high at 77 days and 80 days respectively. Most businesses strive to reduce their inventory turnover without creating a problem with running out of stock.

M is in a better liquidity position with a current ratio of 1.63:1 compared to B's of 1.20:1. Both appear sound but M's higher ratio could highlight it has too much money tied up in current assets that is not being used productively in generating profits; for example, it has £12,300,000 in the bank. However, B's quick ratio appears extremely low as most of its current assets are tied up in the inventory. The quick ratio highlights B has a serious liquidity problem as it is unable to pay its current liabilities without selling inventory, generating a profit or disposing of non-current assets. M's quick ratio of 0.84:1, although less than 1:1, is acceptable in the retail trade, as there are no trade receivables as customers pay in cash.

Although B's earnings per share is currently higher than M's, this may be short lived as the liquidity problems of B may become serious and cause the business to declare itself bankrupt due to a lack of cash.

7.

To: Mr X
From: A student
Re: The benefits and limitations of ratio analysis

Benefits of ratio analysis:

- helps users interpret financial information
- assists users in the decision-making process
- highlights the relationships that exist between different figures on the income statement and statement of financial position
- allows businesses to look at their trends
- provides a basis of comparison between different businesses.

Limitations of ratio analysis:

- ratios are only as good as the information on which they are based; if accounting information has been manipulated, the ratios will be unreliable
- the statement of financial position is only a snapshot of a business on a particular day; it may not be representative of the year-round position
- ratios are a relative measure and so the underlying figures should always be considered to put them into context
- ratio calculations are based upon historical data.

When compared to other businesses, variations in accounting policy may distort the comparison.

8. Tesco

(a) Ratios

	2009			2008	
Gross profit %	$\dfrac{4,218}{54,327} \times 100$		7.76%	$\dfrac{3,630}{47,298} \times 100$	7.67%
Operating profit %	$\dfrac{3,206}{54,327} \times 100$		5.90%	$\dfrac{2,791}{47,298} \times 100$	5.90%
ROCE	$\dfrac{3,206}{(12,995 + 12,391)} \times 100$		12.63%	$\dfrac{2,791}{(11,902 + 5,792)} \times 100$	15.77%
Asset turnover	$\dfrac{54,327}{46,053^*}$		1.18 times	$\dfrac{47,298}{30,164}$	1.57 times
Current ratio	$\dfrac{14,045}{18,040}$		0.78:1	$\dfrac{6,300}{10,263}$	0.61:1
Quick ratio	$\dfrac{(14,045 - 2,669)}{18,040}$		0.63:1	$\dfrac{6,300 - 2,430}{10,263}$	0.38:1

(b) Confidential report

To: CEO Tesco plc
From: A student
Re: Significance of ratios

Tesco plc is a profitable business, generating a profit for the year end 2009 of £2,166,000,000. The basic gross and net profit margins appear to be consistent over the two years, generating margins of approximately 8 per cent and 6 per cent respectively. There appears to be a decline in the return on capital employed (ROCE) which has decreased by 3.14 per cent to 12.63 per cent and it would be useful to explore the possible reasons for this decline.

To do this we should begin by looking at the profit margins. We know that these can be split into two categories, the gross profit margin and the net (operating) profit margin. As we can see from our results there does not appear to have been any drastic changes in either of these ratios. It is therefore unlikely that they are responsible for the lower ROCE. Looking at the other component of the ROCE we can see that the asset turnover has decreased from 2008 to 2009. It is likely therefore that this decrease has fed through to a now reduced ROCE. It shows that Tesco is using its assets less efficiently to generate revenue and earn profits.

Tesco plc has a better liquidity position in 2009 compared to 2008, with both the current and quick ratios showing an improvement. Generally it is argued that the current assets should be able to cover the current liabilities two times, so the ratio should be 2:1. For the quick ratio, 1:1 is considered reasonable. The current ratio for Tesco, 0.78:1 in 2009, is suggesting that its current assets, if need be, cannot cover the current liabilities, so in the short-term Tesco is unable to meet its short-term debts using short-term resources. This would essentially suggest that the company has a poor cash position and could therefore be on its way to becoming insolvent. However, we need to consider the nature of the business and as Tesco is operating in the retail sector, where customers pay in cash, a current ratio of less than 2:1 and a quick (acid test) ratio of less than 1:1 is acceptable. The quick ratio has shown a marked improvement over the two years from 0.38:1 in 2008 to 0.63:1 in 2009.

Case study

Sainbury's plc

$$\frac{22.9 - x}{x} = 7.1\%$$

where x = total sales (including VAT) in the previous year

$$22.9 - x = \frac{7.1\,x}{100}$$

$$22.9 = \frac{7.1\,x}{100} + \frac{100\,x}{100}$$

$$22.9 \times 100 = 107.1x$$

$$x = \frac{2290}{107.1}$$

$$x = 21.38$$

Total sales (including VAT) in 2010 would have been £21.38bn.

Index

Note: page numbers in **bold** refer to keyword definitions, page numbers in *italics* refer to information contained in tables and diagrams.

accounting, definition 2, **2**
accounting concepts
    fundamental 10–12, 15
    underlying 9–10, 15
accounting data 2, **2**
    recording, classifying, reporting and
        identifying 2
accounting equation 19–21, 31
    extended 27
    and the statement of financial position
        39–40, 51
accounting information systems 2–3, **2**, 15
accounting policies 81, 83, 87
accounting standards 8–9, 99
Accounting Standards Board (ASB) 8, 13,
    133, 157
    Statement of Principles 14
accounts 21, 31
accounts payable **39**, 63, 99, 139
accounts receivable 38, **38**
    see also receivables
accruals 98–101
    accounting treatment 100–101
    definition 99–100, **99**
    relating to real company accounts
        104–5, *104*
accruals (matching) concept 11, 58, 100–1,
    113–14, 122, 132
acid test (quick) ratio 162, 163, 168–9
airline industry 130
analyst-advisers 3, 4, 157
Archer, Mary 35
Asda 135
asset accounts, debits/credits 21–3
asset turnover ratio 169–70
assets 19–20, **20**, 36
    capital introduced 27, **43**
    current 38, 41–2, 44–5, 47, *50*, 65, 70,
        77–97, 163
        bank 38, 78, 88–93
        and the current ratio 168
        definition 36, 38, **38**
        inventory 38, 78–83
        and the quick ratio 168–9
        receivables 38, 78, 83–8, 92
    drawings **43**
    income from sale of 49
    net 44, 167, 169
    non-current 38, 41–2, 44–5, 47, *50*, 65,
        70, 108–13

accounting for the sale of 123–5
    and cash flows from investing
        activities 140–1
    definition **36**, 38, **38**
    examples 140
    intangible 111, 113
    level of spend on 147
    tangible 111, 140–1
    valuing 109–25
    on the statement of financial position
        36–45, 47–9, *50*, 51, 65, 70, 78, 88,
        109–19, 123, 140
    total 41–2, 44, 47–8, *50*, 65, 70
audits 14, 16, 174
    external 14
    internal 14
authorized share capital 46, **46**
Average Cost (AVCO) assumption 80,
    81, 92

B&Q 112
bad debt 84, **84**, 85–8, 92
    provision for 85–8, 92
bad debt expense 84, 92
balance carried down (Balance c/d) 24–5
balance sheets 3, 36, **36**
    see also statements of financial position
balancing the accounts 24–6
bank 38, 78, 88–93
    manipulation of the bank figure 91–2
Bank of Credit and Commerce
        International (BCCI) 129–30
Bank of England base rate 167
bank overdraft 39, 88
bank reconciliation 88–91, **89**, 92–3
banking system 110–11
bankruptcy 84, 143
budgets, cash flow 148–150, **148**, 151
business contacts 157, 158
business entity concept 10
business organization *see* entity

capital
    definition **19**, 36
    opening balance 27, **43**
    owner's 19–20, 27–30
    on the statement of financial position
        36–7, 39–45, 65
    working 133, 136, 138–9, 143
    see also share capital

capital accounts 21–3, 25–6
capital employed (CE) **166**
    see also return on capital employed
capital expenditure 12
capital introduced 27, **43**
cash 88, 129, **129**
    functions 133–4
    impact of working capital on 138
    importance of 129–31
    profit versus 132–3, 143, 146
    running out of 143
cash budget statements 148–50
cash equivalents **129**
cash flow statements 71, 128–55, 174
    and cash flow budgets 148–50, **148**,
        151
    cash flows from financing activities 136,
        140–6
    cash flows from investing activities 136,
        140–1, 144–7
    cash flows from operating activities 136,
        137–9, 142–7
    cash versus profit 132–3, 143, 146
    direct method 136
    importance of cash 129–30
    indirect method 136, 144
    interpretation 146–7
    net operating cash flow 137–8
    presentation 135–46
    purpose of 133–5
cash inflows 129, 133, 139, 146
    net 137
cash management 129–30
cash outflows 129, 133, 139
CE *see* capital employed
chairman's statements 174, 176
Chandos, Lord 108
Companies Act 6, 8, 10
competitors 4, 158
consistency 11, 81, 112
corporate governance 14, 16
corporation tax, liability 67–9
cost of inventory 79–81, 92
cost of sales 57–62, **57**, 64, 69, 78
creative accounting 86
'credit crunch' 2007–09 86, 88
credit terms 84, 134–5
credits 21–6, 31, 84–5
    balancing the accounts 24–6
    and the trial balance 26, 40

current ratio 161, 162, 163, 168–9
customers, stakeholder status 5

data
    accounting 2, **2**
    qualitative 3
    quantitative 3
debits 21–6, 31, 84–5
    balancing the accounts 24–6
    and the trial balance 26, 40
debtors *see* receivables
deposits, uncredited 89–91
depreciation 108–9, 113–23, 140
    calculation 116–23, 126
    and cash flow versus profit 132
    definition 113, **113**
    and real company accounts 125
director's reports 174, 176
dividend cover 172–3
dividends 45–6, 68–9, 146, 157, 165
double entries 19, 68–9
    and accruals 100
    and prepayments 101
double-entry bookkeeping 18, 19
doubtful debts 84–8, **84**, 92
    provision for 85–6, 87–8, 92
drawings 27, 42–4, **43**
dual aspect rule 19

earnings available to ordinary shareholders
    172, 172–3
earnings per share (EPS) 171
eBay 135
efficiency ratios 160, 169–74, 177
employees 4, 157
entity 15
    business entity concept 10
    types of 6–8, *7*
entries 21
equity 45–9, *50*, 70
exchange rates 87–8
expenses 27–8
    definition **27**, **57**
    on the income statement 56–8,
        60–4, 66, 69, 71, *71*, 73, 101,
        104–5
expenses ratios 161, 163

fair value accounting approach
    109–11
fashion trade 82–3
FIFO (First in First Out) assumption 80,
    81, 92
Financial Accounting Standards Board
    (FASB) 14, 109–11
financial information
    characteristics of useful 13, *13*
    comparability 13, *13*
    relevance 13, *13*
    reliability 13, *13*
    understandability 13, *13*
financial statements 3, 36
    materiality 12
    standardization 8–9
    Statement of Principles 13

time interval concept 10
    see also cash flow statements; income
        statements; statement of financial
        position (SoFP)
financing activities 19, 36, 147
    cash flow from 136, 141–6
First in First Out (FIFO) assumption 80,
    81, 92

Geneen, Harold S. 128
general reserve 46, 67–70
going concern 10
government
    and business accounts 157
    as business stakeholder 3, 4
gross loss 58
gross profit
    definition **57**, **165**
    on the income statement 56–62, 64,
        69, *71*
    and inventory 78–81
gross profit percentage 161, 163, 165, 170

hire purchases 12
historical cost concept 9, 49

IAS *see* International Accounting
    Standards
IASB *see* International Accounting
    Standards Board
IFRS *see* international financial reporting
    standards
impairment of receivables 84, 92
income, from asset sale 49
income statements 55–76
    accounting transactions that bypass 133
    accruals 101
    basic 56–7
    and cash flow statements 132, 133,
        150–1
    and costing raw materials 80–1
    and depreciation 114–15, 117, 119, 132
    interpretation 157, 158, 159–63, 174
    limitations 72
    limited company 67–70
    non-current asset sale 123–4
    preparation 58–65
    prepayments 102
    profit and loss accounts 60–2, 72
    published 70–1, *71*, 82–3
    purpose of 133
    and service organizations 65–7, 73
    trading account 58–60, 72
    and the trial balance 26, 62–4
Indian airline industry 130
inflation 72
information 2–3
    see also financial information
information management 3
information needs 3–5
International Accounting Standards (IAS)
    IAS 1 Presentation of Financial
        Statements 49
    IAS 7 136
    IAS 16 109

International Accounting Standards Board
    (IASB) 8–9, 110–11
international financial reporting standards
    (IFRSs) 8
interpretation of accounts 156–86
    horizontal analysis 174–5
    limitations of ratio analysis 176
    process 159
    published accounts 164–74
    ratio analysis 157, 159–76
    trend analysis 174, 176
    users of financial statements
        157–8, 177
inventory 38, **38**, 58–64, 68–9, 78–83, 92
    cost of 79–81, 92
    in published financial statements 82–3
    and the quick ratio 168–9
    valuing 78–83, 92
    and working capital 139
    see also stock
inventory turnover period 170
investing activities, cash flow from 136,
    140–1, 144–7
investment ratios 160, 172, 177
investors 3
issued share capital **46**

Johan, Parminder 156

King, Justin 175
Kingfisher plc 112

Last In First Out (LIFO) assumption 92
leases 12
ledgers 21, 23–6
    balancing the accounts 24–6
    nominal 90–1
legislation 8–9, 15
Lehman Brothers 130
Leighton, Alan 135
lenders, stakeholder status 3, 4
Letterman, David Michael 1
liabilities 19–20, **20**, 37
    current **37**, 38–9, **39**, 41–2, 44–5, 47, *50*,
        65, 70, 88, 163, 168–9
    definition **20**, **37**
    greater than the net worth of the
        company 130
    non-current **37**, 38–9, **39**, 41–2, 44–5,
        47, *50*, 65, 70
    and the statement of financial position
        36, 38–45, 47–8, *50*, 51, 65, 70, 88,
        101, 103–4
    total 41–2, 44, 47–8, *50*, 65, 70
    see also accruals
liability
    limited 7, *7*, 10, 45
    unlimited *7*, 45
liability accounts, debits/credits 21–3
LIFO (Last In First Out) assumption 92
'limited by shares' 7
limited companies 6, **6**, *7*
    income statements 67–70
    private 7
    public 7

statements of financial position 45–8
see also public limited companies
liquidity 38, 134, **168**
liquidity ratios 159, 161–3, 168–9, 177
loan creditors 157
loss
    gross 58
    on the income statement 56, 58
    net 58
'lower of cost and net realizable value,
    the' 79

managers 4
mark-to-market (MTM) valuation
    approach 109–11
market capitalization 173–4
market value 109
Marks & Spencer plc 174
materiality 12
Mercury plc 142–3
Mitchells & Butler (M&B) 122–3
money measurement concept 9
Morrison's plc 143, 144–6
MTM (mark-to-market) valuation
    approach 109–11
Monger, Charles Thomas 18

net book value 118–19, 123, 124,
    140, **140**
net loss 58
net operating cash flow 137–8
net (operating) profit 56, 57, **57**, 60–2, 64,
    67, 71, *71*, 82, 137, 145–6, **166**
net (operating) profit percentage (NP%)
    161, 163, 165, 166, 170
net realizable value 79, 81–2, **82**, 83, 92
New York Times Company 147
Next plc 82–3

opening balance 27, **43**
operating activities, cash flow from 136,
    137–9, 142–7
operating (net) profit 56, 57, **57**, 60–2, 64,
    67, 71, *71*, 82, 137, 145–6, **166**
ordinary shares 45–6, **45**
overdraft 39, 88
overtrading 143
owners, stakeholder status 4
owner's capital 19–20, 27–30
owner's interest 19

P/E ratio (price/earnings ratio)
    172, **173**
Pantaloon Retail 130–1
partnerships 6, **6**, *7*
payables **39**, 63, 99, 139
    see also trade payables turnover
    period
payment cycles 131
payments
    late 134
    uncleared 89–91
Polly Peck 129
preference shares 45–6, **46**

prepayments 98–99, 101–7
    accounting treatment 101–4
    definition 101, **101**
    relating to real company accounts 104–5
price/earnings ratio (P/E ratio) 173, **173**
private limited companies 7
profit 174–5
    cash versus 132–3, 143, 146
    gross 56–62, **57**, 64, 69, *71*, 78–81, **165**
    importance of 56
    on the income statement 56–62, 64,
        66–9, 71, *71*, 82
    interpretation of accounts 158
    net/operating 56, **57**, 57, 60–2, 64, 67,
        71, *71*, 82, 137, 145–6, **166**
    paper 143
    pre-tax 137–8
    see also retained earnings
profit and loss accounts 60–2, 72
profitability ratios 159–163, 165–70, 177
property 112, 120
prudence 11
public limited companies 7
    income statements 70–1, *71*, 82–3
    interpretation of accounts 164–74, 175
    receivables 87–8
    statements of financial position 49, *50*,
        83
public, the 5, 157, 158
purchases 27–30, 58–64

qualitative data 3
quantitative data 3
quick ratio (acid test ratio) 162, 163, 168–9

R20 123
ratio analysis 157, 159–77
    efficiency ratios 160, 169–74, 177
    expression of comparative relationships
        159
    investment ratios 160, 172–3, 177
    limitations 176–7
    liquidity ratios 159, 161–3, 168–9, 177
    profitability ratios 159–61, 163,
        165–70, 177
raw materials, costing 79–81
receivable expense 84, 92
receivables 78, 83–8, 92
    definition **20**
    impairment of 84, 92
    in published accounts 87–8
    and working capital 139
    see also accounts receivable; trade
        receivables turnover period
recording transactions 18–34
    accounting equation 19–21, 27, 31
    balancing the accounts 24–6
    credits 21–4, 31
    debits 21–4, 31
    defining accounting transactions 19
    T-accounts 21–4
    trial balance 26–30, 31
reducing balance method (depreciation
    calculation) 116–20, **118**, 123, 125

remuneration, as a percentage of
    revenue 163
rent 27–30, 101
reserves 46–8
    general 46, 67–70
    revaluation 46, 67–8
residual value 116, **116**
retained earnings 46–8, *46*,
    67–9, 70
return on capital employed (ROCE) 161,
    163, 165, 166–70, **166**
revaluation reserve 46, 67–8
revenue 27–30
    definition 27, **57**
    and depreciation 121
    on the income statement 56–9, 61–4, 66,
        69, *71*, 82
revenue expenditure 12
Richard, Doug 134–5
Roddick, Dame Anita 55
Royal Bank of Scotland plc 86

Sainsbury's plc 81, *175–6*
sales
    cost of 57–62, **57**, 64, 69, 78
    and interpretation of accounts 158
Sandhaven plc 164–74, 175
seasonal variation 135
service organizations, income statements
    65–7, 73
share capital 6–7, 45–8, **45**
    authorized 46, **46**
    issued **46**
share premium 6, 7, 46, **46**
shareholders 6–7, 45–6
    definition **45**
    earnings available to ordinary
        172, **172**
    and interpretation of accounts 157
    stakeholder status 3
shares 6–7, *7*
    'limited by shares' 7
    nominal value 6, 7
    ordinary 45–6, **45**
    preference 45–6, **46**
sole traders 6, **6**, 7, 45, **45**
stakeholders 15
    definition 3
    information needs 3–5
    and materiality 12
    and statements of financial
        position 36
    types of 3, 4–5, *5*
Statement of Changes in Income and
    Equity 67
statement of financial position (SoFP) 3,
    35–54, 62–5, 68–70, 78
    accounting equation 39–40, 51
    accruals 100
    basic 36–7
    and cash flow statements 137, 140
    company 45–8
    definition **36**
    and depreciation 115–19

interpretation 157, 159, 161–3, 164, 174, 176
limitations 49–50, 176
non-current asset sale 123
preparation 40–4
prepayments 102–3
published 49, *50*, 71, 83
and the trial balance 26, 40, 42, 43
Statement of Principles 13–14, 16
stock 38
see also inventory
stock exchange 7
stock takes 58
straight line method (depreciation calculation) 116–18, **117**, 120, 123, 125
substance over form 11–12
suppliers 4–5

T-accounts 21–4
tax liability
corporation tax 67–9
and net profit figures 56
Tchenguiz, Robert 122–3
Tesco plc 81, 135, 158
Theobald, Caroline 134
time interval concept 10
trade payables turnover period 171
trade receivables turnover period 170–1
trading account 58–60, 72
transactions 8, 19, 31
see also recording transactions
trial balance 26–30, 31, 99
errors 27

and the statement of financial position 26, 40, 42–3
true and fair view 8

unions 3

Vodafone plc 49, *50*, 70, *71*, 87–8, *104–5*

Wal-Mart 130, 135
'wear and tear' 113
Webvan 135
"what if?" scenarios 134
'window-dressing' 91–2, 93, 176
Winterson, Jeanette 77
working capital 133, 136, 138–9, 143
write-downs 83
'writing off' debts 84, 87–8, 92